Prentice Hall LITERATURE

PENGUIN EDITION

Unit One
Resources

The British Tradition

PEARSON

Upper Saddle River, New Jersey
Boston, Massachusetts
Chandler, Arizona
Glenview, Illinois
Shoreview, Minnesota

13-digit ISBN: 978-0-13-366468-3
10-digit ISBN: 0-13-366468-6

1 2 3 4 5 6 7 8 9 10   12 11 10 09 08

PEARSON

CONTENTS

"The Seafarer" (translated by Burton Raffel), "The Wanderer" (translated by Charles W. Kennedy), "The Wife's Lament" (translated by Ann Stanford)

Contemporary Commentary: Burton Raffel Introduces *from* Beowulf 31

Contemporary Commentary: Burton Raffel Listening and Viewing 32

from Beowulf (translated by Burton Raffel)

The Canterbury Tales by Geoffrey Chaucer

from **The Decameron: Federigo's Falcon by Giovanni Boccaccio**

from **Sir Gawain and the Green Knight (translated by Marie Borroff)**

from **Morte d'Arthur by Sir Thomas Malory**

Letters of Margaret Paston by Margaret Paston, "Twa Corbies" Anonymous, "Lord Randall" Anonymous, "Get Up and Bar the Door" Anonymous, "Barbara Allan" Anonymous

About the Unit Resources

The *Prentice Hall Literature Unit Resources* provide manageable, comprehensive, and easy-to-use teaching materials to support each Student Edition unit. You can use these resources to address your students' different ability levels and learning styles, customize instruction to suit your teaching needs, and diagnose and assess student progress. All of these materials are also available at *PHLitOnline*, a rich, online source of personalized instruction and activities.

Here is a brief description of each element of the *Unit Resources*:

UNIT-LEVEL FEATURES

Big Questions (grades 6–10)

Support for the Big Questions includes complete lyrics to BQ Tunes (engaging songs that incorporate Big Question Vocabulary; available on CD); unit-opener worksheets that practice Big Question Vocabulary, an Applying the Big Question chart, re-rendered from the Student Edition.

Essential Questions (The American Experience; The British Tradition)

Support for the Essential Questions includes unit-opener worksheets that focus on each Essential Question individually and a worksheet to support the end-of-unit Essential Question Workshop.

Skills Concept Maps

Each map presents a graphic look at the relationship between the literature and the skills taught in the unit, with space provided for students' notes.

Vocabulary Workshop, Writing Workshop, and Communications Workshop support

End-of-unit worksheets provide opportunities for students to practice vocabulary, and gather and organize information for their Student Edition assignments.

SELECTION-LEVEL SUPPORT

Vocabulary and Reading Warmups

These exercises and easy reading passages provide selection vocabulary practice for students reading at one or two levels below grade level

Writing About the Big Question (grades 6–10)

These worksheets tie the Big Question to individual selections, while giving students additional practice using the Big Question Vocabulary.

Literary Analysis, Reading, and Vocabulary Builder

A series of worksheets that provide extra practice on each of the main skill strands in the Student Edition. You can find more support for the Literary Analysis and Reading strands in the separate Graphic Organizers Transparencies component.

Integrated Language Skills

The Student Edition Integrated Language Skills features are supported by grammar worksheets and additional pages containing graphic organizers and questions to help students gather and organize information to complete their Student Edition Writing and Listening and Speaking or Research and Technology assignments.

Enrichment

These activities give opportunities for advanced students to focus more closely on topics related to the content or theme of the literature selection.

ASSESSMENT

Diagnostic Tests

The beginning of each Unit 1 Resources book features a Diagnostic Test. Thereafter, each even-numbered Benchmark Test ends with a 20-question diagnostic component called Vocabulary in Context. Teachers desiring a larger sample for measuring students' reading ability can find an additional 20 questions at *PHLitOnline*.

Benchmark Tests

Twelve Benchmark Tests, spaced evenly throughout the year, assess students' mastery of literary, reading, vocabulary, grammar, and writing skills. A diagnostic Vocabulary in Context, described above, ends each even-numbered Benchmark Test.

Open-Book Tests

For every selection or grouping of selections, there is an Open-Book Test featuring short-answer and extended-response questions and opportunities for oral response. Most Open-Book-Tests also contain a question requiring students to represent information in a graphic organizer. These tests are available as a computer test bank on CD-ROM and at *PHLitOnline*.

Selection Tests

For every selection or grouping of selections, there are two closed-book Selection Tests (A and B) featuring multiple-choice and essay questions. Both tests assess essentially the same material; however Test A is designed for lower-level students, and Test B is designed for students average and above.

ADDITIONAL SUPPORT IN *UNIT ONE RESOURCES*

Pronunciation Guide

A two-page student guide to understanding diacritical marks given in standard dictionary pronunciations; includes practice

Form for Analyzing Primary Source Documents

In support of Primary Sources features in *The American Experience* and *The British Tradition*, a form for analyzing various types of primary sources.

Teaching Guides

To support fluency monitoring, Guide for Assessing Fluency; to support vocabulary instruction through music, a Guide for Teaching with BQ Tunes.

Pronunciation Key Practice—1

Throughout your textbook, you will find vocabulary features that include pronunciation for each new word. In order to pronounce the words correctly, you need to understand the symbols used to indicate different sounds.

Short Vowel Sounds

These sounds are shown with no markings at all:

a   as in <u>a</u>t, c<u>a</u>p

i   as in <u>i</u>t, g<u>y</u>m, <u>ea</u>r

e   as in <u>e</u>nd, f<u>ea</u>ther, v<u>e</u>ry

u   as in m<u>u</u>d, t<u>o</u>n, tr<u>ou</u>ble

Long Vowel Sounds

These sounds are shown with a line over the vowel:

ā   as in <u>a</u>te, r<u>ai</u>n, br<u>ea</u>k

ī   as in n<u>i</u>ce, l<u>ie</u>, sk<u>y</u>

ē   as in s<u>ee</u>, st<u>ea</u>m, p<u>ie</u>ce

ō   as in n<u>o</u>, <u>oa</u>t, l<u>ow</u>

A. DIRECTIONS: *Read aloud the sounds indicated by the symbols in each item. Then write the word the symbols stand for.*

1. kap _____
2. kāp _____
3. tīp _____
4. klōz _____
5. tuf _____

6. ker _____
7. wird _____
8. swet _____
9. swēt _____
10. nīt _____

Other Vowel Sounds

Notice the special markings used to show the following vowel sounds:

ä   as in father, far, heart

o͝o   as in look, would, pull

yo͞o   as in cute, few, use

o͝u   as in out, now

ô   as in all, law, taught

o͞o   as in boot, drew, tune

o͝i   as in oil, toy, royal

ʉ   as in her, sir, word

B. DIRECTIONS: *Read aloud the sounds indicated by the symbols in each item. Then write the word the symbols stand for.*

1. bo͝i _____
2. kär _____
3. ko͝od _____
4. lo͞oz _____
5. kro͝un _____

6. wʉrk _____
7. lʉr _____
8. kôt _____
9. myo͞o _____
10. rä _____

Pronunciation Key Practice—2

Some Special Consonant Sounds

These consonant sounds are shown by special two-letter combinations:

hw   as in which, white   zh   as in vision, treasure
sh   as in shell, mission, fiction   th   as in threw, nothing
ŋ   as in ring, anger, pink   *th*   as in then, mother
ch   as in chew, nature

Syllables and Accent Marks

Your textbook will show you how to break a word into syllables, or parts, so that you can pronounce each part correctly. An accent mark (») shows you which syllable to stress when you pronounce a word. Notice the differences in the way you say the following words:

bā´ bē   ō bā´   den´ im   dē nī´

Sounds in Unaccented Syllables

You will often see the following special symbols used in unaccented syllables. The most common is the schwa (ß), which shows an unaccented "uh" sound:

ə   as in ago, conceited, category, invisible
'l   as in cattle, paddle
'n   as in sudden, hidden

Light and Heavy Accents

Some long words have two stressed syllables: a heavy stress on one syllable and a second, lighter stress on another syllable. The lighter stress is shown by an accent mark in lighter type, like this: («)

C. DIRECTIONS: *With a partner, read aloud the sounds indicated by the symbols in each item. Say the words that the symbols stand for.*

1. kôr´əs   5. mezh´ ər   9. fər bid´ 'n
2. kən pash´ ən   6. des´ pər ā´ shən   10. hwim´ pər
3. brē´ *th*iŋ   7. im´ə choor´   11. fun´ də ment´ 'l
4. ig nôrd´   8. plunj´ iŋ   12. rek´ əg nīz«

D. DIRECTIONS: *With a partner, read aloud the sounds indicated by the symbols in the following lines. Each group of lines represent the words of a small poem.*

1. ī ēt mī pēz with hun´ ē.   2. dōnt wʉr´ ē if yoor jäb iz smôl
    īv dun it ôl mī līf.   and yoor ri wôrdz´ är fyoo.
    it māks *th*ə pēz tāst fun´ ē.   ri mem´ bər *th*at *th*ə mīt´ ē ōk
    but it kēps *th*em än *th*ə nīf.   wuz wuns ə nut līk yoo.

Name _____ Date _____

Form for Analyzing Primary Source Documents

1. Type of Document (check one)

   _____ Newspaper   _____ E-Mail

   _____ Letter   _____ Press release

   _____ Map   _____ Report

   _____ Other   _____ Advertisement

   _____ Memorandum   _____ Government Document

2. Date(s) of Document _____

3. Author(s) of Document _____

   _____

   Position or Title of Author(s) _____

4. Audience: *For whom was the document written?*

   _____

5. Purpose and Importance:

   a. Why was this document written?

   _____

   _____

   Write down two details that support your answer:

   _____

   _____

   b. List two important ideas, statements, or observations from this document:

   _____

   _____

   _____

   _____

   c. What does this document show about life in the time and place in which it was written?

   _____

   _____

   _____

   _____

Diagnostic Test

Read the selection. Then, answer the questions that follow.

1. Crystal always felt it was her_____to be a musical-comedy star.
   A. destined
   B. predestined
   C. destiny
   D. deserted

2. Dr. Kumar was a_____expert in the field of child development.
   A. convicted
   B. associated
   C. apprehensive
   D. prominent

3. They couldn't tell, with any_____, what time the family would arrive.
   A. hermit
   B. disorders
   C. certainty
   D. virtues

4. After looking all over the fabric store, Amy finally found a_____of the cloth she wanted.
   A. specator
   B. blunder
   C. remnant
   D. substitute

5. After spending time in the dense jungle forest, he liked the_____beauty of the desert.
   A. stark
   B. realms
   C. favorable
   D. unjust

6. Ray's grandparents faced_____in the 1950s because of the color of their skin.
   A. participation
   B. reign
   C. discrimination
   D. congratulation

7. The Portugese were the_____of the African country of Angola.
   A. colonies
   B. colonial
   C. colonized
   D. colonizers

8. In the night, Alweyn slipped quietly away so as not to wake those_____in the castle.
   A. unprecedented
   B. namely
   C. whitewashed
   D. slumbering

9. When I realized I didn't have my sweater, Mom told me, "You should have thought of that _____."
   A. traditionally
   B. beforehand
   C. unjustly
   D. certifiably

10. The older map showed that the_____between the two counties was not where they thought it was.
    A. ventilation
    B. veranda
    C. biographer
    D. boundary

11. During the basketball game, the referee called three_____against the home team.
    A. penalties
    B. straits
    C. hilts
    D. barbarians

12. Jesse worried that the virus had_____his files and made them unusable.
    A. banished
    B. ransacked
    C. authorized
    D. corrupted

13. Solving world hunger has a_____appeal.
    A. reverent
    B. classical
    C. universal
    D. barbarian

14. When citing facts to back up your point, you must be very_____.
    A. corrupted
    B. specific
    C. deprived
    D. vibrant

15. In English class, we read about Helen of Troy as we studied Greek_____.
   A. publicity
   B. roman
   C. fathom
   D. mythology

16. My friend Eban wrote the music for the songs, and I wrote the_____.
   A. succession
   B. lyrics
   C. valor
   D. occurrences

17. In order to get your real estate license, the board needs to_____you.
   A. certain
   B. certificate
   C. certainly
   D. certify

18. I hope I'll be able to get_____aid to help pay for college.
   A. finances
   B. financial
   C. finally
   D. financially

19. The Colemans came home to mess and found that their apartment had been_____.
   A. specific
   B. deprived
   C. ransacked
   D. blissful

20. The family had moved every few months, and Kyle was tired of all the_____.
   A. upheaval
   B. immunity
   C. reverence
   D. estimation

21. After Napoleon Bonaparte gave up power, he was_____to the island of Elba.
   A. awaked
   B. enforced
   C. departed
   D. exiled

22. Although Anya wanted to get married on a beach, her father was hoping for a more _____ wedding.
    A. traditional
    B. unjust
    C. enforced
    D. swooned

23. Lianne wasn't ready yet to _____ to which college she wanted to attend.
    A. convey
    B. commit
    C. conceive
    D. commotion

24. The dictator's way of dealing with those who disagreed with him was _____.
    A. exiled
    B. awaked
    C. unjust
    D. countless

25. The dectective climbed into his car, started it up, and began to _____ the suspect.
    A. exile
    B. commit
    C. pursue
    D. depart

26. He was eager to find out what rights had been _____ him and his family.
    A. accorded
    B. discriminated
    C. colonized
    D. slumbered

27. They failed to put out the campfire before leaving, _____ starting a forest fire.
    A. thereby
    B. namely
    C. likewise
    D. whereas

28. Don Ramón felt that he lost his fortune because of his enemy's _____.
    A. furnishings
    B. analogy
    C. rendezvous
    D. treachery

29. As Alonzo looked around the room at the smiling faces, he knew he was _____ friends.
   A. thereby
   B. amongst
   C. wholly
   D. moderately

30. Jill had forgotten about the test, and_____ she was unprepared.
   A. consequently
   B. energetically
   C. wholly
   D. fabulously

31. The soldiers dodged the flying arrows as they_____ the castle.
   A. nourished
   B. abstracted
   C. besieged
   D. inflicted

32. Sydney raised her hand and asked, "What does the symbol on the banner_____?"
   A. resign
   B. signaling
   C. signed
   D. signify

33. Bettina felt that the huge fuss they made over her second-place ribbon was_____ unnecessary.
   A. wholly
   B. devoutly
   C. outwardly
   D. universally

34. He kneeled out of respect and_____ for the holiness of the place.
   A. solstice
   B. barbarian
   C. prophet
   D. reverence

35. Felicia added examples to support her argument because she was_____ with her essay.
   A. traditional
   B. dissatisfied
   C. numberless
   D. authorized

36. They stayed on the ship until after it had passed through the _____ between the two bodies of water.
    A. valor
    B. surgeon
    C. strait
    D. tenement

37. If one group controls too much of the food, it _____ others of their fair share.
    A. ransacks
    B. beseiges
    C. deprives
    D. signifies

38. The town hoped that the could raise enough _____ through the campaign to keep the libraries open.
    A. lyrics
    B. constables
    C. confiscation
    D. revenue

39. The punishment for bringing drinks into the stadium was their _____ by the guards.
    A. confiscation
    B. immunity
    C. valor
    D. upbringing

40. Tom put special latches on the cabinets as a _____ against the baby's getting them open.
    A. personhood
    B. safeguard
    C. circumstance
    D. adversary

Name _____

Concept Map Unit 1

From Legend to History: The Old English and Medieval Periods (A.D. 449–1485)

Three Essential Questions serve as lenses through which to view the literature—

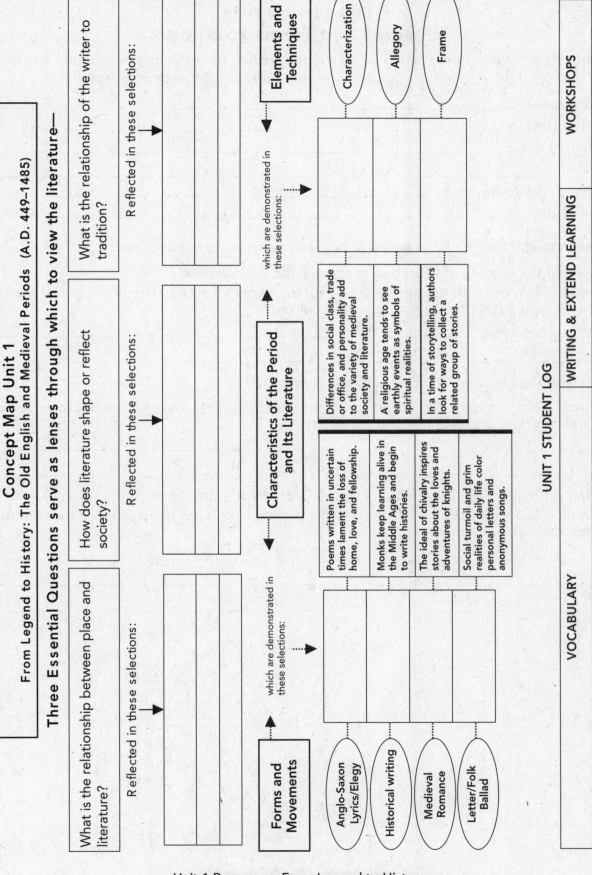

What is the relationship between place and literature?

Reflected in these selections:

How does literature shape or reflect society?

Reflected in these selections:

What is the relationship of the writer to tradition?

Reflected in these selections:

Elements and Techniques

- Characterization
- Allegory
- Frame

which are demonstrated in these selections:

Characteristics of the Period and Its Literature

Poems written in uncertain times lament the loss of home, love, and fellowship.

Monks keep learning alive in the Middle Ages and begin to write histories.

The ideal of chivalry inspires stories about the loves and adventures of knights.

Social turmoil and grim realities of daily life color personal letters and anonymous songs.

Differences in social class, trade or office, and personality add to the variety of medieval society and literature.

A religious age tends to see earthly events as symbols of spiritual realities.

In a time of storytelling, authors look for ways to collect a related group of stories.

Forms and Movements

- Anglo-Saxon Lyrics/Elegy
- Historical writing
- Medieval Romance
- Letter/Folk Ballad

which are demonstrated in these selections:

UNIT 1 STUDENT LOG

VOCABULARY	WRITING & EXTEND LEARNING	WORKSHOPS

Unit 1 Resources: From Legend to History

Unit 1 Introduction
Names and Terms to Know

I. DIRECTIONS: *Write a brief sentence explaining each of the following names and terms. You will find all of the information you need in the Unit Introduction in your textbook.*

1. "Angle land": _____

2. Alfred the Great: _____

3. Magna Carta: _____

4. Bede: _____

5. William the Conqueror _____

6. Henry VII: _____

II. DIRECTIONS: *Use the hints below to help you answer each question.*

1. How did the coming of Christianity change life in England?

   [Hints: When did Christianity arrive? What was English society like before it arrived? What new elements did Christianity bring to England?]

   _____

   _____

2. How did the Norman Conquest change England?

   [Hints: What language did the Normans bring to England? What new social structure did they bring?]

   _____

   _____

3. What difficulties did the English struggle with during the 1300s and 1400s?

   [Hints: What did the Black Death do to the population? What wars afflicted the country? What did Henry VII do?]

   _____

   _____

   _____

Unit 1 Introduction

Essential Question 1: What is the relationship between place and literature?

I. DIRECTIONS: *Answer the questions about the first Essential Question in the Introduction about the relationship between place and literature. All the information you need is in the Unit 1 Introduction in your textbook.*

A. *Responding to Island Environment*

    1. The early English regarded the sea as _____

    _____

    2. Christian monks changed "The Seafarer" and "The Wanderer" by _____

    _____

    3. In *Beowulf* the "sea-road" led to _____

    4. The mead-hall setting represented _____

    _____

B. *Making a Nation of an Island*

    1. Bede portrayed England as _____

    _____

    2. Chaucer's *Canterbury Tales* helped draw together a national identity by _____

    _____

II. DIRECTIONS: *Complete the following sentence stems based on the Essential Question Vocabulary words.*

    1. A magazine article about our state's *geography* would pay a lot of attention to _____

    2. An *invasion* usually involves force, because _____

    3. Someone who is forced into *exile* is forbidden to _____

Unit 1 Introduction

Essential Question 2: How does literature change or reflect society?

I. DIRECTIONS: *On the lines provided, answer the questions about the second Essential Question in the Introduction about writers and social trends All the information you need is in the Unit 1 Introduction in your textbook.*

A. *Capturing a Vanishing Tribal World*

    1. *Beowulf* showed that to become a leader, _____
_____

    2. What world was passing away in *Beowulf*? _____
_____

B. *Chaucer and Social Trends*

    1. What social types did *The Canterbury Tales* represent? _____
_____

    2. What were some of the problems in the Catholic Church during Chaucer's time?
_____

    3. Chaucer portrayed his society without _____

    4. What was a source of political turbulence in the medieval period? _____
_____

    5. Chaucer reflect the rising middle class by _____
_____

    6. In dealing with social change, writers do not act like sociologists; rather they show
_____

II. DIRECTIONS: *Complete the sentence stems based on the Essential Question Vocabulary words.*

    1. One way to settle *controversy* is to _____

    2. A *tribe* is like an extended family because _____

    3. In my family, I often end up in the *role* of the _____

Unit 1 Introduction

Essential Question 3: What is the relationship of the writer to tradition?

I. DIRECTIONS: *On the lines provided, answer the questions about the third Essential Question in the Introduction about the relationship between the writer and tradition. All the information you need is in the Unit 1 Introduction in your textbook.*

A. *Writers and Tradition*

    1. "Tradition" means _____

    2. What did *Sir Gawain and the Green Knight* express through the use of old legends?
    _____

    3. In *Morte D'Arthur* Sir Thomas Malory reworked the story of Arthur in order to
    _____

    4. What are three possible ways in which different tellers changed the story of *Beowulf*?
    _____
    _____

B. *Chaucer's Handling of Tradition*

    1. Chaucer modeled the structure of *The Canterbury Tales* on the earlier _____
    _____

    2. How did Chaucer depart from this model? _____
    _____

    3. Describe the new a new poetic rhythm that Chaucer developed. _____
    _____

    4. *Beowulf, The Canterbury Tales,* and the medieval retellings of the King Arthur stories show how traditions reach both _____

II. DIRECTIONS: *Complete the sentence stems based on the Essential Question Vocabulary words.*

    1. Ernesto loved the *traditional* Thanksgiving dinner, especially _____

    2. Part of Alice's *inheritance* from her grandfather included _____

    3. My little brother's resistance to going to bed took on a new *form*, and he began to _____
    _____

Unit 1 Introduction
Follow-Through Activities

I. CHECK YOUR COMPREHENSION: *Use this chart to complete the Check Your Comprehension activity in the Unit 1 Introduction. In the middle column, list two key concepts for each Essential Question. In the right column, list a work for each concept.*

Essential Question	Key Concept	Work (Author)
Place and Literature	1. Exile to a foreign land 2. _____	1. "Seafarer" (unknown) 2. _____
Literature and Society	1._____ 2. _____	1. _____ 2. _____
Writer and Tradition	1. _____ 2. _____	1. _____ 2. _____

II. EXTEND YOUR LEARNING: *Use this graphic organizer to help plan your research for the Extend Your Learning activity.*

Language Family: _____	
Word	**Etymology : Ango-Saxon or Norman?**
1.	
2.	
3.	
4.	
5.	
6.	
7.	
8.	
9.	
10.	

Vocabulary Warm-up Word Lists

Study these words from the selections. Then, complete the activities.

Word List A

perched [PURCHT] *v.* seated on a high or insecure resting place
The falcon's nest was perched on the edge of the cliff.

whirled [WHURLD] *v.* moved rapidly in a circular manner
The couple whirled around the dance floor as they waltzed.

terns [TURNZ] *n.* any birds of the seagull family
Hundreds of terns flew over the garbage dump.

unfurl [un FUHRL] *v.* to unfold or unroll
The cabin boy learned to unfurl the sails on the ship.

scorch [SKAWRCH] *v.* to shrivel or parch with heat
The sun can scorch fresh paint, causing it to blister.

billowing [BIL oh ing] *adj.* rising and rolling in large waves
The smoke was billowing from the chimney.

smitten [SMITN] *v.* fascinated with someone or something; in love
The young man was smitten with love when he read the girl's poetry.

strive [STRYV] *v.* try very hard
Always strive to do your best.

Word List B

wretched [RECH id] *adj.* deeply distressed
The wretched child could not stop crying.

desolation [DES oh LAY shun] *n.* lonely grief
The survivors of the plane crash were overcome with desolation.

tarnished [TAHR nishd] *adj.* having lost its shine, beauty, or reputation
Since the brass lamp was tarnished, the price was reduced.

decrees [dee KREEZ] *n.* authoritative orders having the force of law
When our team won, the mayor issued decrees renaming streets in the team's honor.

brood [BROOD] *v.* think about something constantly out of worry or anger
Until he failed the test, the student had no reason to brood about his grades.

fleeting [FLEET ing] *adj.* passing quickly
The star was surrounded by bodyguards, so the crowd only got a fleeting glimpse of him.

mournful [MAWRN ful] *adj.* suggesting sadness
Whether played at parades or funerals, the bagpipes have a mournful sound.

naught [NAWT] *n.* nothing
When the rain washed away the seeds, the farmer's work was for naught.

Name _____ Date _____

"The Seafarer," translated by Burton Raffel
"The Wanderer," translated by Charles W. Kennedy
"The Wife's Lament," translated by Ann Stanford
Vocabulary Warm-up Exercises

Exercise A *Fill in each blank in the paragraph with the appropriate word from Word List A.*
Use each word only once.

The first ship builders developed the sail and the oar by trial and error. Their creations were
refined as the need for larger, stronger, and faster vessels increased. At first, sailors would
[1] _____ only one sail per vessel. But over the centuries, a variety of
arrangements and sizes of sails were seen [2] _____ in the wind. With
greater wind power, explorers did [3] _____ to go further into uncharted
waters. Frightened sailors, [4] _____ on top of masts, kept a lookout for the
currents that [5] _____ dangerously, threatening to sink ships. Although
their skin would [6] _____ in the sun, and rations were meager, those
[7] _____ by the ocean were not discouraged. Like the
[8] _____ that accompanied even the earliest vessels, these seamen built
their homes and thrived near the coastlines.

Exercise B *Revise each sentence so that the underlined vocabulary word is used in a logical*
way. Be sure to keep the vocabulary word in your revision.

Example: If you feel <u>wretched</u>, then you will do your best on a test.
   If you feel <u>wretched</u>, then you probably *will* not *do your best on a test.*

1. Determined to spot the <u>fleeting</u> asteroid, the astronomer rarely watched the sky.

   _____

2. The <u>decrees</u> issued by the emperor were easily ignored.

   _____

3. The compliments from readers' <u>tarnished</u> the magazine's reputation.

   _____

4. The director began to <u>brood</u> when his new film was a hit.

   _____

5. When the prince was born, the church bells rang with <u>mournful</u> sounds.

   _____

6. Immigrants rarely experience feelings of <u>desolation</u> after leaving their homeland.

   _____

7. The school cancelled the party, so the preparation was not for <u>naught</u>.

   _____

"The Seafarer," translated by Burton Raffel
"The Wanderer," translated by Charles W. Kennedy
"The Wife's Lament," translated by Ann Stanford
Reading Warm-up A

Read the following passage. Pay special attention to the underlined words. Then, read it again,
complete the activities. Use a separate sheet of paper for your written answers.

Many cultures strive to extend their knowledge of the
world. The Vikings, the Arabs, and the Polynesians are
noteworthy for mapping the world's oceans. These peoples
were the earliest and most successful navigators. From
the end of the eighth century, Scandinavians used the
tides, currents, and stars to explore the rivers of Russia
and the Black Sea. The billowing sails on their longships
also permitted voyages across the freezing Atlantic to
Iceland and North America. Once they arrived, they
attempted early settlements, which quickly failed. The
Norsemen were more successful in the British Isles and
Northern France, where they built thriving kingdoms.

During the same period, the Arabs discovered a sea
route to China, via the Strait of Malacca. This allowed
more goods to be transported to Europeans who were
smitten by the riches of the east.

Meanwhile, the Polynesians colonized the islands of
the Pacific. Perched on their canoes and braving the hot
sun that might scorch them, they trusted the winds to
unfurl their sails and carry them great distances across
empty oceans. Once they were closer to land, oars were
essential. Without them, it was hard to avoid the reefs
that destroyed larger European sailing ships centuries
later.

No matter when they lived, or what part of the world
they explored, these sailors had one thing in common:
the companionship of the terns that hovered and whirled
over their vessels.

1. Circle the words that tell
   what many ancient cultures
   strive to do. Then, explain
   what *strive* means.

2. Circle the word that tells
   what was billowing. Then,
   rewrite the sentence, using a
   synonym for *billowing*.

3. Circle the words that explain
   what had the Europeans
   smitten. Then, describe how
   someone who is *smitten*
   might behave.

4. Circle the words that
   describe where the sailors
   perched. Explain what
   perched means.

5. Underline the word that is a
   clue to the meaning of
   scorch. Describe something
   that might *scorch*.

6. Circle the words that tell
   what the winds unfurl. Then,
   describe something you have
   seen *unfurl*.

7. Circle the phrase that
   describes what the terns did.
   Then, tell where you might
   find *terns*.

8. Describe how something that
   whirled might look.

"The Seafarer," translated by Burton Raffel, **"The Wanderer,"** translated by Charles W. Kennedy, **"The Wife's Lament,"** translated by Ann Stanford

Reading Warm-up B

Read the following passage. Pay special attention to the underlined words. Then, read it again, and complete the activities. Use a separate sheet of paper for your written answers.

Historically, exile was regarded as an exceptionally severe form of punishment. Once sentenced, the <u>wretched</u> person was forced to leave his city or country for years, sometimes for the rest of his life. If he lingered, or returned home prematurely, the penalty was usually death. Those remaining behind suffered too, as they were left to <u>brood</u> over the fate of their banished loved one. To make matters worse, the entire family's reputation was <u>tarnished</u> by the conviction, and often their personal property was seized as well.

Those who were banished faced a life of wandering, which led to loneliness and <u>desolation</u>. People of the time relied on lifetime bonds between family members or between lords and followers. Wandering from place to place, exiles might not have a chance to form more than a <u>fleeting</u> relationship with others. To make matters worse, the exiles were in constant danger from criminals who preyed upon those far from their families and friends.

Sometimes the exiled person's fate was decided by an official and announced by written <u>decrees</u>. In other cases, it was decided by a vote of the citizens. Besides instilling fear, banishment was a useful way for government officials to hold onto power. Removing controversial political figures prevented them from organizing rebellions in their own native lands, or even from becoming martyrs. Exiling rivals was intended to set an example and make further opposition come to <u>naught</u>.

Banishment was such a dominant fear that <u>mournful</u> poetry, music, and dramas were written about it. Shakespeare used banishment in a number of his plays including *Romeo and Juliet* and *A Winter's Tale.* Unfortunately, exile is not only an ancient form of punishment. Recent history gives us many examples of entire populations being dispossessed and banished from their native lands for religious or political reasons.

1. Circle the phrase that explains one reason why an exiled person might be <u>wretched</u>. Then, tell what *wretched* means.

2. Why would those left behind <u>brood</u>? Explain what *brood* means.

3. Circle the words that tell what is <u>tarnished</u>. Rewrite the sentence using a synonym for *tarnished*.

4. Circle the word that is a clue to the meaning of <u>desolation</u>. Explain what *desolation* is.

5. Underline the word that is close to the opposite of <u>fleeting</u>. Describe something that is *fleeting*.

6. Circle the word that tells the action that <u>decrees</u> were used to perform. Describe two *decrees* that you think the government should make.

7. Underline the phrase that tells what comes to <u>naught</u>. Describe something else that comes to *naught*.

8. What have you heard that sounds <u>mournful</u>? Tell what *mournful* means.

Name _____ Date _____

"The Seafarer," translated by Burton Raffel
"The Wanderer," translated by Charles W. Kennedy
"The Wife's Lament," translated by Ann Stanford
Literary Analysis: Anglo-Saxon Lyrics/Elegy

Anglo-Saxon lyrics were recited or chanted aloud to an audience by wandering poets. In order to make the poems easier to listen to and to memorize, they were developed with strong rhythms. Each line has a certain number of beats, or accented syllables—almost always four. Many lines have a **caesura,** or pause, in the middle, after the second beat. Anglo-Saxon poetry also contained **kennings,** two-word metaphorical names for familiar things. Note these examples of rhythm, caesura, and kennings in these lines:

Rhythm: No hárps ríng in his héart, nó rewárds,

Caesura: No pássion for wómen, [pause] no wórldly pléasures,

Kenning: Nóthing, only the oceán's heáve;

An **elegy** is a lyric poem mourning the loss of someone or something. Each of these Anglo-Saxon poems provides an example of an elegy.

1. Mark the syllables that have a strong accented beat (´) in these lines from "The Seafarer."

    But there isn't a man on earth so proud,

    So born to greatness, so bold with his youth,

    Grown so brave, or so graced by God,

    That he feels no fear as the sails unfurl,

2. In the lines in passage 1, how many caesuras are there? Write the word that appears before each caesura.

    _____

3. Mark each syllable that has a strong accented beat (´) in these lines from "The Seafarer."

    Those powers have vanished, those pleasures are dead.

    The weakest survives and the world continues,

    Kept spinning by toil. All glory is tarnished.

4. Underline the kenning in these lines from "The Wife's Lament."

    First my lord went out away from his people

    over the wave-tumult. I grieved each dawn

    wondered where my lord my first on earth might be.

5. Why do these poems qualify as elegies? What kind of loss does each poem lament?

    _____

    _____

    _____

    _____

Name _____ Date _____

"**The Seafarer,**" translated by Burton Raffel
"**The Wanderer,**" translated by Charles W. Kennedy
"**The Wife's Lament,**" translated by Ann Stanford
Reading Strategy: Connect to Historical Context

Recognizing the **historical context** and the characteristics of the period in which a work was written helps you notice relevant details and ideas. For example, if you know that Anglo-Saxon culture was male-dominated, you may be able to understand the poet's line: "My lord commanded me to move my dwelling here."

DIRECTIONS: *Use your understanding of Anglo-Saxon historical context to help you understand the following excerpts. In the right column, record how your comprehension is affected by what you know.*

Excerpt	How Historical Context Aids Understanding
1. **"The Seafarer":** "This tale is true, and mine. It tells/How the sea took me, swept me back/And forth in sorrow and fear and pain,/Showed me suffering in a hundred ships. . . ."	1.
2. **"The Wanderer":** "'So have I also, often in wretchedness/Fettered my feelings, far from my kin,/Homeless and hapless, since days of old,/When the dark earth covered my dear lord's face,/And I sailed away with sorrowful heart,/Over wintry seas, seeking a gold-lord. . . .'"	2.
3. **"The Wife's Lament":** "I must far and near/bear the anger of my beloved./The man sent me out to live in the woods/under an oak tree in this den in the earth./Ancient this earth hall./I am all longing."	3.

"The Seafarer," translated by Burton Raffel
"The Wanderer," translated by Charles W. Kennedy
"The Wife's Lament," translated by Ann Stanford

Vocabulary Builder

Word List

admonish   compassionate   fervent   rancor   rapture   sentinel

A. DIRECTIONS: *On the line, write the letter of the definition for each word in the right column.*

___ 1. fervent   A. ill-will

___ 2. compassionate   B. advise; caution

___ 3. sentinel   C. expression of joy

___ 4. admonish   D. someone who guards

___ 5. rancor   E. having great feeling

___ 6. rapture   F. sympathizing; pitying

B. WORD STUDY: *The Anglo-Saxon suffix* -ness *means "the state of being or quality of." Answer each of the following questions, changing the underlined word to a word with the suffix* -ness.

1. Why did she think the cake was too <u>sweet</u>? _____

   _____

2. How did the <u>bright</u> light affect you? _____

   _____

3. Did you think Ryan was <u>eager</u> enough to convince Mrs. Malone that he should be in the band? _____

   _____

4. What do you think the teacher thought when Alan was so <u>helpful</u> on Thursday?

   _____

   _____

"The Seafarer," translated by Burton Raffel
"The Wanderer," translated by Charles W. Kennedy
"The Wife's Lament," translated by Ann Stanford

Integrated Language Skills: Support for Writing

Use the chart below to organize information for your editorial about the loss of someone or something from your community or school.

Topic	
How the loss made you feel	
Why others should regret the loss	

On a separate page, write a draft editorial that addresses your topic of loss, your feelings about it, and your opinion about why others should regret the loss. Use examples and details to support your opinions.

"The Seafarer," translated by Burton Raffel
"The Wanderer," translated by Charles W. Kennedy
"The Wife's Lament," translated by Ann Stanford

Enrichment: Social Studies

These poems are about exiles—persons who for one reason or another find themselves far from home. During Britain's Anglo-Saxon period, many people became exiles due to various migrations into and out of the British Isles.

DIRECTIONS: *Read the following paragraph about some of these fifth-century migrations. Label and draw lines on the map to illustrate these migrations.*

At the start of the fifth century, England was under Roman rule. In 410, the Romans began leaving England, having been called back to Rome to defend it. This left an opportunity for new groups of people to come and take the land. Beginning in 449, a wave of people came to the British Isles seeking new lands. The three main groups were the Angles, Saxons, and Jutes. The Angles came from southern Denmark, eventually settling in the eastern half of England. The Saxons came from northern Germany and settled in the southern part of England. This part of England is now the counties of Essex, Sussex, and Wessex. The Jutes probably came from northern Denmark and northern Germany, near the mouth of the Rhine River. They settled in an area just south of London, in what is now called Kent, and on the Isle of Wight. Many natives of these lands, the Celtic Britons, were forced to move west and north. Eventually, many of them settled in Wales.

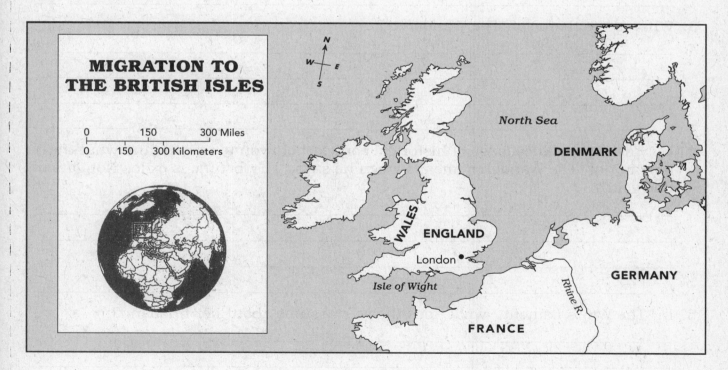

"**The Seafarer**" Translated by Burton Raffel,
"**The Wanderer**" Translated by Charles W. Kennedy,
"**The Wife's Lament**" Translated by Ann Stanford

Open-Book Test

Short Answer *Write your response to the questions in this section on the lines provided.*

1. In "The Seafarer," the phrase "summer's sentinel," meaning a cuckoo, is used. What kind of poetic element is this? Explain.

   _____

   _____

   _____

   _____

2. What is the reason, despite all the hardships he's suffered, that the narrator in "The Seafarer" continues to follow the life of the sea?

   _____

   _____

   _____

   _____

3. What is the theme of "The Wanderer"?

   _____

   _____

   _____

   _____

4. How does your knowledge of historical context help you to understand what the narrator of "The Wanderer" means when he says, "His fortune is exile,/Not gifts of fine gold"?

   _____

   _____

   _____

   _____

5. In "The Wife's Lament," what does the wife assume about her husband?

   _____

   _____

   _____

   _____

6. What is the purpose of the caesura in this line from "The Wife's Lament"?

I had few loved ones/ in this land

or faithful friends.

_____

_____

_____

7. Read each line in the chart below. Then write the element of Anglo-Saxon lyrics it illustrates.

Line	Element
First my lord went out/ away from his people	
The song of the swan/Might serve for pleasure . . .	
ocean's heave	

8. During this time in history, many groups of people left or were sent from their homes. How does knowing this help the reader to understand "The Seafarer," "The Wanderer," and "The Wife's Lament"?

_____

_____

_____

9. In "The Wife's Lament," the narrator says she and her husband were *blithe*. Why did they feel this way?

_____

_____

_____

10. In "The Wanderer," the narrator speaks of *grievous* disasters. What are some of these disasters, and why are they grievous?

_____

_____

_____

Essay

Write an extended response to the question of your choice or to the question or questions your teacher assigns you.

11. Choose one of the Anglo-Saxon poems: "The Seafarer," "The Wanderer," or "The Wife's Lament." In an essay, describe its historical context. Then explain how knowing this context gives you clues to its meaning. Use at least two details from the poem to help you respond.

12. A fundamental Anglo-Saxon belief is that human life is shaped by fate. How is this belief reflected in the poems "The Seafarer," "The Wanderer," and "The Wife's Lament"? Answer this question in an essay, giving examples from one or more of the poems to support your explanation.

13. Most of the poems and stories of the Anglo-Saxon period were passed along by oral tradition. In an essay, tell how the use of features such as the kenning and caesura may have helped maintain this oral tradition. Illustrate your explanation with examples from "The Seafarer," "The Wanderer," and "The Wife's Lament."

14. **Thinking About the Essential Question: Does a sense of place shape literature or does literature shape a sense of place?** In the three texts, "The Seafarer," "The Wanderer," and "The Wife's Lament," the speaker has lost his or her home. Choose one poem, and in an essay describe the home the speaker has lost. Then explain how the imagined home influences the poem as a whole.

Oral Response

15. Go back to questions 1, 2, 4, or to the question your teacher assigns to you. Take a few minutes to expand your answer and prepare an oral response. Find additional details in "The Seafarer," "The Wanderer," or "The Wife's Lament" that will support your points. If necessary, make notes to guide your response.

"The Seafarer," translated by Burton Raffel
"The Wanderer," translated by Charles W. Kennedy
"The Wife's Lament," translated by Ann Stanford

Selection Test A

Critical Reading *Identify the letter of the choice that best answers the question.*

____ 1. In "The Seafarer," the phrase "summer's sentinel" is used to mean a cuckoo. "Summer's sentinel" is an example of what kind of Anglo-Saxon lyric?
   A. caesura
   B. predicate
   C. kenning
   D. scop

____ 2. These lines from "The Seafarer" illustrate what characteristic of Anglo-Saxon poetry?

   The song of the swan / Might serve for pleasure. . . .

   A. caesuras
   B. alliteration
   C. assonance
   D. kennings

____ 3. What is the subject of the first part of "The Seafarer"?
   A. living a life at sea
   B. a man's longing for his wife
   C. how a sailor became a Christian
   D. surviving a life in exile

____ 4. What is the speaker's final message in "The Seafarer"?
   A. Life at sea is a great experience.
   B. Those faithful to God will be rewarded.
   C. The glories of earth are past.
   D. Gold will not purchase a place in heaven.

____ 5. Many poems of this period are about wandering and exile. Why do you think these are such common subjects?
   A. Many people dreamed of adventure.
   B. Only these poems survived.
   C. Many people were poor and homeless.
   D. Many people ending up leaving home.

____ 6. Why did the speaker in "The Wanderer" leave his home?
 A. His lord died.
 B. His wife died.
 C. He was a coward in battle.
 D. He wanted to go to sea.

____ 7. What is the theme of "The Wanderer"?
 A. old age and illness
 B. everyday dangers of life
 C. the sorrow of being homeless
 D. a need for adventure

____ 8. What does the narrator of "The Wanderer" miss the most?
 A. his wife
 B. peace
 C. food
 D. his friends

____ 9. Why did Anglo-Saxon poetry use the caesura?
 A. to make the poetry more musical
 B. to give the storyteller breathing spaces
 C. to fool the audience with a trick
 D. to add drama to the storytelling

____ 10. What does the wife think her husband is doing in "The Wife's Lament"?
 A. hurrying home to her
 B. living in comfort
 C. suffering great sadness
 D. having great adventures

____ 11. What aspect of Anglo-Saxon life does this line from "The Wife's Lament" suggest?

 My lord commanded me / to move my dwelling here.

 A. Women followed their husbands in wartime.
 B. Women were often ruled by their husbands.
 C. People built new houses wherever they traveled.
 D. People were not happy staying in one place.

Vocabulary and Grammar

___ **12.** What is the correct vocabulary word to complete this sentence?

The seafarer had no _____ toward the lord he served.

A. rapture

B. winsomeness

C. rancor

D. sentinel

___ **13.** What is the correct vocabulary word to complete this sentence?

The _____ stood watch over the entrance to the castle.

A. admonish   C. rapture

B. rancor   D. sentinel

___ **14.** What is the correct vocabulary word to complete this sentence?

For the wife in "The Wife's Lament," life in exile was a _____ experience.

A. grievous

B. fervent

C. blithe

D. compassionate

Essay

15. Knowing the historical context of a piece of poetry can help you understand many poems. Choose one of the Anglo-Saxon poems in this group. In an essay, explain how knowing the historical context of the poem gives you clues to its meaning. Answer these questions: What historical points are mentioned in the poem? How is the speaker affected by these historical points? How do you feel about the speaker and the events he or she experiences? Use at least two details from the poem to help you respond.

16. Anglo-Saxons believed that human life is shaped by fate. An individual's wishes and actions could not always change a person's fate. Choose one of the poems in this group. Explain how the speaker is influenced by a belief in fate. Give at least two examples from the poem to support your ideas.

17. **Thinking About the Big Question: Does a sense of place shape literature or does literature shape a sense of place?** In the three texts, "The Seafarer," "The Wanderer," and "The Wife's Lament," the speaker has lost his or her home. Choose one poem, and in an essay, describe the home the speaker has lost.

"The Seafarer," translated by Burton Raffel
"The Wanderer," translated by Charles W. Kennedy
"The Wife's Lament," translated by Ann Stanford

Selection Test B

Critical Reading *Identify the letter of the choice that best completes the statement or answers the question.*

____ 1. The phrase "summer's sentinel," meaning a cuckoo, is an example of
    A. a kenning.
    B. a predicate.
    C. a scop.
    D. an exile.

____ 2. What does the author of "The Wanderer" seem to miss most?
    A. material possessions
    B. religion
    C. adventure
    D. companionship

____ 3. During this time in history, many groups of people left or were sent from their homes. Knowing this helps the reader understand why
    A. each person was sent away.
    B. each person was lonely.
    C. the theme of "exile" was so common.
    D. the lyric poem was popular.

____ 4. Which of the following best describes the speaker's message at the end of "The Seafarer"?
    A. Life at sea is both exhilarating and wearisome.
    B. Gifts of gold for heaven will not redeem a sinful soul.
    C. Those who walk with God shall be rewarded.
    D. The earth no longer flourishes in glory.

____ 5. Read this sentence from "The Wife's Lament":
    Be he outlawed far/in a strange folk-land—that my beloved sits/under a rocky cliff rimed with frost/a lord dreary in spirit.

    What words or phrases help you to recognize the historical context of the line?
    A. rocky cliff
    B. outlawed; strange folk-land
    C. dreary in spirit
    D. my beloved

____ 6. The main theme of "The Wanderer" involves the
    A. value of friendship.
    B. need for safety.
    C. importance of traditions.
    D. pain of homelessness.

____ 7. In "The Wife's Lament," the wife assumes her husband is now
   A. on an exciting adventure and does not think of her.
   B. on his way home for a reconciliation.
   C. married to someone else.
   D. melancholy, as she is.

____ 8. Which characteristic of Anglo-Saxon poetry is illustrated by "The Seafarer"?
   A. celebration of heroic achievements
   B. use of caesura
   C. rhymed couplets
   D. Caedmonian verse

____ 9. The first part of "The Seafarer" is the story of
   A. a man's life on the sea.
   B. a sailor's conversion to Christianity.
   C. an exile's lament for his country.
   D. an ocean storm off the coast of England.

____ 10. The purpose of a caesura in a line of Anglo-Saxon poetry is to
   A. remind a scop what to say.
   B. provide a metaphorical name for something.
   C. indicate a pause for breath.
   D. mark the four beats in the line.

____ 11. What initiated the wife's exile in "The Wife's Lament"?
   A. her husband's long absence
   B. a plot by her husband's kinsmen
   C. her traveling in spite of her husband's wishes
   D. the lord of that region issuing a formal decree

____ 12. When reading Anglo-Saxon poetry, how does recognizing historical context help a reader understand why certain things occur?
   A. It gives the reader clues about the situation in the time period in which it was written.
   B. It helps readers restate in their own words what the poem says.
   C. It requires readers to use a dictionary to find the meaning of complicated words.
   D. It shows the reader how important correct spelling and grammar are.

____ 13. What is the reason, despite all the hardships he's suffered, that the narrator in "The Seafarer" continues to follow the life of the sea?
   A. weary fatalism
   B. passionate curiosity
   C. religious vision
   D. material need

____ 14. Which element in "The Seafarer" is most characteristic of lyric poetry?
   A. regular rhythm and rhyme
   B. strong reliance on figurative language
   C. intense personal emotion
   D. narrative structure

Vocabulary and Grammar

____ 15. Which is the best meaning of the italicized word in this sentence?
   The Wife initially felt *rapture* when she was with her husband.

   A. joy   C. fear
   B. anxiety   D. boredom

____ 16. An appropriate word to describe the disasters the Wanderer experienced is _____.
   A. grievous   C. compassionate
   B. rancor   D. admonish

____ 17. Which is the best meaning of the italicized word in the phrase "Are *fervent* with life"?
   A. frightful   C. cautious
   B. cowardly   D. passionate

____ 18. The word that means the same as *admonish* is _____.
   A. scold   C. counsel
   B. remove   D. replace

Essay

19. A fundamental Anglo-Saxon belief is that human life is shaped by fate. How is this belief reflected in the poems in this section? Answer this question in an essay, giving examples from one or more of the poems to support your explanation.

20. Most of the poems and stories of the Anglo-Saxon period were passed along by the oral tradition. In an essay, tell how the use of features such as the kenning and caesura may have helped maintain this oral tradition. Illustrate your explanation with examples from the selections.

21. **Thinking About the Essential Question: Does a sense of place shape literature or does literature shape a sense of place?** In the three texts, "The Seafarer," "The Wanderer," and "The Wife's Lament," the speaker has lost his or her home. Choose one poem, and in an essay, describe the home the speaker has lost. Then explain how the imagined home influences the poem as a whole.

Name _____ Date _____

From the Translator's Desk
Burton Raffel Introduces *Beowulf*

DIRECTIONS: *Use the space provided to answer the questions.*

1. According to Burton Raffel, who or what drives the plot of *Beowulf*?

   _____

   _____

2. What are two magical qualities that the hero Beowulf possesses?

   _____

   _____

3. What are three ways that Beowulf's name tells us that he is no mere human being?

   _____

   _____

   _____

   _____

4. According to Raffel, how does the author of *Beowulf* create suspense at the start of the poem?

   _____

   _____

   _____

   _____

5. Why does Grendel's mother enter the narrative?

   _____

   _____

6. According to Raffel, how does the fire-breathing dragon contrast with a good king like Beowulf?

   _____

   _____

7. What arguments does Raffel use to support his claim that *Beowulf* is "very much an Old Testament poem"? Do you find these arguments persuasive? Why or why not?

   _____

   _____

   _____

   _____

   _____

   _____

Burton Raffel
Listening and Viewing

Segment 1: Meet Burton Raffel
- What does Burton Raffel attempt to do to a poem that he translates?
- When discussing translation, Raffel quotes Ezra Pound: "You don't translate what a man says; you translate what a man means." Do you agree or disagree with Pound? Explain.

_____

_____

_____

_____

Segment 2: Burton Raffel on Beowulf
- Why is *Beowulf* a culturally significant poem that we still read today?

_____

_____

_____

_____

Segment 3: The Writing Process
- What are the steps that Burton Raffel goes through while translating a text into English?
- Why do you think it is important to follow such a rigorous method when translating?

_____

_____

_____

_____

Segment 4: The Rewards of Writing
- According to Burton Raffel, why are translations important to society?
- What do you think you could learn from translated literature?

_____

_____

_____

_____

Vocabulary Warm-up Word Lists

Study these words from the selection. Then, complete the activities.

Word List A

mail [MAYL] *n.* armor made of connected metal rings, or loops of chain
   The museum displayed chain <u>mail</u> that was designed to protect a horse.

fleeing [FLEE ing] *adj.* running away; vanishing
   When it rained on the baseball field, the <u>fleeing</u> players ran to the dugouts.

boast [BOHST] *v.* speak with excessive pride; brag
   The team captain told his players not to <u>boast</u> even though they were undefeated.

inherited [in HER i tid] *v.* received property from a person by a will
   Mary <u>inherited</u> an antique silver tea service from her grandmother.

feud [FYOOD] *n.* a long, bitter quarrel, especially between families
   The man refused to enter the store because his family was in a <u>feud</u> with the owner's family.

protector [proh TEK ter] *n.* someone or something who guards others from harm
   Joe never got into any fights at school because his older brother was his <u>protector</u>.

truce [TROOS] *n.* an agreement to stop fighting
   The two countries signed a <u>truce</u> agreeing not to fight during the holiday.

swayed [SWAYD] *v.* shifted from side to side; rocked back and forth
   The dancers <u>swayed</u> with the music, moving back and forth.

Word List B

deserted [de ZURT id] *v.* abandoned; empty of people
   After the guests all left the party, the house felt <u>deserted</u>.

threshold [THRESH ohld] *n.* an entranceway
   The guide welcomed the visitors from the <u>threshold</u> of the restored Victorian house.

relished [REL ishd] *v.* enjoyed; found pleasure in
   The restaurant critic <u>relished</u> the opportunity to write a favorable review.

groped [GROHPD] *v.* reached or felt around uncertainly, as in a search
   After the lights went out, they <u>groped</u> around in the dark trying to find a candle.

comrades [KAHM radz] *n.* companions; friends
   Soldiers sometimes refer to each other as "<u>comrades</u> in arms."

sought [SAWT] *v.* looked for
   The librarian <u>sought</u> an out-of-print book by a local author.

dissolved [di ZAHLVD] *v.* melted away; transformed into liquid
   The lemonade mix <u>dissolved</u> quickly when water was added to it.

uttered [UHT terd] *v.* spoke; expressed verbally
   No one in the group <u>uttered</u> a word as they recorded the music tracks for their demo.

from Beowulf, translated by Burton Raffel
Vocabulary Warm-up Exercises

Exercise A *Fill in each blank in the paragraph with the appropriate word from Word List A.*

Many illustrations depict dragons as green, scaly reptiles with wings and claws. Typically, they are shown battling medieval knights that are dressed in chain

[1] _____. Sometimes these mythological creatures perched on top of a

priceless, stolen treasure, acting as its [2] _____. According to legend,

attacking the dragon was tricky, since it moved quickly. You can imagine its hypnotic

movements as it [3] _____ from side to side. Dragons liked to

[4] _____ about their incredible strength, hoping to frighten the hero.

Once angered, the creature sought revenge, breathing fire and chasing after

[5] _____ villagers. If the dragon could not be overpowered, it had to be

outsmarted. However, negotiating a [6] _____ with the dragon was

almost impossible. Defeating the dragon could be part of a larger battle or an ongoing

[7] _____ that has raged for centuries. Often, the hero had

[8] _____ his mission from previous generations.

Exercise B *Decide whether each statement below is true or false. Circle* T *or* F, *and explain your answers.*

Example: T / F The actor relished the role, so he did not mind the pay cut.
  T If the actor relished the role, then he might not mind a pay cut.

1. After all visitors left the museum, it was no longer deserted.
   T / F _____

2. The chlorine dissolved quickly when added to the water in the pool.
   T / F _____

3. It was easy to see the exit, so they groped their way out of the theater.
   T / F _____

4. Traditionally, the groom carries his bride over the threshold of their new home.
   T / F _____

5. The students uttered their thoughts while they kept silent.
   T / F _____

6. The decorator sought brand-new furniture at antique shops.
   T / F _____

7. The recruit's comrades were all much older and more experienced than he was.
   T / F _____

Name _____ Date _____

from **Beowulf,** translated by Burton Raffel
Reading Warm-up A

Read the following passage. Pay special attention to the underlined words. Then, read it again, and complete the activities. Use a separate sheet of paper for your written answers.

Mail is body armor made from chain links woven together to form a metal fabric. It is then fashioned into gloves, hoods, shirts, and leggings that cover the entire body from head to toe. From the time of the Roman conquest until the mid-fourteenth century, mail was the best available defense against the sword and lance that dominated hand-to-hand combat.

The metal mesh allowed the warrior flexibility as he lifted his weapon or swayed to avoid an enemy's blade. However, mail was not a protector from the piecing power of a crossbow bolt or a bullet. By the end of the 1600s, mail was no longer used for protection.

Because it was so expensive, mail was worn only by the wealthiest warriors. The cost did not come from the material, but from the time required to assemble it. Tiny rings made from short lengths of iron or steel wire were fastened together with a small rivet. Next, the clusters of rings were attached together to form a seamless garment. The typical knight also wore a solid helmet and a breastplate, and carried a shield.

Knights would boast about ornate armor since it indicated wealth and position. Mail might be something a knight inherited from his father and then passed on to his own offspring. However, armor was also taken as bounty or offered as part of a truce when a battle or feud ended.

The knights of the Crusades wore chain mail armor. Although it wasn't as heavy as plate armor, it still weighed more than the leather armor worn by the Moors. The lighter leather gave the Moors and their horses much greater mobility on the battlefield. Even when fleeing, they had an advantage.

1. Circle the words that describe what mail is made of. Then, explain why *mail* offered a good defense.

2. Rewrite the sentence using a phrase that means the same as swayed. Then, tell what *swayed* means.

3. What is a likely reason mail did not serve as a protector from a bullet? Explain what *protector* means.

4. Circle the words that tell why knights would boast about their ornate armor. Then, tell what *boast* means.

5. Circle the words that tell from whom a knight inherited mail. Why might it be helpful to have *inherited* mail?

6. Underline the phrase that is a clue to the meaning of truce. Why might some battles end with a *truce* instead of a victory?

7. Circle the word that is a clue to the meaning of feud. Explain how a *feud* might differ from a war.

8. Rewrite the sentence using a synonym for fleeing. Describe something you have seen *fleeing*.

from **Beowulf,** translated by Burton Raffel
Reading Warm-up B

Read the following passage. Pay special attention to the underlined words. Then, read it again, and complete the activities. Use a separate sheet of paper for your written answers.

Brian and his brother Brendan were on a family vacation in Ireland when they came upon a magnificent medieval castle in the city of Trim. The enormous fortress had been featured in a Hollywood film, and they <u>relished</u> the chance to explore it.

They approached its thick, stony walls and entered, crossing its massive <u>threshold</u>. To their surprise, there were no guards on duty and no admission fee. The castle was open to the public and treated as a local park with plaques describing the various battles that had been fought there. The castle itself was almost <u>deserted</u>, with no one around except for the neighborhood dogs playing in the wide courtyard and the horses taking a leisurely drink from the river that flowed nearby.

Sections of the castle had been authentically restored, making it easier for Brian and his brother to imagine what it might have been like to defend it. As they wandered through storage rooms, barracks, and kitchens, neither <u>uttered</u> a word for almost an hour. They were overwhelmed by the amount of history that had taken place in that one stronghold.

Next, they <u>groped</u> their way up a narrow, winding, stone stairway, wondering how hordes of armed soldiers and their <u>comrades</u> could have navigated these steps while a battle raged. Brendan decided that accidents had to have been a common occurrence.

Moving further inside the castle, they <u>sought</u> and then found the lavish private chambers that had been occupied by royalty. Once they took in the simple, wooden furnishings that decorated these rooms, all the images of grandeur in their heads quickly <u>dissolved</u>. They were convinced that life in this rugged castle was like life on the frontier: a constant struggle with hardships, enemies, and nature.

1. Tell why Brian and Brendan <u>relished</u> the chance to explore the medieval castle. Then, tell what *relished* means.

2. Circle the words that are a clue to the meaning of <u>threshold</u>. Describe something that might cover or mark a *threshold*.

3. Circle the phrase that is a clue to the meaning of <u>deserted</u>. Use *deserted* in a sentence.

4. Circle the sentence that explains why neither boy <u>uttered</u> a word. Then, explain what *uttered* means.

5. Why might the boys have <u>groped</u> their way up the staircase? Define *groped*.

6. Who were the soldiers' <u>comrades</u>? Use the word *comrades* in a sentence of your own.

7. Circle the words that show the boys were successful as they <u>sought</u> the chambers. What might you have *sought* in the castle?

8. Circle the words that tell what <u>dissolved</u> when the boys saw the furnishings. Then, tell what *dissolved* means.

from **Beowulf,** translated by Burton Raffel
Literary Analysis: The Epic/The Legendry Hero

The **epic** *Beowulf* is a long narrative poem that recounts the exploits of the legendary warrior Beowulf. Like other **legendary heros,** Beowulf represents good and earns glory by struggling against the forces of evil represented by several monstrous creatures. He represents the values of his nation, culture, and religion. *Beowulf* is a typical epic poem in its serious tone and elevated language, which portrays characters, action, and setting in terms larger and grander than life. The use of **kennings,** two-word metaphorical names for familiar things, is also a particular characteristic of Anglo-Saxon poetry.

DIRECTIONS: *Read each passage from* Beowulf. *Then list the characteristics of epic poetry and legendary hero represented in it.*

1. So mankind's enemy continued his crimes, / Killing as often as he could, coming / Alone, bloodthirsty and horrible. Though he lived / In Herot, when the night hid him, he never / Dared to touch king Hrothgar's glorious / Throne, protected by God—God, / Whose love Grendel could not know. . . .

_____

_____

_____

_____

2. "Hail Hrothgar! / Higlac is my cousin and my king; the days / Of my youth have been filled with glory. Now Grendel's / Name has echoed in our land: sailors / Have brought us stories of Herot, the best / Of all mead-halls, deserted and useless when the moon / Hangs in skies the sun had lit, / Light and life fleeing together. / My people have said, the wisest, most knowing / And best of them, that my duty was to go to the Danes' / Great king. They have seen my strength for themselves, / Have watched me rise from the darkness of war. . . ."

_____

_____

_____

_____

3. "Grant me, then, / Lord and protector of this noble place, / A single request! I have come so far, / O shelterer of warriors and your people's loved friend, / That this one favor you should not refuse me— / That I, alone and with the help of my men, / May purge all evil from this hall."

_____

_____

_____

_____

from **Beowulf,** translated by Burton Raffel
Reading Strategy: Paraphrase

Long sentences and difficult language can make a piece of writing hard to follow. When you encounter such passages, it is important to determine the main ideas. In order to do so, you can **paraphrase** the passage, or restate the main ideas in your own words. Paraphrasing will help you make sure you understand the main point of the passage. Look at this example:

Passage from *Beowulf*	Paraphrased
"I've never known fear, as a youth I fought In endless battles. I am old, now, But I will fight again, seek fame still, If the dragon hiding in his tower dares To face me."	I have been fearless throughout life and will continue to fight if the dragon dares to face me.

DIRECTIONS: *Use this graphic organizer to help you paraphrase difficult passages in* Beowulf. *Each time you come across a difficult passage, write it in the column labeled "Passage from* Beowulf." *Then, write any difficult words from that passage in the appropriate column. Define each difficult word, either by using the words surrounding it to piece together its meaning or by looking it up in the dictionary. Next, determine the key ideas in the passage, and jot these down in the appropriate column. Finally, use the key ideas, along with your understanding of the difficult words, to paraphrase the passage. One passage has already been paraphrased for you.*

Passage from *Beowulf*	Difficult Words	Key Ideas	Paraphrase
No one waited for reparation from his plundering claws: That shadow of death hunted in the darkness, . . .	reparation (making up for wrong or injury) plundering (taking by force, theft, or fraud)	No one expected to be repaid for what Grendel took in his claws. Grendel was a shadow of death hunting in the darkness.	No one expected to be repaid for what Grendel took. He hunted in the darkness.

from **Beowulf,** translated by Burton Raffel
Vocabulary Builder

Word List

loathsome   massive   purge   reparation   solace   writhing

A. DIRECTIONS: *For each underlined word, substitute a word or phrase with the same meaning. Write it in the blank following the sentence.*

1. Only a hero of Beowulf's strength could hope to lift the <u>massive</u> sword in Grendel's battle hall.

   _____

2. The third monster, most <u>loathsome</u> of all, had eight eyes on stalks and was covered with slime.

   _____

3. Most epic heroes strive to <u>purge</u> the world of wicked beings.

   _____

4. Snakes can move rapidly with their <u>writhing</u> form of locomotion.

   _____

5. The badly defeated warrior found <u>solace</u> in the affection of his family.

   _____

6. The captured bandits were ordered to give gold to their victims as <u>reparation</u>.

   _____

B. WORD STUDY: *The root -sol- comes from the Latin* solari, *meaning "to comfort." Explain how the root -sol- influences the meaning of the underlined word in each sentence.*

1. Before Beowulf arrived, Hrothgar and his Danes were <u>disconsolate</u> over the deeds of Grendel.

   _____

2. He <u>consoled</u> his little daughter for the loss of her goldfish by promising to buy her a new one.

   _____

3. The Geats grieved <u>inconsolably</u> when the dragon killed their once mighty king, Beowulf.

   _____

4. Although she won the <u>consolation</u> tournament, Allison was disappointed in her performance.

   _____

from **Beowulf,** translated by Burton Raffel

Grammar and Style: Coordinating Conjunctions

A **coordinating conjunction** links two of the same grammatical sentence parts. For example, a coordinating conjunction may link two subjects, two predicates, or two independent clauses. There are seven coordinating conjunctions: *and, but, or, nor, yet, so,* and *for.* Look at these uses of coordinating conjunctions from *Beowulf.*

Passage	Conjunction and Use
. . . The Almighty drove Those demons out, and their exile was bitter, . . .	The coordinating conjunction **and** connects two independent clauses.
. . . [T]heir ears could not hear His praise nor know His glory. . . .	The coordinating conjunction **nor** connects two predicates.

The coordinating conjunctions *yet, so,* and *for* also serve other functions in sentences. To identify them as coordinating conjunctions, make sure they are used to connect two of the same kinds of sentence parts.

Example	Use
Beowulf was brave, yet he was also smart.	*Yet* is used as a coordinating conjunction to connect two independent clauses.
I have not read *Beowulf* yet.	*Yet* is used as an adverb to modify *have read.*
Beowulf volunteers to fight Grendel, for he sees it as his destiny.	*For* is used as a coordinating conjunction to connect two independent clauses.
I bought a copy of *Beowulf* for two dollars.	*For* is used as a preposition in the phrase *for two dollars.*

A. PRACTICE: *Underline each coordinating conjunction in these lines from* Beowulf. *Tell what sentence parts it connects.*

1. The high hall rang, its roof boards swayed,/And Danes shook with terror.

   _____

2. . . . [T]hey could hack at Grendel/From every side, trying to open
   A path for his evil soul, but their points/Could not hurt him. . . .

   _____

3. . . . [T]he sharpest and hardest iron/Could not scratch at his skin, for that sin-stained demon
   Had bewitched all men's weapons. . . .

   _____

B. Writing Application: *Write a sentence for each of the coordinating conjunctions* for, so, *and* yet. *Make sure you use each as a coordinating conjunction.*

1. _____

2. _____

3. _____

Name _____ Date _____

from **Beowulf**, translated by Burton Raffel
Integrated Language Skills: Support for Writing

Use the chart below to organize your ideas for creating your job application. Think about the qualifications for the job. Also, consider the characteristics Beowulf possesses that fit the job.

Job Description	
Qualifications Required	
Beowulf's Characteristics	

On a separate page, draft a job application as Beowulf's. Highlight qualifications that are required for the job of battling Grendel. Keep in mind that your audience is a king.

Name _____ Date _____

from **Beowulf,** translated by Burton Raffel
Enrichment: Film Portrayals of Monsters

For thousands of years, evil monsters have played an important role in the world's literature. Today, monsters continue to thrive—until a hero comes along—on movie screens and television sets. You have probably enjoyed a number of frightening monster films and videos from the safety of your living room or local movie theater. You may even have your own favorite monsters—ones that were effectively presented and gave you a particularly "good scare."

DIRECTIONS: *Think about the creatures of doom and darkness that you have seen in films and videos. Include aliens from outer space and psychological human monsters, as well as the more "old-fashioned" sort. Make a chart like the one shown here. List your favorite monsters in the first column. Then fill in the other columns with information about each monster. Use the information in your chart to help you consider how you would present Grendel in a film or video version of* Beowulf. *Write a description using scenes from the poem in which you present your ideas. You may also want to add sketches showing Grendel's appearance, as well as viewpoints and camera angles.*

Movie Monster	How shown? A clear image or a shadowy impression?	From what point of view is it filmed? Hero's? Victim's? Monster's?	How is sound used to present the monster?	Why is the monster frightening and effective?

Name _____ Date _____

from **Beowulf** Translated by Burton Raffel
Open-Book Test

Short Answer *Write your response to the questions in this section on the lines provided.*

1. How can you tell that Beowulf is a legendary hero?

   _____

   _____

2. In *Beowulf,* what does the poet mean when he says that the monster's "Thoughts were as quick as his greed or his claws"?

   _____

   _____

   _____

3. What aspect of Beowulf's battle with Grendel tells you that Beowulf is honorable?

   _____

   _____

4. Beowulf gives Wiglaf his gold necklace. What does this gesture mean? Explain.

   _____

   _____

   _____

5. In *Beowulf,* the poet states that the warriors fighting Grendel are "trying to open/A path for his evil soul." What is the poet saying?

   _____

   _____

6. In the Venn diagram below, compare and contrast the characters of Beowulf and Wiglaf. Write their differences in the parts of the circles that do not overlap. Write their similarities in the parts of the circles that overlap.

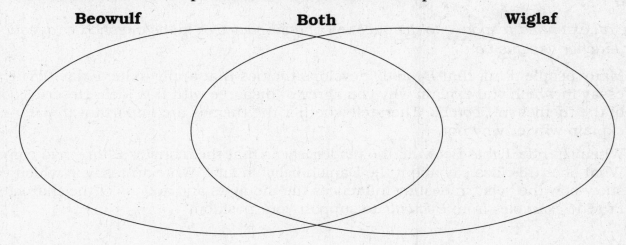

Beowulf   **Both**   **Wiglaf**

43

7. How does the watchman's opinion of Beowulf in lines 158–165 illustrate the warrior's role as a legendary hero?

_____

_____

_____

_____

8. After Beowulf's death, the Geats build a tower to memorialize him. Why is this action ironic?

_____

_____

_____

_____

9. What provides *solace* for the characters in *Beowulf*, according to the poet? Focus on the meaning of *solace* in your response.

_____

_____

_____

_____

10. Beowulf requests that he alone "*purge* all evil from this hall." What does he want to do?

_____

_____

_____

_____

Essay

Write an extended response to the question of your choice or to the question or questions your teacher assigns you.

11. Many people think that *Beowulf* develops themes that apply to life today. Write an essay in which you explain why you agree or disagree with this idea. Describe some of the themes in *Beowulf*. Then tell whether the themes are important to you and explain why or why not.

12. When Grendel fights Beowulf, the reader learns that the monster's "time had come." What does this idea say about the Danish belief in fate? Write an essay in which you show how the belief in destiny influences the thoughts and actions of the characters. Provide examples from *Beowulf* to support your position.

13. The hero of an epic poem usually embodies the ideals of conduct that are valued by the culture in which the epic was composed. Write an essay in which you show how Beowulf embodies the ideas of Anglo-Saxon culture. Mention at least four of Beowulf's virtues, citing the part or parts of the epic in which the virtue is displayed.

14. **Thinking About the Essential Question: Do writers influence social trends or just reflect them?** Beowulf's behavior tells readers much about the way Anglo-Saxons viewed heroism. In an essay, explain whether you think the author of the work intended the portrayal of Beowulf as a reflection of the culture's idea of heroism or as a lesson on how heroes should behave. Use examples from the poem to support your opinion.

Oral Response

15. Go back to questions 2, 6, 7, or to the question your teacher assigns to you. Take a few minutes to expand your answer and prepare an oral response. Find additional details in *Beowulf* that will support your points. If necessary, make notes to guide your response.

from **Beowulf,** translated by Burton Raffel
Selection Test A

Critical Reading *Identify the letter of the choice that best answers the question.*

____ 1. How can you tell that Beowulf is a legendary hero?
  A. He is the son of a Geat ruler who came to fight in England.
  B. He is a soldier who fought in battles long ago.
  C. He is larger than life and is remembered in tales from long ago.
  D. He believes in honor and loyalty.

____ 2. What does the poet mean in this line from *Beowulf*?
  The monster's / Thoughts were as quick as his greed or his claws. . . .
  A. The monster's thoughts are kind.
  B. The monster thinks very quickly.
  C. The monster has long claws.
  D. The monster is hungry.

____ 3. Why does Beowulf come to see Hrothgar?
  A. He wants to help Hrothgar by killing Grendel.
  B. He has been sent into exile by the king of Geatland.
  C. He needs Hrothgar's help against an enemy.
  D. He comes to seek shelter in Hrothgar's hall.

____ 4. How do you know that Beowulf is an honorable man?
  A. He is willing to risk his life in order to earn fame by killing Grendel.
  B. He is known as a follower and cousin of Higlac.
  C. His father was the great Edgetho, a famous warrior.
  D. He refuses to use a sword to fight Grendel because Grendel has none.

____ 5. What weapon does Beowulf use to kill Grendel?
  A. his sword
  B. his hands
  C. a dagger
  D. a lance

____ 6. To what does the poet give credit for Beowulf's victory over Grendel's mother?
  A. God's judgment
  B. Beowulf's kindness
  C. good luck
  D. Beowulf's powerful grip

Unit 1 Resources: From Legend to History
46

____ 7. What is the theme of *Beowulf*?
   A. The strongest always win.
   B. Evil can never be defeated.
   C. Good always triumphs in the end.
   D. Sometimes everyone needs help.

____ 8. Why does Wiglaf tell his comrades they should help Beowulf fight the dragon?
   A. They had promised to help Beowulf when he needed them.
   B. Together they can win and get the dragon's gold.
   C. Beowulf is too old to fight anymore on his own.
   D. They can share Beowulf's fame if they kill the dragon.

____ 9. What does it mean when Beowulf gives Wiglaf his gold necklace?
   A. Beowulf wants Wiglaf to kill his cowardly companions.
   B. Beowulf realizes Wiglaf is the strongest warrior.
   C. Beowulf is making Wiglaf ruler of Geatland.
   D. Beowulf is rewarding Wiglaf for saving his life.

____ 10. How do you know that *Beowulf* is an epic poem?
   A. It is a poem about terrible monsters and dragons.
   B. It is a long poem that tells a story about a legendary hero.
   C. It tells about real events and real people of long ago.
   D. It was not written down at first but told by storytellers.

____ 11. Read the following quotation from *Beowulf*. What is the best paraphrase for the underlined part of the quotation?

   Their courage / Was great but all wasted: they could hack at Grendel / From every side, trying to open / A path for his evil soul, but their points / Could not hurt him. . . .

   A. opening a door so he could escape
   B. trying to save his soul
   C. stopping him from escaping
   D. attempting to kill him

____ 12. Why does Beowulf want a tower built for him?
   A. to remind people of his life and famous deeds
   B. to warn people not to make war on Geatland
   C. to serve as a landmark for sailors from afar
   D. to protect the treasure that came from the dragon's tower

Vocabulary and Grammar

____ 13. Which word best describes the reason that Beowulf hangs Grendel's arm in Hrothgar's mead-hall?

    A. solace

    B. writhing

    C. reparation

    D. massive

____ 14. In which situation might someone most need *solace*?

    A. a victory over a monster

    B. the discovery of a great treasure

    C. the sight of Grendel's head

    D. the death of a loved one

____ 15. Which of these quotations from the poem contains a coordinating conjunction?

    A. "Then when the darkness had dropped, Grendel . . ."

    B. "Remember,/Hrothgar, O knowing king . . . "

    C. "And sometimes they sacrificed to the old stone gods,"

    D. "How the monster relished his savage war/On the Danes."

Essay

16. Many people think that *Beowulf* develops themes that apply to life today. Write an essay in which you explain why you agree or disagree. Respond to these questions: What are some of the themes in *Beowulf*? Can you see ways in which these themes might be important to you? Why or why not?

17. Some ancient peoples, such as the Germans and Greeks, believed that only by achieving fame and glory will a person be remembered after death. In an essay, tell whether you think this belief is reflected in *Beowulf*. Give at least two examples from *Beowulf* to support your opinion.

18. **Thinking About the Essential Question: Do writers influence social trends or just reflect them?** Beowulf's behavior tells readers much about the way Anglo-Saxons viewed heroism. In an essay, explain the ways the author portrays Beowulf as a hero. Use examples from the poem to support your opinion.

from **Beowulf**, translated by Burton Raffel
Selection Test B

Critical Reading *Identify the letter of the choice that best completes the statement or answers the question.*

____ 1. How can the reader tell that *Beowulf* is a legendary story?
A. It takes place a long time ago.
B. The story involves warriors and battles.
C. The hero is described as someone greater than all other men.
D. The people in the story are called Geats and Danes.

____ 2. Why does Beowulf sail with his chosen companions to Hrothgar's kingdom?
A. to bring home treasures from that rich kingdom
B. to help Hrothgar by destroying a monster
C. to win glory by slaying a fire-breathing dragon
D. to take over Higlac's throne

____ 3. Which of the following lines from *Beowulf* contains an example of kenning?
A. "'Higlac is my cousin and my king; the days/Of my youth have been filled with glory.'"
B. "Their guide reined in his horse, pointing/To that hall, built by Hrothgar for the best / And bravest of his men . . ."
C. "The high hall rang, its roof boards swayed,/And Danes shook with terror."
D. "'. . . I have come so far,/Oh shelterer of warriors and your people's loved friend,/ That this one favor you should not refuse me. . . .'"

____ 4. From which fact can the reader infer that Beowulf is honorable?
A. Beowulf refuses to use weapons because Grendel uses none.
B. Higlac is Beowulf's cousin.
C. Beowulf is the strongest of the Geats.
D. Beowulf vows to ambush Grendel and destroy the monster.

____ 5. What does this line mean?
The monster's/Thoughts were as quick as his greed or his claws. . . . .
A. He is hungry.
B. He has intelligence.
C. He has sharp claws.
D. He is not trustworthy.

____ 6. Which of the following best summarizes the theme of *Beowulf*?
A. Might makes right.
B. Brains are superior to brawn.
C. Wickedness cannot be defeated.
D. Valor will triumph.

____ 7. Which is the best paraphrase of the following passage from the poem?

> So the living sorrow of Healfdane's son/Simmered, bitter and fresh, and no wisdom/Or strength could break it: that agony hung/On king and people alike. . . .

A. Hrothgar felt a strong and unending sorrow that he had no power to overcome. It affected both him and his subjects.

B. The king was in agony and out of his mind because of what his people had done to him.

C. Grendel was furious at the Danes, and so he inflicted great pain on the king and his people.

D. Hrothgar felt an endless sorrow he couldn't get rid of.

____ 8. Wiglaf thinks he and his comrades should help Beowulf fight the dragon because

A. Beowulf is too old and sick to fight.

B. it will increase Beowulf's chance of victory.

C. then Beowulf's comrades can claim the monster's treasure.

D. in the past they had promised to repay Beowulf's kindness with their lives.

____ 9. When the dying Beowulf gives Wiglaf his gold necklace, the gesture means that

A. Beowulf has captured the monster's treasure.

B. Beowulf wants Wiglaf to kill his comrades.

C. Beowulf recognizes Wiglaf's superior strength in battle.

D. Beowulf is passing on the rulership of Geatland to Wiglaf.

____ 10. Which of the following lines from *Beowulf* contains an example of a caesura?

A. ". . . Hidden evil before hidden evil."

B. ". . . Burns like a torch. No one knows its bottom . . ."

C. ". . . And golden cups and the glorious banner . . ."

D. ". . . And struck at the dragon's scaly hide."

____ 11. Why is it ironic that after his death the Geats build a tower to memorialize Beowulf?

A. Beowulf requested that the tower be built.

B. The treasure is left in the tower.

C. Beowulf's body has been cremated.

D. Most of the Geats had deserted him in battle.

____ 12. Which phrase best paraphrases the underlined words in this quotation from the poem?

> . . . they could hack at Grendel/From every side, trying to open/A path for his evil soul, but their points/Could not hurt him. . . ."

A. to kill him

B. to drive him out of the hall

C. to turn his soul to God

D. to help him escape

____ 13. When used to describe Beowulf, the phrase "noble protector of all seamen" is an example of

A. a caesura.

B. a wyrd.

C. a kenning.

D. an alliteration.

Unit 1 Resources: From Legend to History

Vocabulary and Grammar

____ 14. When Beowulf requests that he alone "May purge all evil from this hall," what does he mean by *purge*?
A. drive out
B. overcome
C. cleanse
D. bury

____ 15. Which of the following passages contains a coordinating conjunction?
A. "A powerful monster, living down/In the darkness, growled in pain, impatient/As day after day the music rang/Loud in that hall. . . ."
B. And sometimes they sacrificed to the old stone gods,/Made heathen vows, hoping for Hell's/Support. . . ."
C. ". . . sailors/Have brought us stories of Herot, the best/Of all mead-halls, deserted and useless . . ."
D. ". . . He was spawned in that slime,/Conceived by a pair of those monsters born/Of Cain. . . ."

____ 16. Which of the following passages contains a coordinating conjunction?
A. "Hrothgar's wise men had fashioned Herot/To stand forever . . . ."
B. "The monster's hatred rose higher,/But his power had gone."
C. "He came to, ripped him apart . . ."
D. "Beowufl,/A prince of the Geats, had killed Grendel. . . ."

____ 17. Which of these words best fits the image of the dragon presented in this quotation?
. . . The dragon/Coiled and uncoiled, its heart urging it/Into battle. . . .
A. writhing
B. purging
C. massive
D. loathsome

Essay

18. The pagan Germans, Greeks, and other ancient peoples believed that fame and glory are the only things that will survive a human being's death. What evidence do you find in this poem of the importance placed on a person's public reputation? Write an essay in which you use examples from the poem to support your answer.

19. The hero of an epic poem normally embodies the ideals of conduct that are most valued by the culture in which the epic was composed. Write an essay in which you show how Beowulf embodies the ideals of conduct in the Anglo-Saxon culture. You should mention at least four of Beowulf's virtues. For each one, cite the part or parts of the epic where the virtue is displayed.

20. **Thinking About the Essential Question: Do writers influence social trends or just reflect them?** Beowulf's behavior tells readers much about the way Anglo-Saxons viewed heroism. In an essay, explain whether you think the author of the work intended the portrayal of Beowulf as a reflection of the culture's idea of heroism or as a lesson on how heroes should behave. Use examples from the poem to support your opinion.

Study these words from the selections. Then, complete the activities.

Word List A

amber [AM ber] *n.* hard, semiclear yellow or orange natural resin
Her yellow bracelet is made of amber, not plastic.

breadth [BREDTH] *n.* width
The breadth of many doorways is 30 inches.

climate [KLY muht] *n.* ordinary or average weather conditions of a place
The mild, rainy climate in England is perfect for growing roses.

extracted [ek STRAK tid] *v.* drew out; pulled out
He extracted a confession from the criminal.

fortified [FAWRT uh fyd] *adj.* strengthened against military attack
The fortified walls of the castle were three feet thick.

horizon [huh RY zuhn] *n.* the line where the earth and sky seem to meet
At sunset, the sun appears to move below the horizon.

lingers [LIN guhrz] *v.* continues to stay
Sometimes a customer lingers and must be asked to leave when a shop is closing.

twilight [TWY lyt] *n.* early evening; the soft light at the end of the day
After sunset, I could barely see my friend's face in the dim twilight.

Word List B

abounding [uh BOWND ing] *adj.* plentiful; having great numbers
After all the rain this summer, my garden is abounding with tomatoes.

boundary [BOWN dree] *n.* border; edge; thing separating two places
That river is the boundary between Texas and Mexico.

consequently [KAHN si kwent lee] *adv.* as a result
The movie received good reviews; consequently, people wanted to see it.

corrupted [kuh RUPT id] *v.* deteriorated from what is good, normal, or standard
People corrupted the phrase for "day's eye" into the word "daisy."

immunity [i MYOON uh tee] *n.* protection from being punished or harmed
The prosecutor offered the criminal immunity from the charges.

migrated [MY grayt id] *v.* moved from one place to settle in another
Millions migrated from Europe to the United States.

pasturage [PAS che rij] *n.* pasture; food like hay or grass for cattle and other farm animals
Sky Ranch has a hundred acres of good pasturage for its sheep.

scalding [SKAWLD ing] *adj.* heated almost to the boiling point
When the scalding coffee spilled, the waitress jumped back to avoid getting burned.

from A History of the English Church and People by Bede
Vocabulary Warm-up Exercises

Exercise A *Fill in the blanks, using each word from Word List A only once.*

The Age of the Vikings began in the late 700s when raiding Norwegians began attacking Scotland and Ireland. During these raids, the Vikings looted monasteries and [1] _____ valuable objects from them, including some decorated with pearls, [2] _____, and other precious stones. It was the custom to bury a Viking with his possessions, so evidence of these long-ago thefts [3] _____ in Viking burial sites. Successful Viking attacks required fast ships and a favorable [4] _____. The eighth century had mild winters that made long sea voyages possible. Vikings found their way across the [5] _____ of the ocean by using a few different techniques, such as observing the point where the sun rose and set on the [6] _____. As soon as [7] _____ came, they would land, leaving their boats. After conquering an area, the Vikings established their own [8] _____ settlements.

Exercise B *Answer each question in a complete sentence. In each answer, use the word from Word List B that means the same as the underlined word or words.*

Example: Does the milk have to be <u>near boiling</u> before you can make pudding? (scalding) *The milk should be <u>scalding</u> before you make pudding.*

1. Why did the farmer put "No Hunting" signs along the <u>border</u> of his property?

   _____

2. Did American pioneers use covered wagons as they <u>moved</u> west?

   _____

3. Are some criminals given <u>protection from punishment</u>?

   _____

4. If you never water your garden, is it likely to be <u>filled</u> with flowers?

   _____

5. If a judge accepts a bribe or payoff, has he been <u>changed from what is good</u>?

   _____

6. If you witness a car accident, are you, <u>as a result</u>, expected to wait to tell police what you saw?

   _____

7. Could livestock thrive without <u>grasslands to eat</u>?

   _____

Name _____ Date _____

from A History of the English Church and People by Bede
Reading Warm-up A

Read the following passage. Then, complete the activities.

Early British peoples have left behind relics of their communities, including tools, silver, gold, and <u>amber</u> jewelry, pottery, and other objects. But perhaps the most famous remainder of Britain's early peoples is the remarkable Stonehenge.

Stonehenge is a combination of manmade mounds and a circle of huge stones. It was built in stages between 3000 B.C. and 1600 B.C. on Salisbury Plain in southern England.

No explanation of the original purpose served by Stonehenge has been conclusively verified. But scholars have <u>extracted</u> a lot of information about Stonehenge, drawing out their facts from studying the position of its stones. It is clear this was not intended to be a <u>fortified</u> place, strengthened against attack from a warring people. Instead, the stones were arranged to mark events in the sky. On the summer solstice, one stone lines up with the rising sun just as the sun crosses the <u>horizon</u> and becomes visible over the rim of the Earth. The stones also line up with the moon and the stars at various times. Stonehenge may also have been used as a temple for ceremonies held in the dim light of <u>twilight</u>. However, the mystery of Stonehenge has not yet been solved and <u>lingers</u> still, continuing to puzzle scientists.

What is certain is that the construction process required great labor, time, and skill. Stones had to be transported for miles across the land, an incredible feat. Many of the stones were more than thirteen feet in height, seven feet in <u>breadth</u>, and more than three feet thick.

Over time, some stones have been stolen and put to other uses. The rainy <u>climate</u> and the thousands of visitors have caused additional damage. Access to the site is now regulated. Stonehenge has been designated a World Heritage Site by the United Nations.

1. Circle the word that tells what was made of <u>amber</u>. Then, describe *amber*.

2. Underline the words that tell what was <u>extracted</u>. Write a sentence using the word *extracted*.

3. Underline the words that give a clue to the meaning of the word <u>fortified</u>. What is the opposite of *fortified*?

4. Circle the word that tells what crosses the <u>horizon</u>. Then, tell what *horizon* means.

5. Underline the words that describe <u>twilight</u>. Then, explain what *twilight* is.

6. Circle the words that tell what <u>lingers</u>. Then, underline the words that tell why it *lingers*.

7. Circle the words that describe the <u>breadth</u> of many stones. Give a synonym for *breadth*.

8. Circle the word that is a clue to the meaning of the word <u>climate</u>. What word could be substituted for the word *climate* in this sentence?

from **A History of the English Church and People** by Bede
Reading Warm-up B

Read the following passage. Then, complete the activities.

Experts believe that people of the Stone Age <u>migrated</u> to Britain by crossing a land bridge that joined the island to the rest of Europe. When the land bridge was eventually submerged under the Atlantic Ocean, Britain became isolated from Europe. Access to the island was available to outsiders only by sea. <u>Consequently</u>, the developing culture of the new inhabitants was less apt to be <u>corrupted</u> or otherwise altered, for better or worse, by foreign influences.

The original settlers were mainly hunters and gatherers, but some were sophisticated enough to build the great stone circle at Stonehenge. By 1100 B.C., the inhabitants of Britain had developed permanent settlements. The stone circles were abandoned, and hill forts were constructed to protect villages.

Cultivating fields <u>abounding</u> with crops, so there was plenty of food, became the mainstay of daily life. Livestock in these agricultural communities grazed on abundant <u>pasturage</u>. The introduction of iron tools made farming easier. Iron pots facilitated treatment of animal skins so they could be made into clothing, shoes, and pouches. The skins were plunged into <u>scalding</u> hot liquid and then scraped free of flesh.

By the first century A.D., Britain consisted of a series of small kingdoms. Lacking unity, it was vulnerable to the invasion by Roman soldiers in 43 A.D. The Romans quickly established a civil government, which meant that many Britons were probably able to live with <u>immunity</u> from war, safe from violence and disorder. The Romans built a network of well-engineered roads across the country. They also constructed a fortification, called Hadrian's Wall, to guard the northern border and mark the <u>boundary</u> between territory ruled by Rome and the dangerous, untamed territory to the north. The wall was started in 122 A.D., but parts of it still stand today.

1. Circle the word that tells where people <u>migrated</u>. Then, rewrite the sentence using a word or phrase that means the same as *migrated*.

2. Underline the sentence that provides a reason for using the word <u>consequently</u> in this passage. Write a new sentence, or a pair of sentences, using the word *consequently*.

3. Underline what was less likely to be <u>corrupted</u>. Then, write down one or two words that mean the opposite of *corrupted*.

4. Circle the word that tells what was <u>abounding</u> in the fields. Then, give a synonym for *abounding*.

5. Circle the words that explain what <u>pasturage</u> was used for. Do you think agricultural *pasturage* has changed much since then? Write a sentence explaining why or why not.

6. Underline the word that is a clue to <u>scalding</u>. Then, explain why *scalding* liquid might be used to clean skins.

7. Circle the word that is a key to the meaning of <u>immunity</u>. Then, give a synonym for *immunity*.

8. Underline the word that has the same meaning as <u>boundary</u>. Then, explain what the Romans did to mark the *boundary*.

Unit 1 Resources: From Legend to History
55

from **A History of the English Church and People** by Bede
Literary Analysis: Historical Writing

A **historical writing** is a factual narrative or record of past events, gathered through observation and outside, or secondary, sources. In the excerpts from *The History of the English Church and People*, the author does not reveal his sources, but most probably used his own observations, documents in court or monastic libraries, and stories he heard from others (many probably handed down orally for generations).

DIRECTIONS: *On the lines following each quotation, write what source or sources the author might have used to gather information. Comment on the probable accuracy of the quotation.*

1. "The original inhabitants of the island were the Britons, from whom it takes its name, and who, according to tradition, crossed into Britain from Armorica. . . ."

   _____

   _____

   _____

2. ". . . it is said that some Picts from Scythia put to sea in a few long ships and were driven by storms around the coasts of Britain, arriving at length on the north coast of Ireland. Here they found the nation of the Scots, from whom they asked permission to settle, but their request was refused."

   _____

   _____

   _____

3. In agreeing to allow the Picts to take Scottish wives, the Scots said that ". . . they (Picts) should choose a king from the female (Scottish) royal line rather than the male."

   _____

   _____

   _____

4. "In fact, almost everything in this isle enjoys immunity to poison, and I have heard that folk suffering from snakebite have drunk water in which scrapings from the leaves of books from Ireland had been steeped, and that this remedy checked the spreading poison and reduced the swelling."

   _____

   _____

   _____

from **A History of the English Church and People** by Bede
Reading Strategy: Achieving a Purpose in Nonfiction

Authors of nonfiction write to **achieve a purpose,** whether it be to persuade, to entertain, or to inform. As a reader, your job is to determine the nonfiction writer's purpose and decide whether the author achieves that purpose. To evaluate the author's work, you must look at the way he or she uses language, style, syntax, and rhetorical devices. Consider how these elements of nonfiction contribute to expressing the author's purpose.

A. DIRECTIONS: *Read the first paragraph of the excerpt from* A History of the English Church and People. *Answer the following questions about the paragraph to determine and evaluate the author's purpose.*

1. What kind of content does Bede include in this paragraph? _____
   _____

2. How would you describe his language choice and style? _____
   _____

3. How does his use of rhetorical devices, for example, a quotation of Saint Basil, contribute to his purpose? _____
   _____

B. DIRECTIONS: *Use a graphic organizer like the one here as you read the excerpt from* A History of the English Church and People. *Record elements that strike you as you read. Explain how these elements contribute to or distract from Bede's purpose.*

Purpose:		
Nonfiction Element	**Example**	**Contribution**
Language and Style	Britain, formerly known as Albion, is an island in the ocean. . . .	Provides straightforward information in a formal style
Syntax		
Rhetorical Devices		

from A History of the English Church and People by Bede
Vocabulary Builder

Word List

cultivated   immunity   innumerable   migrated   promontories

A. DIRECTIONS: *Write the word from the Word List that best completes each sentence.*

1. _____ people lined up to shake the king's hand.
2. Some plants provide _____ against particular diseases.
3. Lookouts were posted at all the _____.
4. The farmer _____ the land to ensure a high yield of crops.
5. Many people _____ south during the winter to avoid the cold.

B. DIRECTIONS: *Put a check mark in the blank next to the synonym for the underlined word or phrase in the sentence.*

___ 1. According to Bede there were <u>a vast number of</u> wonderful things in Ireland.
  A. hallowed
  B. ravaged
  C. innumerable
  D. stranded

___ 2. Many people <u>moved</u> to other countries during World War II.
  A. promontories
  B. cultivated
  C. migrated
  D. immunity

___ 3. The lighthouses were perched along the <u>cliffs above the ocean</u>.
  A. promontories
  B. furlongs
  C. cockles
  D. barricades

___ 4. The doctor showed his <u>resistance</u> to the disease by remaining healthy through the epidemic.
  A. promontories
  B. innumerable
  C. migrated
  D. immunity

Name _____ Date _____

from **A History of the English Church and People** by Bede
Integrated Language Skills: Support for Writing

Use the web below to organize your information about the history of Britain and your ideas for development based on Bede's report in *A History of the English Church and People*. Consider the country's population, resources, and geography as you gather ideas for your business memo.

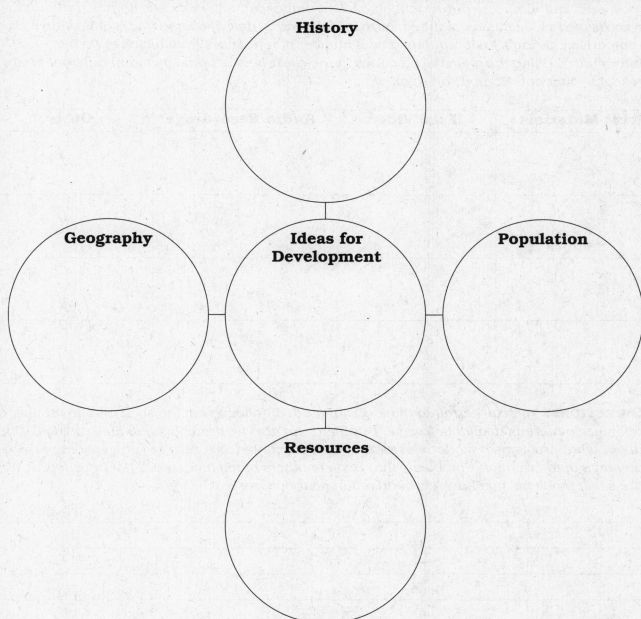

Use a separate page to draft a business memo that clearly and succinctly states your proposal for Britain's development. Be sure to use the proper memo format for your draft.

Name _____ Date _____

Enrichment: Career as a Historian

A. DIRECTIONS: *When historical works such as Bede's* A History of the English Church and People *were being written, historians had few reference materials at their disposal. For the most part, authors were dependent on ancient manuscripts in monastic libraries; annual records of such events as planting, births, and deaths; and of course, the oral tradition. By comparison, today's historian has a vast number of references from which to gather information. Using the general categories in the chart below, name as many different kinds of resource materials as you can think of.*

Print Materials	Film/Video	Audio Recordings	Other

B. DIRECTIONS: *You can certainly think of many advantages to having such a large number of reference materials available for use. But there can also be drawbacks to the situation. Think about what problems a modern historian might encounter as a result of easy access to large amounts of information—problems that Bede or others of his time would not have faced. What are some problems you have encountered in your own research?*

_____

_____

_____

_____

_____

_____

_____

_____

Name _____ Date _____

from A History of the English Church and People by Bede
Open-Book Test

Short Answer *Write your response to the questions in this section on the lines provided.*

1. What was Bede's main reason for writing *A History of the English Church and People*?
   How do you know?

   _____

   _____

   _____

2. In *A History of the English Church and People*, Bede is not completely accurate.
   What keeps him from being accurate?

   _____

   _____

3. Cite two examples from the end of the passage that reflect Bede's idealized view of
   Ireland.

   _____

   _____

4. Consider the time in which Bede wrote *A History of the English Church and People*.
   Which source would probably have provided Bede with the most reliable information
   that Britain had "twenty-eight noble cities"? Explain.

   _____

   _____

5. In *A History of the English Church and People*, Bede writes that "all are united in
   their study of God's truth." What can the reader infer about Bede's attitude toward
   the English Church from this statement?

   _____

   _____

   _____

6. In the chart below, write four facts and four opinions from *A History of the English
   Church and People*.

Facts	Opinions

7. What aspect of *A History of the English Church and People* seems to lend the greatest credibility to Bede's work? Explain.

_____

_____

_____

_____

8. Why might historians hesitate to believe Bede when he states in *A History of the English Church and People* that the Scots said, "We can give you good advice. There is another island not far to the east. . . . Go and settle there if you wish"?

_____

_____

_____

_____

9. In *A History of the English Church and People*, Bede describes *innumerable* castles in Britain. How many are there?

_____

_____

_____

_____

10. In *A History of the English Church and People*, Bede claims the Irish had *immunity* from poison. Do you think this is likely? Focus on the meaning of *immunity* in your response.

_____

_____

_____

Essay

Write an extended response to the question of your choice or to the question or questions your teacher assigns you.

11. Bede had very limited resources from which to gather facts for *A History of the English Church and People*. In an essay, discuss his limited resources and how they may have affected the story he wrote. Could he always be sure he had accurate information? Did he have all the information he needed? Use examples from the text as well as your own reasons to support your statements.

12. Modern historians use new technological tools such as DNA analysis and computers to conduct their research. In an essay, discuss three modern technological devices that would have helped Bede in recording *A History of the English Church and People*. Support your ideas with specific references to the text.

13. As the British shifted their allegiance from lord and town to king and nation, they experienced a new sense of regional identity. In an essay, explain how *A History of the English Church and People* reflects this nationalism. Use examples from Bede's history to support your ideas.

14. **Thinking About the Essential Question: Does a sense of place shape literature or does literature shape a sense of place?** *A History of the English Church and People* tells a great deal about a specific place and time. In an essay, explain some of the things we can learn about the subject, Britain, from the text. Then describe some of the things we can learn about the text from its subject. Use examples from the text to support your ideas.

Oral Response

15. Go back to questions 3, 5, 8, or to the question your teacher assigns to you. Take a few minutes to expand your answer and prepare an oral response. Find additional details in *A History of the English Church and People* that will support your points. If necessary, make notes to guide your response.

from **A History of the English Church and People** by Bede
Selection Test A

Critical Reading *Identify the letter of the choice that best answers the question.*

_____ 1. What was Bede's main reason for writing *A History of the English Church and People*?
    A. to compare Britain and Ireland
    B. to identify the languages spoken
    C. to describe the geography of Britain
    D. to record the history of Britain

_____ 2. According to Bede, what was the greatest thing that Britain had to offer?
    A. It had many natural resources.
    B. It had a very warm climate.
    C. It had a powerful navy.
    D. It operated under one government.

_____ 3. Read these quotations from *A History of the English Church and People*. Based on the details they provide, which quotation is probably the most historically accurate?
    A. "I have heard that folk suffering from snakebite have drunk water in which scrapings from the leaves of books from Ireland have been steeped . . ."
    B. "On the opposite side of Britain, which lies open to the boundless ocean, lie the isles of the Orcades."
    C. "As Saint Basil says: 'Water receives its heat when it flows across certain metals, and becomes hot . . .'"
    D. ". . . almost everything in this isle enjoys immunity to poison . . ."

_____ 4. According to Bede, what is true of Ireland?
    A. It is the largest island.
    B. It gets lots of snow.
    C. It does not have any snakes.
    D. The climate is too warm.

_____ 5. What keeps Bede from being completely accurate in his *A History of the English Church and People*?
    A. He sometimes accepted unlikely stories as true.
    B. He usually did not tell where he got information.
    C. Much of his information comes from his own observations.
    D. He used the limited resources available to him at the time.

____ 6. Why does Bede go into such detail in *A History of the English Church and People* to describe the kinds of shellfish found in Britain?

A. He knows his readers are interested in the fish of the seacoast.

B. He wants to show how varied and rich the waters of Britain are.

C. He wants readers to know the Britons are well nourished.

D. He is stressing the importance of the seacoast.

____ 7. Why does Bede include a quotation from the Scots in *A History of the English Church and People*?

A. He is trying to flatter the Scots.

B. He wants to show how unreasonable the Scots were.

C. He wants to make it seem that he was present at the time.

D. He has read the quotation in another work.

____ 8. How does Ireland's climate compare to Britain's in *A History of the English Church and People*?

A. It is much colder.

B. It is much wetter.

C. It is more variable.

D. It is superior.

____ 9. What attitude toward women is Bede expressing in this quotation from *A History of the English Church and People*?

> Having no women with them, these Picts asked wives of the Scots, who consented on condition that, when any dispute arose, they should choose a king from the female royal line rather than the male.

A. Picts believed Scots women brought a higher social status.

B. Picts held little respect for Scots women.

C. Scots women were eager to marry Pict men.

D. Scots wanted political influence in the Pict royal court.

____ 10. What does Bede feel most unifies the people of Britain in *A History of the English Church and People*?

A. their love of the land

B. their fear of the Picts

C. their desire for peace

D. their belief in and study of God's truth

Vocabulary and Grammar

____ **11.** What does *innumerable* mean in this line from *A History of the English Church and People*?

> In old times, the country had twenty-eight noble cities, and innumerable castles. . . .

A. several   C. strong

B. countless   D. stone

____ **12.** What are the *promontories* that Bede describes in *A History of the English Church and People*?

A. peaks of high coastal land

B. castles with strong walls

C. gently rolling hills

D. a kind of shellfish

____ **13.** What word means the same as the italicized word in this sentence from *A History of the English Church and People*?

> . . .vines are *cultivated* in various localities.

A. cut   C. grown

B. picked   D. burned

Essay

14. The oral tradition preserves the past while entertaining listeners. Write an essay in which you explain how Bede uses literary techniques, such as imagery, detail, and tone, to hold the people's interest. Use examples from *A History of the English Church and People* to support your opinion.

15. Bede did not have many resources from which to gather facts for *A History of the English Church and People*. He got some information from oral traditions. He used manuscripts from monasteries, but these were few in number. He also had records of local events, such as when crops were planted. He could also see things for himself. In an essay, discuss Bede's limited resources and how they may have affected the history he wrote. For instance, could he always be sure he had accurate information? Did he have all the information he needed to tell about the settlement of Britain? How could he test information about the snakes in Ireland? Give at least two examples from the text, as well as your own reasons, to support your statements.

16. Thinking About the Essential Question: Does a sense of place shape literature or does literature shape a sense of place? *A History of the English Church and People* tells a great deal about a specific place and time. In an essay, explain some of the things we can learn about the subject, Britain, from the text. Use examples from the text to support your ideas.

from **A History of the English Church and People** by Bede
Selection Test B

Critical Reading *Identify the letter of the choice that best completes the statement or answers the question.*

____ 1. Bede's main purpose in writing *A History of the English Church and People* was to
   A. describe Britain's geography.
   B. provide a factual narrative of past events in Britain.
   C. delineate the languages and nations within Britain.
   D. compare Britain and Ireland.

____ 2. Considering the time in which he wrote, which source would probably have provided Bede with the most reliable information that Britain had "twenty-eight noble cities"?
   A. personal experience
   B. testimony from sailors
   C. records from a monastic library
   D. accounts in letters

____ 3. From his phrase "all are united in their study of God's truth," what can be inferred about Bede's attitude toward the English Church?
   A. He believed in its teachings.
   B. He was aware of its influence.
   C. He questioned its sovereignty.
   D. He reluctantly obeyed its mandates.

____ 4. Bede's account suggests that Britain had
   A. an ideal climate.
   B. a powerful navy.
   C. abundant natural resources.
   D. a unified government.

____ 5. Which of the following lines probably reflects the greatest degree of historical accuracy?
   A. "'Go and settle there if you wish; should you meet resistance, we will come to your help.'"
   B. "Ireland is broader than Britain, and its mild and healthy climate is superior."
   C. ". . . it is said that some Picts from Scythia put to sea in a few long ships and were driven by storms around the coasts of Britain . . ."
   D. "On the opposite side of Britain, which lies open to the boundless ocean, lie the isles of the Orcades."

____ 6. According to Bede, in which of the following ways are the four British nations different?
   A. They worship differently.
   B. Not all study the scriptures in Latin.
   C. They speak different languages.
   D. They have very different climates.

_____ 7. Which of the following seems to lend the greatest credibility to Bede's work?
A. the large amount of factual, specific information
B. his personal observations on climate
C. the references to religion in Britain
D. his descriptions of different customs

_____ 8. The line "almost everything in this isle enjoys immunity to poison" suggests that Bede
A. had a very high opinion of Ireland.
B. originally lived in Ireland.
C. traveled frequently to Ireland.
D. preferred Britain to Ireland.

_____ 9. In writing *A History of the English Church and People*, Bede was not completely scholarly or accurate because he
A. made extensive use of the limited resources of his time.
B. sometimes accepted unlikely tales as truth.
C. relied heavily on his own observations.
D. did not cite his sources.

_____ 10. Why does Bede describe the colors of the dye made from cockles and the waters of the salt and hot springs in *A History of the English Church and People*?
A. He wants to make the Picts jealous of what they do not have.
B. He wants to appeal to the senses to create a vivid image of the land.
C. He wants to make people proud of the land in which they live.
D. He wants to entice readers to visit Britain.

_____ 11. Why does Bede include a quotation from the Scots in *A History of the English Church and People*?
A. He wants to show how deceitful the Scots are.
B. He is being factual, having heard the statement himself.
C. He wants to make it seem as if he were actually present at the time.
D. He wants to show the Scots as helpful and kind.

_____ 12. Which of the following sentences about *A History of the English Church and People* is unbiased?
A. The weather in Ireland is healthy and pleasant.
B. The Picts are a wild and ungovernable people.
C. The Scots' requests were unreasonable.
D. The nights are short in summer in Britain.

Vocabulary and Grammar

_____ 13. If a person has *immunity*, he or she has _____.
A. great strength
B. the ability to read
C. the ability to speak Latin
D. freedom from disease

____ 14. Which word or phrase is most nearly the same in meaning as *promontories*?
   A. large waves
   B. fields
   C. deep caves
   D. rocky outcroppings

____ 15. One would have trouble counting the castles in Britain because they are _____.
   A. cultivated
   B. migrated
   C. innumerable
   D. promontories

Essay

16. This selection tells a great deal about the now-distant past. What are some of the things we can learn from the events of the past? Write about some examples of historical literature or documents that affect the way people live today.

17. Research materials for people writing in Bede's time were restricted to the oral tradition, manuscripts in monastic libraries, and records of such events as planting crops and other community events. In an essay, discuss why such resources might make it difficult to get a completely accurate account of the past.

18. **Thinking About the Essential Question: Does a sense of place shape literature or does literature shape a sense of place?** *A History of the English Church and People* tells a great deal about a specific place and time. In an essay, explain some of the things we can learn about the subject, Britain, from the text. Then describe some of the things we can learn about the text from its subject. Use examples from the text to support your ideas.

Unit 1: From Legend to History
Benchmark Test 1

MULTIPLE CHOICE

Literary Analysis and Reading Skills *Answer the following questions.*

1. Which is the best definition of an epic?
   A. a long narrative poem that tells a romantic story
   B. a long narrative poem that tells a heroic story
   C. a long narrative poem that includes kennings and caesuras
   D. a long narrative poem from ancient Greece

2. Which of these is a characteristic of most epics?
   A. a hero who goes against cultural traditions
   B. a romance that leads to marriage
   C. serious, elevated language
   D. alliteration

3. Which statement is true of most Anglo-Saxon lyrics?
   A. They were originally composed and passed along in the oral tradition.
   B. They were composed by monks in Latin and translated into Old English.
   C. They can be read in the original by most readers of Modern English.
   D. They are lighthearted, escapist fare designed to entertain listeners at dinner.

4. Which phrase best describes the mood of an elegy?
   A. cheerful and carefree
   B. angry and bitter
   C. puzzling or questioning
   D. serious and mournful

5. What is the main purpose of the caesura that appears in most lines of Anglo-Saxon verse?
   A. It elevates the heroic language.
   B. It adds a sense of mourning or sadness.
   C. It provides the speaker with a place to pause.
   D. It provides the speaker with directions regarding tone of voice.

6. Which statement is true of historical writing from early times?
   A. It presents facts objectively, with no indication of the writer's beliefs.
   B. Beliefs and superstitions of the era tend to color the facts.
   C. None of the facts can be verified.
   D. All of the writing is in Latin.

Read this description of the Danes' reaction to the death of Grendel. Then, answer the questions that follow.

Many at mornings, as men have told me,
warriors gathered the gift-hall round,
folk-leaders faring from far and near,
o'er wide-stretched ways, the wonder to view

5 trace of the traitor. Not troublous seemed
   the enemy's end to any man
   who saw by the gait of the graceless foe
   how the weary-hearted, away from thence,
   baffled in battle and banned, his steps
10 death-marked dragged to the devil's mere.°   °**mere** marsh.
   Bloody the billows° were boiling there,   °**billows** surging waters; waves.
   turbid° the tide of tumbling waves   °**turbid** churned up and muddy.
   horribly seething, with sword-blood hot,
   by the doomed one dyed, who in den of the moor
15 aid forlorn his life adown,
   his heathen soul, and hell received it.
   Home then rode the hoary° clansmen   °**hoary** gray- or white-haired.
   from that merry journey, and many a youth,
   on horses white, the hardy warrior,
20 back from the mere. Then Beowulf's glory
   eager they echoed, and all averred°   °**averred** declared to be true.
   that from sea to sea, or south or north,
   there was no other in earth's domain,
   under vault° of heaven, more valiant found,   °**vault** arched space.
25 of warriors none more worthy to rule!
         from *Beowulf*, translated by Francis Gummere

7. Which statement accurately paraphrases the first sentence of the passage from *Beowulf* and most clearly illuminates its main idea?
   A. People have told me what happened on the morning after the battle with Grendel.
   B. We are filled with wonder at the feats of warriors who are leaders of their folk.
   C. Warriors came from all over to view with wonder the evidence of Grendel's death.
   D. The warriors who fought the traitor Grendel came from far and near.

8. In what action typical of epic heroes has Beowulf recently engaged?
   A. preparing a banquet   C. battling with evil forces
   B. amassing a treasure   D. telling his own story

9. Based on the passage, how do most members of Beowulf's society feel about him?
   A. They like him but do not trust him.   C. They are very jealous of his powers.
   B. They fear him greatly.   D. They admire him deeply.

10. What quality does Beowulf share with most other legendary heroes?
    A. He is very strong.
    B. He is exceedingly wise.
    C. He is partly divine, with one parent who is a god.
    D. He is humorously extreme in his thoughts and actions.

11. Where does the first caesura in this passage from *Beowulf* occur?
    A. after *mornings* in line 1   C. after *gathered* in line 2
    B. after *me* in line 1   D. after *traitor* in line 5

12. This translation of *Beowulf* tries to follow as closely as possible the style of the original poem. Based on this passage, what can you conclude about the alliteration in Anglo-Saxon verse?

    A. It is used sparingly.

    B. It is generally used to create kennings.

    C. The alliterated sound generally changes with each new line.

    D. All the alliterated words in a line are generally the same part of speech.

13. Which of these details in the passage from *Beowulf* is an example of assonance?

    A. the repeated *b* sound in line 9   **C.** the adjective *death-marked* in line 10

    B. the repeated short *a* sound in line 9   **D.** the phrase *devil's mere* in line 10

14. Which phrase in the passage from *Beowulf* is an example of a kenning?

    A. *many at mornings* in line 1   **C.** *tumbling waves* in line 12

    B. *enemy's end* in line 6   **D.** *sword-blood* in line 13

Read this passage from a historical work compiled in late Anglo-Saxon times. Then, answer the questions that follow.

    Sixty winters ere that Christ was born, Caius Julius, emperor of the Romans, with eighty ships sought Britain. There he was first beaten in a dreadful fight, and lost a great part of his army. Then he let his army abide with the Scots, and went south into Gaul. There he gathered six hundred ships, with which he went back into Britain. When they first rushed together, Caesar's tribune, whose name was Labienus, was slain. Then took the Welsh sharp piles, and drove them with great clubs into the water, at a certain ford of the river called Thames. When the Romans found that, they would not go over the ford. Then fled the Britons to the fastnesses of the woods; and Caesar, having after much fighting gained many of the chief towns, went back into Gaul.

from *The Anglo-Saxon Chronicle*

15. Which statement most accurately paraphrases the last three sentences in the passage and best clarifies their essential message?

    A. By placing wooden piles at the ford in the river, the Britons (Welsh) prevented further advances of the Romans and were able to escape to the woods. Julius Caesar, having conquered many British towns, then returned to Rome.

    B. The Britons (Welsh), after using piles to prevent the Romans from crossing the river, were fast enough to escape to the woods. Julius Caesar, having conquered many British towns, then returned to Rome.

    C. Because they could afford to use wooden piles in the river, the Britons (Welsh) outmaneuvered the Romans and hid in the woods until Julius Caesar, defeated at last, returned to Rome.

    D. The Britons (Welsh) were not as smart as Julius Caesar, who knew enough not to cross a river filled with piles and instead concentrated on capturing many British towns before returning to Rome.

16. Which detail relating to the historical context is most useful in understanding the passage?
   A. Julius Caesar traveled to Britain in about 55 B.C.
   B. The Romans often used warships propelled by slave rowers.
   C. Julius Caesar would later be assassinated by senators in Rome.
   D. Troops on horseback crossed rivers in shallow places known as fords.

17. Which of the following graphic aids would be most helpful in explaining the historical context of the passage from *The Anglo-Saxon Chronicle?*
   A. a topographical map showing the mountains and rivers of Britain
   B. a diagram of a Roman aqueduct built during the reign of Julius Caesar
   C. a historical map showing Roman routes and conquests in Britain under Julius Caesar
   D. a bar graph showing the population of the cities of Britain in the time of Julius Caesar

18. *The Anglo-Saxon Chronicle* includes both eyewitness accounts and accounts of events written long after they happened. How might an eyewitness account of an event differ from an account of the same event written years later?
   A. It would tend to be less interesting to modern readers.
   B. It would tend to be more detailed, immediate, and exciting.
   C. It would be mostly objective, showing all sides of the issues and situations.
   D. It would not be as accurate because it would lack support from historic documents.

19. Based on the passage, which of these stylistic effects helps *The Anglo-Saxon Chronicle* achieve its purpose?
   A. Simple, direct language makes it seem like an accurate, believable history.
   B. Flowery, poetic language makes it seem like a highly imaginative account.
   C. An elevated academic vocabulary makes it seem like a scholarly work.
   D. Emotionally charged language makes it seem like a persuasive essay.

Read this passage from an anonymous Anglo-Saxon poem in modern translation. Then, answer the questions that follow.

> He told me to come that carved this letter,
> And bid thee recall, in thy costly array,
> Ye gave to each other in days of old,
> When still in the land ye lived together,
> 5 Happily mated, and held in the mead-halls
> Your home and abode. A bitter feud
> Banished him far. He bids me call thee,
> Earnestly urge thee overseas.
> . . . A home he hath found in a foreign land,
> 10 Fair abode and followers true,
> Hardy heroes, though hence he was driven;
> Shoved his boat form the shore in distress,
> Steered for the open, sped o'er the ocean,
> Weary wave-tossed wanderer he.

15   Past are his woes, he has won through his perils,
       He lives in plenty, no pleasure he lacks;
       Nor horses nor goods nor gold of the mead-hall;
       All the wealth of earls upon earth
       Belongs to my lord, he lacks but thee.

from The Husband's Message

20. Based on the passage, what would you say makes "The Husband's Message" an elegy?
  A. The husband mourns the death of his wife.
  B. The husband mourns the absence of his wife.
  C. The husband celebrates his new life in a new land.
  D. The husband is angry that his wife cannot be with him.

21. Which is a good example of alliteration in the passage?
  A. the phrase *thy costly array* in line 2   **C.** the repeated *h* sounds in line 11
  B. the repeated long *o* sounds in line 6   **D.** the word *mead-hall* in line 17

22. Which of these historical details about the early Anglo-Saxons is most useful in clarifying the passage from "The Husband's Message"?
  A. They believed strongly in the workings of fate, or *wyrd*.
  B. They spoke a Germanic language now called Old English.
  C. They were a seafaring people who often settled in new lands.
  D. They converted to Christianity after settling in present-day England.

23. The early Anglo-Saxons used a system of writing known as the runic alphabet, sometimes carving messages in wood. What aspect of the passage does this historical context help explain?
  A. the husband's ability to send a letter
  B. the husband's success in his new location
  C. the wife's need to have someone read the letter to her
  D. the wife's inability to receive the letter directly from her husband

Vocabulary

24. Based on your knowledge of the root *-sol-*, in which situation would you offer someone *solace?*
  A. He or she lives in a sunny climate.   **C.** He or she has gone to sleep.
  B. He or she has talked for hours.   **D.** He or she has lost a loved one.

25. Based on your knowledge of the Latin root *-sol-*, choose the best paraphrase of this sentence.

    I tried to *console* Aunt Betty during her illness.

  A. I tried to entertain Aunt Betty during her illness.
  B. I tried to comfort Aunt Betty during her illness.
  C. I tried to cure Aunt Betty during her illness.
  D. I tried to visit Aunt Betty during her illness.

Grammar

26. Which coordinating conjunction best completes this sentence?

I thought it might rain later. "Take an umbrella," my mother suggested, , __ risk getting soaking wet."

A. and   **B.** but   **C.** or   **D.** for

27. Which sentence below best combines these two sentences using a conjunction?

Celia may be in the lead. Soon Mary will overtake her.

A. Celia may be in the lead, and soon Mary will overtake her.
B. Celia may be in the lead, but soon Mary will overtake her.
C. Celia may be in the lead, or soon Mary will overtake her.
D. Celia may be in the lead, for soon Mary will overtake her.

ESSAY

28. Imagine that you are the director of a company that provides services to the early Anglo-Saxons or you are the owner of a farm that provides them with products. In a business memo, discuss one of the products you sell, a service you provide, or a practice that is relevant to the sale of your product or service.

29. Imagine that the early Anglo-Saxons publish a newspaper for which you work. Write an editorial for the paper about a practice of early Anglo-Saxon society that you think should change. Present a reasoned argument with examples or other details to support your opinion.

30. Create a job-application form for a legendary or epic hero. On the form, request the kind of information that is typical of most job-application forms (name and address, for example), as well as questions designed to obtain appropriate information about the hero's background and achievements.

Vocabulary Warm-up Word Lists

Study these words from the selection. Then, complete the activities.

Word List A

adversity [ad VER si tee] *n.* great hardship; misfortune
    Forest fires, droughts, and mudslides can cause <u>adversity</u> for people.

courteous [KUR tee us] *adj.* considerate of others; polite
    It is important for a receptionist to be <u>courteous</u> to visitors.

devout [di VOWT] *adj.* extremely religious; pious
    The <u>devout</u> woman could be seen going to church every day.

dispense [di SPENS] *v.* administer; distribute in portions
    It was the head nurse's responsibility to <u>dispense</u> the medicine.

distinguished [di STING gwisht] *adj.* marked by excellence; well-known
    All the world leaders respected the <u>distinguished</u> diplomat.

pilgrimages [PIL gruhm ij iz] *n.* journeys to shrines or sacred places
    The man has made <u>pilgrimages</u> to Mecca and other religious cities.

prudent [PROOD uhnt] *adj.* using good judgment; acting wisely
    The <u>prudent</u> shopper spends less than he or she earns.

repented [ree PENT id] *v.* felt remorse or regret; resolved to reform
    The thief <u>repented</u> and returned the stolen items.

Word List B

agility [uh JIL i tee] *n.* ability to move with ease and speed
    The player's <u>agility</u> allowed her to return the ball after a difficult serve.

dainty [DAYN tee] *adj.* tiny and delicately beautiful
    The <u>dainty</u> teapot, made of fine china, held only one cup of tea.

diligent [DIL uh juhnt] *adj.* marked by effort and care
    The <u>diligent</u> employee was valued for her careful, dependable work.

dispatch [di SPACH] *v.* send to a destination or on specific business
    The need to <u>dispatch</u> a messenger showed that the matter was urgent.

frugal [FROO guhl] *adj.* thrifty; economical; inexpensive
    Her <u>frugal</u> lunch consisted of a peanut butter sandwich and an apple.

prompt [PRAHMPT] *adj.* acting or arriving on time or without delay
    If you are <u>prompt</u> and arrive on time, we won't have to wait for you.

sundry [SUHN dree] *adj.* miscellaneous; various
    The boy's pockets contained string, rocks, and <u>sundry</u> other items.

unanimously [yoo NAN uh muhs lee] *adv.* with everyone agreeing
    The candidate was elected <u>unanimously</u>; not one person voted against her.

The Prologue *from* The Canterbury Tales by Geoffrey Chaucer
Vocabulary Warm-up Exercises

Exercise A *Fill in each blank in the paragraph with the appropriate word from Word List A. Use each word only once.*

During the eleventh and twelfth centuries, kings often commissioned the construction of cathedrals—they thought it would be [1] _____ to be seen as supporters of the church. The builders were not generally important or [2] _____ people. Instead, they were ordinary people who contributed their labor and skill. Often progress was slowed by hardships, but despite the [3] _____, the workers dedicated themselves to these stone masterpieces. In cathedrals, [4] _____ Christians prayed piously and [5] _____ their sins. Some cathedrals were not just places of worship but also the destination of [6] _____. In addition, they were centers of learning. They explored subjects from serious philosophy to the rules of [7] _____ behavior. To students who met the requirements, they would [8] _____ degrees. In many ways, then, the cathedral was the center of medieval society.

Exercise B *Revise each sentence so that the underlined vocabulary word is used in a logical way. Be sure to keep the vocabulary word in your revision.*

Example: Because the cook was <u>frugal</u>, he never bought ingredients that were on sale.
Because the cook was <u>frugal</u>, he always *bought ingredients that were on sale.*

1. Because Will was <u>diligent</u>, his parents nagged him to finish his homework.
   _____

2. The gymnast's natural <u>agility</u> kept her from becoming a finalist in the competition.
   _____

3. The manager fired any worker who was consistently <u>prompt</u>.
   _____

4. The teammates could not agree on a captain, so they chose Lauren <u>unanimously</u>.
   _____

5. The college offered <u>sundry</u> courses in science, so biology was the only choice.
   _____

6. The operator will <u>dispatch</u> the messenger to make sure he has no work to do.
   _____

7. The <u>dainty</u> statuette was huge and solidly made.
   _____

The Prologue *from* The Canterbury Tales by Geoffrey Chaucer
Reading Warm-up A

Read the following passage. Pay special attention to the underlined words. Then, read it again, and complete the activities. Use a separate sheet of paper for your written answers.

Travel in the Middle Ages was slow and difficult, and travelers were subject to <u>adversity</u>. People who were well-known and excellent in their field—<u>distinguished</u> scholars, for example—as well as pilgrims and actors moved freely through Europe. Most people, however, never wandered more than a few miles from their birthplace. If they did go on journeys or <u>pilgrimages</u>, they were guided by the advice of other travelers. This advice was not reliable, however, because travel conditions changed constantly. Maps did not offer much help either, because they were often inaccurate.

Medieval travelers usually set off on foot or by oxcart, since horses were a luxury reserved for the wealthy. If conditions were favorable, a traveler could walk about twenty miles a day. Conditions were rarely favorable, however. Even the main roads were little more than paths that became impassable during snowstorms and rainstorms. Dense woods hid thieves and bandits who preyed on passersby. Inns offered meals and beds, but they were not pleasant places. Sometimes guests were not <u>courteous</u>—they might treat a fellow traveler rudely. Not infrequently, too, guests might be dishonest. Therefore, <u>prudent</u> travelers set forth in groups, hoping to find protection in numbers.

A ship or riverboat was a quicker, less expensive option for traveling a long distance. Travel by water had its own perils, however. Storms and pirates made it just as dangerous as travel by land. Still, many <u>devout</u> Christians, who valued religious acts more than personal safety, undertook journeys to the Holy Land or to shrines closer to home. There, wishing to cleanse themselves of remorse, they <u>repented</u> their sins. They believed that the church would <u>dispense</u> spiritual pardons, granting forgiveness because of the severe hardships they endured.

1. Circle the words that hint at the meaning of <u>adversity</u>. Write a sentence about overcoming *adversity*.

2. Underline the words that explain what might make a person <u>distinguished</u>. Describe someone who is *distinguished*.

3. Underline the words that tell what travelers relied on when they went on <u>pilgrimages</u>. Define *pilgrimages* in your own words.

4. Underline the words that describe the opposite of <u>courteous</u> behavior. Describe a *courteous* person.

5. Circle the words that explain why <u>prudent</u> travelers set forth in groups. Then, tell what *prudent* means.

6. Circle the words that suggest the meaning of <u>devout</u>. Use *devout* in a sentence of your own.

7. Underline the words that are a clue to the meaning of <u>repented</u>. Tell what *repented* means.

8. Circle the word that suggests the meaning of <u>dispense</u>. What is a synonym for *dispense*?

Name _____ Date _____

The Prologue *from* The Canterbury Tales by Geoffrey Chaucer
Reading Warm-up B

Read the following passage. Pay special attention to the underlined words. Then, read it again, and complete the activities. Use a separate sheet of paper for your written answers.

Thomas Becket was born in 1118 in London. Handsome, athletic, and well educated, he proved to be a charming, <u>diligent</u> administrator and diplomat, putting great effort and care into his work. He therefore pleased the archbishop, who appointed him to an important post in the church. The king, Henry II, also named Becket to an important post, so that Becket might use his <u>sundry</u> skills—in law, religion, and matters of state—to carry out delicate missions. Becket was expected to represent the church but instead used his verbal <u>agility</u>, speaking with ease and speed, to support the king's interests. Henry rewarded Becket with wealth and lavish entertainments. In 1162, the king nominated his friend to the position of archbishop, a post Becket was reluctant to accept. The king insisted, however, and Becket was made a priest and, in an unusually <u>prompt</u> manner—with hardly any delay—named archbishop of Canterbury.

Almost at once, Becket became pious and <u>frugal</u>, refusing the <u>dainty</u>, delicately beautiful luxuries he had previously enjoyed. He infuriated Henry by making the church his priority. A series of minor disputes developed into a major quarrel, and fearing for his life, Becket fled to France, where he remained for six years. In 1170, the two men appeared to have <u>unanimously</u> agreed to resolve their differences, and Becket returned to Canterbury. Nevertheless, he refused to pardon the bishops who had taken the king's side in the quarrel. When Henry learned about this, he is said to have shouted, "Who will rid me of this meddlesome priest?"

The king's anger inspired four knights to <u>dispatch</u> themselves to Canterbury and murder Becket in the cathedral there. Becket's death outraged the kingdom, and Henry repented publicly.

1. Underline the words that describe Becket's <u>diligent</u> habits. Define *diligent* in your own words.

2. Underline the words that tell about Becket's <u>sundry</u> skills. What is a synonym for *sundry*?

3. Circle the words that hint at the meaning of <u>agility</u>. Use *agility* in a sentence of your own.

4. Circle the words that hint at the meaning of <u>prompt</u>. Use *prompt* in a sentence.

5. Underline the words that tell how a <u>frugal</u> person might act. Then, tell what *frugal* means.

6. Circle the words that define <u>dainty</u>. Use *dainty* in a sentence.

7. Circle the words that tell what the two former friends resolved <u>unanimously</u>. Then, tell what *unanimously* means.

8. Circle the words that tell what inspired the knights to <u>dispatch</u> themselves. Then, explain what *dispatch* means.

The Prologue *from* The Canterbury Tales by Geoffrey Chaucer
Geoffrey Chaucer: Biography

Possibly the greatest impact Chaucer made with his writing career was in writing in the English language. At the time, literacy was mostly for the upper classes, who deemed Latin the language of text. Even though he chose to write in English, he was also familiar with Latin, French, and Italian. Much that we know about his life is circumstantial or conjecture because of a lack of records. A very learned man and talented poet, Chaucer set the stage for English literature to come.

A. DIRECTIONS: *Use the following outline to take notes on Geoffrey Chaucer's life.*

I. Geoffrey Chaucer (1343?–1400)

A. The Poet's Beginnings

    1. _____

    2. _____

    3. _____

B. The Poet Matures

    1. _____

    2. _____

    3. _____

C. *The Canterbury Tales*

    1. _____

    2. _____

D. The Father of English Poetry

    1. _____

    2. _____

B. DIRECTIONS: *Answer the following questions as if you were Geoffrey Chaucer. Make inferences from your prior knowledge of the author.*

1. Your first major work was written as an elegy for John Gaunt's wife. What challenges did you face writing about a duchess for her husband?

_____

2. What is your most memorable experience as a young man?

_____

3. How did that experience affect your writing?

_____

4. What inspired you to write *The Canterbury Tales*?

_____

_____

The Prologue *from* **The Canterbury Tales** by Geoffrey Chaucer
Literary Analysis: Characterization

Characterization is the writer's act of creating and developing the personality traits of a character. Chaucer uses both **direct characterization**—that is, stating facts about a personality directly—and **indirect characterization**—that is, revealing personality through details of appearance, thoughts, speech, and/or actions—to develop the vivid personalities of the pilgrims in *The Canterbury Tales*.

DIRECTIONS: *Read the following passages from the Prologue. In each passage, circle any direct statements about the character's personality. Underline statements about the character's appearance, speech, and/or behavior that reveal his or her personality indirectly. Then, on the lines that follow, summarize what the passage conveys about the character's personality.*

1. There was also a Nun, a Prioress, / Her way of smiling very simple and coy. / Her greatest oath was only "By St. Loy!" / And she was known as Madam Eglantyne. / And well she sang a service, with a fine / Intoning through her nose, as was most seemly, / And she spoke daintily in French, extremely, / After the school of Stratford-atte-Bowe; / French in the Paris style she did not know. / At meat her manners were well taught withal / No morsel from her lips did she let fall, / Nor dipped her fingers in the sauce too deep; / But she could carry a morsel up and keep / The smallest drop from falling on her breast.

_____

_____

2. A Sergeant at the Law who paid his calls, / Wary and wise, for clients at St. Paul's / There also was, of noted excellence. / Discreet he was, a man to reverence, / Or so he seemed, his sayings were so wise.

_____

_____

3. A worthy woman from beside Bath city / Was with us, somewhat deaf, which was a pity. / In making cloth she showed so great a bent / She bettered those of Ypres and of Ghent. / In all the parish not a dame dared stir / Towards the altar steps in front of her. / And if indeed they did, so wrath was she / As to be quite put out of charity. / Her kerchiefs were of finely woven ground; / I dared have sworn they weighed a good ten pound, / The ones she wore on Sunday on her head. / Her hose were of the finest scarlet red / And gartered tight; her shoes were soft and new.

_____

_____

4. The Miller was a chap of sixteen stone, / A great stout fellow big in brawn and bone. / He did well out of them, for he could go / And win the ram at any wrestling show. / Broad, knotty and short-shouldered, he would boast / He could heave any door off hinge and post, / Or take a run and break it with his head.

_____

_____

Unit 1 Resources: From Legend to History
81

The Prologue *from* The Canterbury Tales by Geoffrey Chaucer
Literary Analysis: Social Commentary

Social commentary is writing that offers insight into society, its values, and its customs. The writer of social commentary often expresses his or her opinion about society through his or her portrayals of characters and descriptions of events. Chaucer's characters each represent a different segment of society, such as a wife, a knight, a merchant, and a nun, to name a select few. Through his observations and through the words he has his characters say, Chaucer provides a commentary on his society.

A. *Read each passage from Chaucer's* Prologue. *Provide an analysis of each passage. Identify the characters, the details, and the opinions Chaucer directly and indirectly expresses through his writing.*

Passage	Analysis
There was a *Knight*, a most distinguished man, Who from the day on which he first began To ride abroad had followed chivalry, Truth, honor, generousness, and courtesy.	
There also was a *Nun*, a Prioress, Her way of smiling very simple and coy. . . At meat her manners were well taught withal; No morsel from her lips did she let fall, Nor dipped her fingers in the sauce too deep; But she could carry a morsel up and keep The smallest drop from falling on her breast.	
This estimable Merchant so had set His wits to work, none knew he was in debt, He was so stately in negotiation, Loan, bargain and commercial obligation.	

Unit 1 Resources: From Legend to History
82

Name _____ Date _____

The Prologue *from* The Canterbury Tales by Geoffrey Chaucer
Reading Strategy: Analyze Difficult Sentences

When you encounter long or involved sentences that seem too difficult to understand, asking yourself *who, what, when, where, why,* and *how* questions can help you figure out their meaning.

DIRECTIONS: *Read the following sentences from the* Prologue. *Then, answer the* who, what, when, where, why, *and/or* how *questions following them to decode their meaning.*

He knew the taverns well in every town / And every innkeeper and barmaid too / Better than lepers, beggars and that crew, / For in so eminent a man as he / It was not fitting with the dignity / Of his position, dealing with a scum / of wretched lepers; nothing good can come / Of dealings with the slum-and-gutter dwellers, / But only with the rich and victual-sellers.

1. What and whom did he know well? _____

2. Whom didn't he know as well? Why? _____

_____

If, when he fought, the enemy vessel sank, / He sent his prisoners home; they walked the plank.

3. What did he do? _____

4. How did he do this? _____

They had a Cook with them who stood alone / For boiling chicken with a marrow-bone, / Sharp flavoring-powder and a spice for savor.

5. Who "stood alone"? _____

6. For what did he stand alone? _____

A Doctor too emerged as we proceeded; No one alive could talk as well as he did / On points of medicine and of surgery, / For, being grounded in astronomy, / He watched his patient's favorable star / And, by his Natural Magic, knew what are / The lucky hours and planetary degrees / For making charms and magic effigies.

7. Whom is this about? _____

8. What can he do? _____

9. How does he treat his patients? _____

_____

But best of all he sang an Offertory, / For well he knew that when that song was sung / He'd have to preach and tune his honey-tongue / And (well he could) win silver from the crowd, / That's why he sang so merrily and loud.

10. What does he do best? _____

11. What does he know he'll have to do when he's done singing? _____

_____

12. Why does he sing so merrily and loud? _____

The Prologue *from* **The Canterbury Tales** by Geoffrey Chaucer
Vocabulary Builder

Word List

absolution   commission   garnished   prevarication   sanguine   solicitous

A. DIRECTIONS: *Write the word from the Word List that best completes each of the following sentences.*

1. The Franklin is probably most _____ when he is dining, since eating well gives him tremendous pleasure.

2. The Friar believes that _____ should come at a price so that people experience painful consequences for their sinful actions.

3. The Knight's son's garments are _____ with embroidery.

4. The innkeeper is a _____ host, doing all he can to make sure his guests are comfortable and happy.

5. A Pardoner given to _____ ought to be afraid of excommunication.

6. The Friar claims to have a _____ from the Pope to hear confessions.

B. WORD STUDY: *Change each verb into a noun with the suffix -tion. Then, fill in each blank in the sentences with the appropriate noun.*

contribute _____   navigate _____

recreate _____   decorate _____

1. The Knight has in his possession fine horses but wears clothes lacking _____.

2. The Monk prefers hunting for _____ to poring over books and tilling the soil.

3. The Friar gives absolution and an easy penance to those who accompany their confessions with a large financial _____.

4. When it comes to getting a boat from one destination to another, apparently none can compare with the Skipper at _____.

The Prologue *from* **The Canterbury Tales** by Geoffrey Chaucer
Integrated Language Skills: Support for Writing

Use the chart to organize your ideas to include on your homepage as the host of the Canterbury Blog.

Background Information	
Possible Links	
Advertisements	
Artwork	
Topics of Discussion	
Other	

Use the chart to help you form ideas about the possible posting the characters might make to the blog.

Character	Character's Qualities	Possible Blog Ideas

On a separate page, draw a design of your homepage for the Canterbury Blog incorporating the ideas you listed in the first chart. Then, write several blog entries in character based on your observations of Chaucer's descriptions.

Name _____ Date _____

The Prologue *from* The Canterbury Tales by Geoffrey Chaucer
Enrichment: Career as a Travel Agent

The characters described in the Prologue are embarking on a pilgrimage to the cathedral in Canterbury where the saint, Archbishop Thomas à Becket, was murdered. During the Middle Ages, Christians often went on such pilgrimages, and Canterbury was a popular destination. The pilgrims planned their journeys themselves but often banded together rather than travel alone. Today, many people still like to travel in groups. Travel agents usually make the trip arrangements.

DIRECTIONS: *Suppose you are a travel agent planning a group trip for a modern pilgrimage to Canterbury. Plan a travel package that you think would appeal to a group of tourists from the United States. Work out the important details, such as who might be interested in such a trip; where they might stay; what they should pack; and how much money the trip will cost. Do a little investigating to get the information you need as well as the actual costs of airfare, car rental, bus or rail transportation, hotels, and other elements of the trip. You may want to use the Internet or guidebooks to research this information. Then write the travel plans in the space below.*

People who might be interested in the trip: _____

_____

Weather in Canterbury at this time of year: _____

_____

What people should pack: _____

_____

Transportation to and from Canterbury: _____

_____

Transportation while in Canterbury: _____

_____

Projected cost of transportation: _____

_____

Lodgings: _____

_____

Projected cost of lodgings: _____

_____

Other things to reserve or apply for ahead of time: _____

_____

Projected cost of food, gas, admission fees, permits, and/or other expenses: _____

_____

Prologue *from* **The Canterbury Tales** by Geoffrey Chaucer

Open-Book Test

Short Answer *Write your response to the questions in this section on the lines provided.*

1. What is Chaucer's primary theme in the Prologue from *The Canterbury Tales*, and how does he reveal it?

   _____

   _____

   _____

   _____

2. What is Chaucer's attitude toward the Nun in the Prologue from *The Canterbury Tales*? Explain.

   _____

   _____

   _____

3. Summarize the meaning of this passage from the Prologue from *The Canterbury Tales* using the *who, what, when, why,* and *how* questioning strategy.

   > Whatever money from his friends he took/He spent on learning or another book/And prayed for them most earnestly, returning/Thanks to them thus for paying for his learning.

   _____

   _____

   _____

   _____

4. In the Prologue from *The Canterbury Tales*, Chaucer describes the Cook as having "an ulcer on his knee." What does this tell you about the Cook?

   _____

   _____

   _____

5. In the Prologue from *The Canterbury Tales*, Chaucer describes the woman from Bath. He says that "In all the parish not a dame dared stir/Towards the altar steps in front of her." What does this tell you about the woman? Explain.

   _____

   _____

   _____

6. In the Prologue from *The Canterbury Tales*, what does Chaucer accentuate by placing his description of the Miller almost immediately after that of the Plowman?

_____

_____

_____

7. How would you best describe the narrator in the Prologue from *The Canterbury Tales*? Explain.

_____

_____

_____

8. In the chart, list three pilgrims from different social classes in the Prologue from *The Canterbury Tales*. Briefly describe each character, and tell which level of society each represents.

Character	Brief Description	Level of Society

9. In the Prologue from *The Canterbury Tales*, Chaucer describes the Franklin as a *sanguine* man. What kind of man is he, and how does Chaucer show it?

_____

_____

_____

10. In the Prologue from *The Canterbury Tales*, how does the young Squire show himself to be *solicitous* of his father? Focus on the meaning of *solicitous* in your response.

_____

_____

_____

Essay

Write an extended response to the question of your choice or to the question or questions your teacher assigns you.

11. In the Prologue from *The Canterbury Tales*, Chaucer's narrator introduces many different characters traveling to Canterbury. Choose one of these characters, and write an essay explaining the nature of his or her personality. Tell what the key details and statements in the Prologue reveal about this individual's personality.

12. Consider the many characterizations of the men and women associated with the church in the Prologue from *The Canterbury Tales*. From these portraits, what conclusion might you draw about Chaucer's attitude toward the Church and/or religious practitioners? Write an essay in which you present your conclusion and support it with evidence from the Prologue.

13. As the father of English poetry, Chaucer is well known for his insight into human character. In an essay, explain how Chaucer's expertise with characterization is evident in the Prologue from *The Canterbury Tales*. Use specific examples from the poem to elaborate on your thoughts.

14. **Thinking About the Essential Question: Do writers influence social trends or just reflect them?** Chaucer says the Knight in the Prologue "was a true, a perfect gentle-knight." In an essay, explain how his description of the Knight reflects the social ideal of knighthood. Then describe how such a description might influence readers to think in a certain way about knights. Use details from the poem to support your response.

Oral Response

15. Go back to questions 1, 3, 4, or to the question your teacher assigns to you. Take a few minutes to expand your answer and prepare an oral response. Find additional details in the Prologue from *The Canterbury Tales* that will support your points. If necessary, make notes to guide your response.

The Prologue *from* **The Canterbury Tales** by Geoffrey Chaucer
Selection Test A

Critical Reading *Identify the letter of the choice that best answers the question.*

_____ 1. What is Chaucer's main reason for writing about the pilgrimage in the Prologue?
   A. to reveal the characters' beliefs about their religion
   B. to create a setting for telling stories by different characters
   C. to describe medieval life from different points of view
   D. to create a colorful setting in which to reveal his characters

_____ 2. Use the strategy for analyzing difficult sentences to analyze the following lines from the Prologue. What was the purpose of the trip?

   It happened in that season that one day / In Southwark, at The Tabard, as I lay / Ready to go on pilgrimage and start / For Canterbury, most devout at heart, / At night there came into that hostelry / Some nine and twenty in a company / Of sundry folk happening then to fall / In fellowship, and they were pilgrims all / That towards Canterbury meant to ride.

   A. to stay at the Tabard
   B. to go on a pilgrimage
   C. to meet twenty-nine people
   D. to enjoy the spring season

_____ 3. In the Prologue, what does the narrator think of the Monk?
   A. He is humble.
   B. He is courageous.
   C. He cares about others.
   D. He cares about himself.

_____ 4. What is Chaucer's primary theme in the Prologue?
   A. the dangers of pleasure
   B. the great variety of human nature
   C. the evil of humankind
   D. the inability of people to get along

_____ 5. What do you know about the woman from Bath, based on these lines from the Prologue?

   In all the parish not a dame dared stir / Towards the altar steps in front of her. . . .

   A. She does not go to church.
   B. She always sits when praying.
   C. She is proud and demanding.
   D. She does not like other women.

____ **6.** According to the Prologue, how many tales will each pilgrim tell on the journey?
   A. two going there and two coming back
   B. as many as they wish
   C. one for the entire trip
   D. however many the Host decides

____ **7.** Which of these quotations from the Prologue is an example of direct characterization?
   A. "The man who draws the shortest straw shall start."
   B. "Her greatest oath was only 'By St. Loy!'"
   C. "Children were afraid when he appeared."
   D. "He was an honest worker, good and true. . . ."

____ **8.** Where are the pilgrims going in the Prologue?
   A. to The Tabard, a famous inn
   B. to a church in London
   C. to a village in Southwark
   D. to the cathedral in Canterbury

____ **9.** What does the narrator mean in saying these lines from the Prologue?
   But first I beg of you, in courtesy, / Not to condemn me as unmannerly / If I speak plainly and with no concealings / And give account of all their words and dealings.

   A. Please do not blame me if I tell you the truth about what they said and did.
   B. Forgive me for making up details to make what they said more interesting.
   C. I am embarrassed to admit it, but I don't always stick to the truth.
   D. I apologize for leaving out things that they said and did that are rude.

____ **10.** Which word best describes the narrator in the Prologue?
   A. judgmental   **C.** shy
   B. sneaky   **D.** innocent

____ **11.** Whom do the pilgrims accept as their leader in the Prologue?
   A. the Host   **C.** the Nun
   B. the Knight   **D.** the Oxford Cleric

____ **12.** What does the narrator mean in the Prologue when he says the following about the Friar?
   But anywhere a profit might accrue / Courteous he was and lowly of service too.

   A. The Friar helps people make money by providing his services.
   B. The Friar helps people by giving them his time and money.
   C. The Friar helps people when he can make money doing it.
   D. The Friar helps people by teaching them how to use money.

Vocabulary

____ 13. What word means almost the same as *sanguine*?
- A. decorated
- B. untruthful
- C. cheerful
- D. respectful

____ 14. Which word most appropriately completes the following sentence? the artist has a _____ from the city council to complete the mural.

A. absolution	C. prevarication
B. commission	D. solicitous

Essay

15. Chaucer introduces many different travelers in the Prologue. Choose one and describe the person's character. In your essay, answer these questions: What does the person do? What kind of personality does the character have? Is the person essentially admirable, or does he or she do things that are not admirable? Finally, explain whether the character is someone you would like to travel with and why. Give at least two details from the Prologue to support your ideas.

16. In an essay, describe the arrangement the pilgrims have agreed upon in the Prologue. Explain why they will be traveling together. Who suggests telling stories? Why does the suggestion make sense to the travelers? Who do they put in charge of their story-telling, and why do they accept this person? What will be the reward for the person who tells the best story? In your response to these questions, use at least two examples from the Prologue.

17. **Thinking About the Essential Question: Do writers influence social trends or just reflect them?** Chaucer says the Knight in the Prologue "was a true, a perfect gentle-knight." In an essay, explain how his description of the Knight reflects the social ideal of knighthood. Use details from the poem to support your response.

The Prologue *from* The Canterbury Tales by Geoffrey Chaucer
Selection Test B

Critical Reading *Identify the letter of the choice that best completes the statement or answers the question.*

____ 1. Chaucer uses the pilgrimage primarily as a device to
   A. emphasize the characters' religious aspirations.
   B. frame the stories told by individual characters.
   C. describe the rigors of medieval life.
   D. create a vivid and realistic setting.

____ 2. The narrator is portrayed as
   A. stern and judgmental.
   B. sophisticated and worldly.
   C. robust and merry.
   D. naive and observant.

____ 3. The narrator says he plans to "give account of all their words and dealings, / Using their very phrases as they fell." For which kind of characterization would an author provide such details?
   A. direct characterization
   B. indirect characterization
   C. direct and indirect characterization
   D. dramatic characterization

____ 4. Which best describes Chaucer's attitude toward the Nun?
   A. amused tolerance
   B. polite detachment
   C. marked scorn
   D. weary reproachfulness

____ 5. Using the *who, what, where, when, why,* and *how* questioning strategy, write the letter of the phrase that best summarizes the meaning of the following passage.

   He was an easy man in penance-giving/Where he could hope to make a decent living;/It's a sure sign whenever gifts are given/To a poor Order that a man's well shriven,/And should he give enough he knew in verity/The penitent repented in sincerity.

   A. He gave out easy penances and absolution in exchange for gifts.
   B. He gave out easy penances and absolution in exchange for gifts whenever he thought he could get gifts from the confessors.
   C. He gave out easy penances and absolution in exchange for gifts whenever he thought he could get gifts from the confessors. He knew that if he exacted a large enough price for the sin that the penitent person would feel truly sorry for what he'd done.
   D. He gave out easy penances and absolution in exchange for gifts whenever he thought he could get gifts from the confessors. He knew that if he exacted a large enough price for the sin that the penitent person would feel truly sorry for what he'd done. In fact, whenever a poor group of friars receives gifts, you can be sure that someone has just received absolution for his sins.

_____ 6. What can the reader infer about the Friar from these lines?

But anywhere a profit might accrue / Courteous he was and lowly of service too.

A. He helps others make money.
B. He is humble and servile.
C. He has aspirations to be a merchant.
D. He will use people for money.

_____ 7. Chaucer describes the Pardoner's hair as "rat-tails" primarily to
A. furnish realistic detail.
B. provide comic relief.
C. suggest the Pardoner's obsession with current fashions.
D. imply moral corruption.

_____ 8. What do the following lines suggest about the woman from Bath?

In all the parish not a dame dared stir / Towards the altar steps in front of her

A. She is a religious fanatic.
B. She abhors the Christian church.
C. She is selfish and arrogant.
D. She disdains the company of women.

_____ 9. Chaucer calls the Franklin's girdle "white as morning milk" to
A. reiterate the Franklin's obsession with food.
B. emphasize the Franklin's personal cleanliness.
C. symbolize the Franklin's purity of heart.
D. show the Franklin's weakness for fancy clothes.

_____ 10. Using the *who, what, where, when, why,* and *how* questioning strategy to understand the following passage, write the letter of the phrase that best summarizes its meaning.

Whatever money from his friends he took / He spent on learning or another book / And prayed for them most earnestly, returning / Thanks to them thus for paying for his learning.

A. He stole his friends' money, spent it on books, and then prayed his friends would return.
B. Whatever money he borrowed from his friends he spent on his studies and books, prayed for more books, and then sent his friends thank-you notes for paying for his learning.
C. Whatever money he could get from his friends he spent on his studies and books, prayed for his books, and then returned thanks to his friends for paying for his learning.
D. Whatever money he borrowed from his friends he spent on his studies and books and then prayed earnestly for his friends as a way of giving them thanks.

_____ 11. Which of the following is *not* an example of direct characterization?
A. "He was an honest worker, good and true . . ."
B. ". . . His mighty mouth was like a furnace door."
C. "Children were afraid when he appeared."
D. "He wore a fustian tunic stained and dark . . ."

____ 12. By positioning his description of the Miller almost immediately after that of the Plowman, Chaucer accentuates
   A. the virtues of the Plowman.
   B. the buffoonishness and criminality of the Miller.
   C. the kinship between these two laborers.
   D. the virtues of the Plowman as well as the buffoonishness and criminality of the Miller.

____ 13. What theme does Chaucer convey in the Prologue to *The Canterbury Tales*?
   A. the conflicts inherent in society
   B. the basic evil of mankind
   C. the infinite variety of human nature
   D. the pitfalls of sensual pleasure

Vocabulary

____ 14. In standing by to carve meat for his father at the table, the young Squire is showing himself to be _____.
   A. garnished   C. solicitous
   B. prevaricating   D. sanguine

____ 15. A *sanguine* person is usually _____.
   A. cautious   C. cheerful
   B. angry   D. bored

____ 16. Which word is most nearly the same in meaning as *garnished*?
   A. tasted   C. caught
   B. said   D. decorated

Essay

17. In the Prologue to *The Canterbury Tales*, Chaucer's narrator introduces many different characters traveling to Canterbury. Choose one of these characters, and write an essay explaining the nature of his or her personality and what the key details and statements reveal about this individual's personality.

18. Consider the many characterizations of the men and women associated with the church. From these portraits, what conclusion might you draw about Chaucer's attitude toward the church and/or religious practitioners? Write an essay in which you present your conclusion and support it with evidence from the Prologue.

19. **Thinking About the Essential Question: Do writers influence social trends or just reflect them?** Chaucer says the Knight in the Prologue "was a true, a perfect gentle-knight." In an essay, explain how his description of the Knight reflects the social ideal of knighthood. Then describe how such a description might influence readers to think in a certain way about knights. Use details from the poem to support your response.

Vocabulary Warm-up Word Lists

Study these words from the selection. Then, complete the activities.

Word List A

congregation [kahn gre GAY shun] *n.* people gathered for religious worship
  The rabbi asked his <u>congregation</u> to hold a fundraiser for homeless people.

discourse [DIS kawrs] *n.* a complete or thorough discussion of a topic
  The professor gave a long <u>discourse</u> explaining the reasons for the Civil War.

dignity [DIG ni tee] *n.* honor; self-respect; the quality of deserving esteem or respect
  The singer ignored the boos and walked off the stage with <u>dignity</u>, holding his head high.

pulpit [PUHL pit] *n.* a platform from which a religious leader speaks to worshipers
  The preacher spoke to the crowd from the <u>pulpit</u> at the front of the church.

sermon [SUR muhn] *n.* a lecture on right and wrong, often by a religious leader
  The preacher spoke for half an hour; his <u>sermon</u> was about forgiveness.

vanity [VAHN i tee] *n.* too much pride in your appearance or accomplishments
  Out of <u>vanity</u>, the ninety-year-old movie star had surgery to remove his wrinkles.

vice [VYS] *n.* bad or evil habit
  I think lying is a <u>vice</u> worse than laziness.

wary [WAYR ee] *adj.* on guard; watchful
  They told me their dog was friendly, but I was still <u>wary</u> of it and kept my distance.

Word List B

adversary [AHD vuhr ser ee] *n.* enemy; opponent
  The wrestler stood in the ring facing his <u>adversary</u>.

betray [bee TRAY] *v.* be unfaithful or disloyal; break someone's trust
  Do not <u>betray</u> your friends by telling their secrets to others.

counsel [KOWN suhl] *n.* advice; guidance
  When buying a used car, it is a good idea to get the <u>counsel</u> of a mechanic.

cultivate [KUHL ti vayt] *v.* help something grow or develop; nurture
  To <u>cultivate</u> good manners in yourself, always consider the feelings of others.

deceive [di SEEV] *v.* fool; mislead
  My friends tried to <u>deceive</u> me about the box, but I knew that it was my birthday present.

hypocrisy [hi POK ruh see] *n.* false appearance of being good or of following a belief
  She says that television is junk, but I realized her <u>hypocrisy</u> when I found her watching.

prudent [PROO duhnt] *adj.* using good judgment or common sense; careful
  He was <u>prudent</u> and checked if the lightbulb was still hot before he tried to unscrew it.

slandering [SLAN duhr ing] *adj.* spreading nasty rumors about someone
  In the politician's <u>slandering</u> speech, he said that his opponent did not know how to read.

Name _____ Date _____

from "The Pardoner's Tale" *from* **The Canterbury Tales** by Geoffrey Chaucer
Vocabulary Warm-up Exercises

Exercise A *Fill in each blank in the paragraph using the appropriate word from Word List A.*
Use each word only once.

When giving a speech, a public speaker often stands on a raised platform before a desk
of some kind. A religious leader, for example, may speak from a [1] _____
when he or she addresses the [2] _____ of worshipers. Speaking from a
formal platform adds to the speaker's [3] _____ and helps ensure that
the audience listens with respect. Whether the speech is a humorous toast to an hon-
ored guest or a religious [4] _____ on a bad habit or
[5] _____, the best speeches are short and simple. Listeners are
[6] _____ of long speeches and will avoid a speaker who always gives a
lengthy [7] _____ explaining his or her topic. If nothing else, a speaker's
pride and [8] _____ should make the speaker take care not to be boring!

Exercise B *For each vocabulary word below, write a sentence using the word that makes its*
meaning clear. Then, give a word or phrase that means the same as the vocabulary word.

Example: *Vocabulary word:* prudent
   Be prudent *and lock your car when you park it. (Word that means the same:* careful*)*

1. adversary
_____

2. betray
_____

3. counsel
_____

4. cultivate
_____

5. deceive
_____

6. hypocrisy
_____

7. slandering
_____

Name _____ Date _____

Read the following passage. Pay special attention to the underlined words. Then, read it again, and complete the activities. Use a separate sheet of paper for your written answers.

The parish priest was a central figure in the lives of medieval Christian Europeans. He was obliged to set a moral example for his parishioners by working hard and leading his life with <u>dignity</u> and self-respect.

By most accounts, the priest's life was not an easy one. His duties included presiding at weddings, funerals, baptisms (name-giving ceremonies), as well as giving the Sunday <u>sermon</u> from the <u>pulpit</u> at the front of the church. Many of his parishioners relied on this weekly speech for inspiration and guidance. The priest also celebrated mass, a daily Catholic ceremony, and heard people's confessions of their sins. In addition, the priest was responsible for running the local school, tending the sick, and providing hospitality to travelers. He also collected taxes called *tithes*.

Tithing was a system in which every member of the <u>congregation</u> was expected to give a tithe, or one-tenth of yearly earnings, to support the church. Parishioners could pay either in cash or in grain. The tithe income was shared among the parish priest, the church maintenance fund, the poor, and the bishop (the church official who oversaw the priest). Tithes could be a burden on the people, but village folk may have been <u>wary</u> of complaining too freely about them for fear of the authorities. Tithing was considered part of leading a moral life and could even be required by law.

Since most of the population could not read, people relied upon the priest for religious instruction. They also learned lessons from miracle and morality plays. These were short dramas that were acted out in the churchyards, usually on feast days. Miracle plays were based on biblical stories. A morality play might present a conflict between a virtue, such as charity, and a <u>vice</u>, such as <u>vanity</u>, or excessive pride. Instead of explaining religious ideas in a lengthy <u>discourse</u>, a play told a story—it entertained listeners even as it taught them.

1. Circle the word that is a clue to the meaning of <u>dignity</u>. Explain what a person needs to do to live with *dignity*.

2. Underline the phrase in the next sentence that helps explain what a <u>sermon</u> is. What might be the topic of a medieval *sermon*?

3. Circle the words that tell where you are likely to find a <u>pulpit</u>. Then, explain what a *pulpit* is.

4. Underline the words that show that a <u>congregation</u> is made up of more than one person. Rewrite the sentence using a phrase that means the same as *congregation*.

5. Underline the phrase that tells what folk were <u>wary</u> of. Explain whether people today are *wary* of similar things.

6. Circle the word that means the opposite of <u>vice</u>. Then, explain what *vice* means.

7. Underline the words that define <u>vanity</u>. Give an example that demonstrates *vanity*.

8. Circle the word that tells what a <u>discourse</u> is meant to do. Explain why simple folk might prefer a play to a *discourse*.

from "The Pardoner's Tale" *from* **The Canterbury Tales** by Geoffrey Chaucer
Reading Warm-up B

Read the following passage. Pay special attention to the underlined words. Then, read it again, and complete the activities. Use a separate sheet of paper for your written answers.

When people became sick in medieval times, they usually attempted to cure themselves with home remedies. If these remedies failed, though, they turned to an expert for advice. The expert whose <u>counsel</u> they sought was often an apothecary, the medieval equivalent of a town pharmacist. Lives could depend on his quick diagnosis of an illness and his careful intervention with the proper medicine. Like today's doctors, apothecaries had to be <u>prudent</u> in administering cures, taking care not to intervene unnecessarily if the patient was likely to heal all by himself or herself.

Apothecaries were respected professionals, not con artists or swindlers who set out to <u>deceive</u> those who came to them for help. Becoming a master apothecary required a seven-year apprenticeship and a great deal of dedication and discipline. An apothecary would not wish to <u>betray</u> a patient by promising a cure he could not deliver. Apothecaries did charge for their services, though, and it would have been <u>hypocrisy</u> for most apothecaries to claim that they worked only out of a sense of duty.

Besides dispensing drugs, ointments, and potions, apothecaries needed to obtain the ingredients for their medications. To do this, they would plant and <u>cultivate</u> the right herbs and other plants, watering and tending them. Then, they would collect and dry the needed roots, barks, and seeds. It was essential that an apothecary learn which part of the plant to harvest, and exactly when it should be cut or dug up. A mistake in this area could be devastating or even fatal, since one part of the plant could be edible and another part poisonous.

Of course, treatments did not always provide a cure. If an apothecary had too many failures, his business would suffer. If unsatisfied, a customer could easily become an <u>adversary</u>, seeking to harm the apothecary with <u>slandering</u> remarks that would damage his reputation.

1. Circle the word that is a clue to the meaning of <u>counsel</u>. Name two experts modern people go to for **counsel**.

2. Underline the phrase that is a clue to the meaning of <u>prudent</u>. Why do doctors need to be **prudent** in treating illness?

3. Circle the words that name people who <u>deceive</u> others. Then, give a synonym for **deceive**.

4. Circle the words that tell what would <u>betray</u> a patient. Explain why this act would **betray** the patient.

5. Underline what it would be <u>hypocrisy</u> to claim. Then, circle the phrase that shows why it would be **hypocrisy**.

6. Underline the phrase that tells what you do to <u>cultivate</u> a plant. Then, use the word **cultivate** in a sentence of your own.

7. Underline the phrase that tells what an <u>adversary</u> may seek to do. Tell what **adversary** means.

8. Circle the words that tell what <u>slandering</u> remarks would damage. Describe a defense against **slandering** remarks.

Unit 1 Resources: From Legend to History
99

"The Pardoner's Tale" *from* **The Canterbury Tales** by Geoffrey Chaucer
Literary Analysis: Allegory/Archetypal Narrative Elements

An **allegory** is a narrative that has both a literal meaning and a deeper, symbolic meaning. On the literal level, it tells a story. On the symbolic level, many or all of its characters, events, settings, and objects symbolize, or represent, abstract ideas and work to teach a moral message. Allegory uses **archetypal narrative elements,** particular basic storytelling patterns, to express common morals and ideas. Such elements include tests of characters' moral fiber, mysterious guides, groups of three, and just endings that reward good and punish evil.

A. DIRECTIONS: *Answer these questions about "The Pardoner's Tale."*

1. What vices do the rioters seem to represent? _____

2. What might the old man represent? _____

3. Which character has a name indicating the abstract idea he represents? _____

4. What might the gold florins represent? _____

5. Consider the events near the end of the tale. What might the revelers' actions toward one another represent? _____

6. What is the moral message that the Pardoner's allegory attempts to teach? _____

_____

B. DIRECTIONS: *On the lines below or on a separate sheet, write your ideas for a modern allegory illustrating the same message as "The Pardoner's Tale" or another moral message. Be sure to include archetypal narrative elements.*

_____

_____

_____

_____

_____

_____

_____

_____

_____

"The Pardoner's Tale" *from* The Canterbury Tales by Geoffrey Chaucer
Reading Strategy: Reread for Clarification

Rereading can often help clarify characters' identities and relationships, the sequence or cause of events, unfamiliar language, and other puzzling information. Often, earlier passages provide the key to understanding the puzzling information. Study this example:

> **Passage**
> They made their bargain, swore with appetite,
> These three, to live and die for one another
> As brother-born might swear to his born brother.

> **Puzzling Detail**
> What bargain did the three men make?

> **Reread Earlier Passage**
> Hold up your hands, like me, and we'll be brothers
> In this affair, and each defend the others,
> And we will kill this traitor Death, I say!

> **Clarification**
> They made a bargain to kill Death.

DIRECTIONS: *For each item below, reread earlier passages of "The Pardoner's Tale" to clarify the possibly puzzling information about which the question asks. On the lines provided, write the details that clarify the information.*

1. In line 102, the publican tells the rioters, "Be on your guard with such an adversary." What adversary is he talking about?

   _____

2. In lines 174–175, one rioter tells the old man, "I heard you mention, just a moment gone, / A certain traitor Death. . . ." What did the old man say earlier about Death?

   _____

3. In line 213, one of the rioters says that they must bring the gold back at night. What reason did he give earlier for doing this?

   _____

4. In lines 260–262, the Pardoner tells us that the youngest rioter "Kept turning over, rolling up and down / Within his heart the beauty of those bright / New florins. . . ." Does the rioter have any florins with him? If not, what does this passage mean?

   _____

5. In lines 304–305, the Pardoner tells us, "Exactly in the way they'd planned his death/They fell on him and slew him. . . ." What was the plan?

   _____

"The Pardoner's Tale" *from* **The Canterbury Tales** by Geoffrey Chaucer
Vocabulary Builder

Word List

apothecary   deftly   hoary   pallor   sauntered   tarry

A. DIRECTIONS: *Read each series of words. Write the word from the Word List that best fits with the other words in the series.*

1. linger, hang behind _____

2. pharmacist, medical person _____

3. ambled, meandered _____

4. paleness, white skin, deathly hue _____

5. ancient, gray, white _____

6. skillfully, cleverly, nimbly _____

B. WORD STUDY: *In each sentence, underline the word that contains the prefix* apo-. *Then, use your knowledge of the prefix to define the word you underlined.*

1. After insulting the group of businessmen, the engineer apologized.

_____

2. The apothegm the gambler used when he lost was: "You win some, you lose some."

_____

3. The minister read the apocryphal writings before the New Testament.

_____

"The Pardoner's Tale" *from* **The Canterbury Tales** by Geoffrey Chaucer

Integrated Language Skills: Support for Writing

Use the following outline to help you organize your sermon on greed. Remember that you are addressing a contemporary audience and should use present-day examples to support your main ideas. Continue the outline on a separate sheet if necessary.

I. Main Argument: _____

_____

   A. Supporting Idea: _____

_____

      1. Detail or Example: _____

_____

      2. Detail or Example: _____

_____

   B. Supporting Idea: _____

      1. Detail or Example: _____

_____

      2. Detail or Example: _____

_____

On a separate sheet, write a draft of your sermon on greed. Follow the ideas as you organized them in your outline. Be sure to clearly support your argument with your ideas and examples.

"The Pardoner's Tale" *from* **The Canterbury Tales** by Geoffrey Chaucer

Enrichment: Plague

Plague is a serious disease caused by *Yersinia pestis*, a bacteria found in rodents and the fleas that live on them. The disease can spread to human beings if they are bitten by the infected fleas, if they come in direct contact with infected body tissues or body fluids, or if they breathe in the bacteria through the air. In human beings, plague has three forms. In bubonic plague, the bacteria settles in the lymph nodes, causing painful lumps called buboes. Other symptoms include fever, headache, chills, tiredness, and stomach upset. If left untreated, the bacteria can multiply in the bloodstream to cause septicemic plague, which adds the symptoms of severe abdominal pain and bleeding in the skin and internal organs. If the bacteria infects the lungs, the person develops pneumonic plague, breathing with great difficulty and coughing up blood. In this stage, one person can spread the plague to another by coughing at close range.

Without early treatment, septicemic plague and pneumonic plague are usually fatal. However, plague today can be effectively treated with several kinds of antibiotics, as long as they are started early in the course of the disease. Antibiotics will usually work even for someone exposed to pneumonic plague if they are given quickly enough.

In times past, there was no known treatment for the plague, and periodic outbreaks were devastating. Probably the most famous outbreak was the one during Chaucer's childhood called the Black Death, which swept from Asia to Europe in the mid-1300s, killing as much as a third of the population.

DIRECTIONS: *Answer these questions based on the information above and the details in "The Pardoner's Tale."*

1. What are the three stages of plague, and what part of the body does each one attack?

   _____

   _____

2. Can someone with bubonic plague transmit it by breathing on someone else? Explain.

   _____

   _____

3. Why do you think plague spread so rapidly in medieval cities?

   _____

   _____

   _____

4. How do you think readers in Chaucer's day felt when they read about the plague? Why?

   _____

   _____

5. What attitude toward death evident in the "The Pardoner's Tale" might be partly explained by the frequent outbreaks of plague in Chaucer's day?

   _____

   _____

Name _____ Date _____

"The Pardoner's Tale" *from* **The Canterbury Tales** by Geoffrey Chaucer
Open-Book Test

Short Answer *Write your response to the questions in this section on the lines provided.*

1. What is the allegory that the Pardoner teaches in "The Pardoner's Tale" from *The Canterbury Tales*? Focus on the meaning of *allegory* in your answer.

   _____

   _____

   _____

   _____

2. What do you learn about the time in which "The Pardoner's Tale" from *The Canterbury Tales* is set by rereading these lines? Explain.

   > And then Death went his way without a word. / He's killed a thousand in the present plague, / And, sir, it doesn't do to be too vague / If you should meet him; you had best be wary.

   _____

   _____

   _____

   _____

3. In "The Pardoner's Tale" from *The Canterbury Tales*, which character or characters does the Pardoner himself most closely resemble? Explain.

   _____

   _____

   _____

   _____

4. The rioters represent certain qualities in "The Pardoner's Tale" from *The Canterbury Tales*. What qualities would you say they represent and why?

   _____

   _____

   _____

5. Reread this passage from "The Pardoner's Tale" from *The Canterbury Tales*. What is the speaker trying to do in his speech?

   > . . ."if it be your design / To find out Death, turn up this crooked way / Towards that grove, I left him there today / Under a tree, and there you'll find him waiting."

   _____

   _____

   _____

   _____

6. In "The Pardoner's Tale" from *The Canterbury Tales*, the three rioters pledge "to live and die for one another / As brother-born might swear to his born brother." What is ironic about this pledge?

_____

_____

_____

7. The three rioters reveal their characters through their actions in "The Pardoner's Tale" from *The Canterbury Tales*. In the chart, write what they do to show each trait.

Trait	Action
Greed	
Treachery	
Contempt	

8. The Pardoner often tells his tale to listeners in *The Canterbury Tales*. What is his usual reason for telling it?

_____

_____

_____

9. In "The Pardoner's Tale" from *The Canterbury Tales* the man whom the rioters meet has a *hoary* head. How old would you guess he was? Why?

_____

_____

_____

10. In "The Pardoner's Tale" from *The Canterbury Tales*, the *apothecary* sold the young rioter a poison. What does an apothecary do? What would he be called today?

_____

_____

_____

Essay

Write an extended response to the question of your choice or to the question or questions your teacher assigns you.

11. Write an essay in which you analyze the characters of the old man and the three rioters from "The Pardoner's Tale" from *The Canterbury Tales*. Describe how they are alike and different. Then decide which is the least trustworthy. Consider what evil each commits and their motives for their actions. Give examples that support your opinion.

12. In "The Pardoner's Tale" from *The Canterbury Tales,* what is the moral message that the allegory conveys? In an essay, state the moral message of the tale. Then use information from "The Pardoner's Tale" to show how several details work together to help build and convey the message.

13. In "The Pardoner's Tale" from *The Canterbury Tales,* who is the old man? Is he a spy for Death? Is he an innocent bystander? Is he Death itself? Write an essay in which you assert your position. Use examples from the text to support your claim.

14. **Thinking About the Essential Question: Do writers influence social trends or just reflect them?** Many of Chaucer's characters reflect the social issues of his time. In an essay, describe the Pardoner's job and how it reflects society's attitudes toward the Church and toward Death. Use examples from "The Pardoner's Tale" from *The Canterbury Tales* to support your ideas.

Oral Response

15. Go back to questions 2, 4, 6, or to the question your teacher assigns to you. Take a few minutes to expand your answer and prepare an oral response. Find additional details in "The Pardoner's Tale" that will support your points. If necessary, make notes to guide your response.

Name _____ Date _____

"The Pardoner's Tale" *from* **The Canterbury Tales** by Geoffrey Chaucer
Selection Test A

Critical Reading *Identify the letter of the choice that best answers the question.*

____ 1. What can you infer from these words of the Pardoner in "The Pardoner's Tale"?

For my exclusive purpose is to win / And not at all to castigate their sin. / Once dead what matter how their souls may fare? / They can go blackberrying, for all I care!

A. He wants his parishioners to seek forgiveness for their sins.

B. He wants his parishioners to work harder at farming for blackberries.

C. He wants his parishioners to think about what will happen when they die.

D. He wants his parishioners to give him plenty of their money.

____ 2. What is the allegory that the Pardoner teaches in "The Pardoner's Tale"?

A. People are not always what they seem.

B. Evil men will get what they deserve.

C. Greed is the root of all evil.

D. Even the best of friends cannot be trusted.

____ 3. What do you learn about "The Pardoner's Tale" by rereading these lines?

And then Death went his way without a word. / He's killed a thousand in the present plague, / And, sir, it doesn't do to be too vague / If you should meet him; you had best be wary.

A. Death would rather not speak.

B. This is a story about the plague.

C. The rioters should stay away from death.

D. Death can be avoided if you are careful.

____ 4. Which words best describe the three rioters in "The Pardoner's Tale"?

A. friendly and fun-loving

B. greedy and rough

C. smart and dangerous

D. cautious and sneaky

____ 5. Reread these lines that are spoken by the old man in "The Pardoner's Tale." What does he mean?

About the earth, which is my mother's gate, / Knock-knocking with my staff from night to noon / And crying, 'Mother, open to me soon! / Look at me, mother, won't you let me in?'

A. He wants to find his mother.

B. He is tired of wandering.

C. He wants to die.

D. He wants a place to live.

_____ 6. Why does the old man send the three rioters to the tree in "The Pardoner's Tale"?

A. so the three rioters will not kill him

B. so the three rioters will go to their own deaths

C. so the three rioters can find gold

D. so he will have time to escape

_____ 7. What is one characteristic of an allegory that is found in "The Pardoner's Tale"?

A. a story that occurs within the story

B. rhyming of every two lines

C. a tale that is told as a long prose poem

D. the use of characters to stand for ideas

_____ 8. In "The Pardoner's Tale," what do the two rioters decide to do after they have sent their friend for food and wine?

A. to take the money while he is gone

B. to carry away the money that night

C. to give some money to the old man

D. to kill their friend when he returns

_____ 9. What does the young rioter decide while on his way into town for food and wine in "The Pardoner's Tale"?

A. to poison his friends

B. to look for Death on his way

C. to find the old man and warn him

D. to tell the old man what they found

_____ 10. Who is the old man in "The Pardoner's Tale"?

A. Death

B. Hope

C. a thief and wanderer

D. a mean-spirited villager

_____ 11. In "The Pardoner's Tale," which character or characters does the Pardoner most closely resemble?

A. the old man

B. Death

C. the three rioters

D. his parishioners

___ 12. Which character trait leads to the downfall of the three rioters in "The Pardoner's Tale"?
   A. innocence   C. jealousy
   B. greed   D. pride

Vocabulary and Grammar

___ 13. Which vocabulary word correctly completes this sentence?
   The _____ sold the young rioter a strong poison that he mixed with wine.
   A. pallor   C. prating
   B. tarry   D. apothecary

___ 14. Which word is closest in meaning to *deftly*?
   A. skillfully   C. quickly
   B. awkwardly   D. eagerly

___ 15. Which vocabulary word correctly completes this sentence?
   The old man's beard was thick and _____.
   A. pallor   C. hoary
   B. tarry   D. sauntered

Essay

16. In "The Pardoner's Tale," the Pardoner says that he uses this story of the three rioters to get his congregation to give him their money. In an essay, explain how this process works. Why do his parishioners give him money? How does this story help the Pardoner achieve his goal? Use information from "The Pardoner's Tale" to help you in your response.

17. Write an essay in which you analyze the characters of the old man and the three rioters from "The Pardoner's Tale." Then decide who is less trustworthy. As you write, tell how they are alike and how they are different. Think about these questions: What evil do they commit? What are their motives for their actions? Give at least two examples to support your opinion.

18. **Thinking About the Essential Question: Do writers influence social trends or just reflect them?** Many of Chaucer's characters reflect the social issues of his time. How does the Pardoner reflect the condition of the Catholic Church? In an essay, describe the Pardoner's job and how it reflects society's attitudes toward the Church. Use examples from "The Pardoner's Tale" to support your ideas.

Name _____ Date _____

"The Pardoner's Tale" *from* The Canterbury Tales by Geoffrey Chaucer
Selection Test B

Critical Reading *Identify the letter of the choice that best completes the statement or answers the question.*

_____ 1. When "The Pardoner's Tale" opens, what has caused Death to stalk the land?
   A. a terrible flood
   B. an outbreak of plague
   C. a riot
   D. greed

_____ 2. What is ironic about the pledge the rioters make in these lines of "The Pardoner's Tale"?
   They made their bargain, swore with appetite. / These three, to live and die for one another / As brother-born might swear to his born brother.

   A. They really are brothers but have forgotten.
   B. They have only just met.
   C. They do not realize that Death is listening.
   D. They later plot to kill one another to get a larger share of the gold.

_____ 3. On the symbolic level of the allegory of "The Pardoner's Tale," which of these qualities might the rioters represent?
   A. old age and death
   B. courage and greed
   C. greed and treachery
   D. fame and fortune

_____ 4. At one point in "The Pardoner's Tale," the publican says, "This very year he killed, in a large village a mile away, man, woman, serf and tillage." Reread these lines that precede the publican's remark, and then decide what most likely happened in the village.

   There came a privy thief, they call him Death,

   Who kills us all round here, and in a breath

   He speared him through the heart, he never stirred.

   And then Death went his way without a word.

   He's killed a thousand in the present plague,

   And, sir, it doesn't do to be too vague

   A. Thieves robbed the village and killed the inhabitants.
   B. A strong wind blew through the village, killing everyone there.
   C. Everyone in the village died with a spear in his or her heart.
   D. Plague claimed the lives of the people in the village.

_____ 5. In "The Pardoner's Tale," how do the rioters treat the old man when they first meet him?
   A. with contempt
   B. with kindess
   C. with false flattery
   D. with polite disinterest

_____ 6. In "The Pardoner's Tale" the three rioters are sure that they can destroy Death, and yet they fail to see that they are falling into his trap. This is an example of _____.
A. irony
B. heroism
C. hedonism
D. flattery

_____ 7. What becomes clearer when rereading the following passage from "The Pardoner's Tale"?
. . . if it be your design / To find out Death, turn up this crooked way / Towards that grove, I left him there today / Under a tree, and there you'll find him waiting.

A. There is a hooded figure near the grove awaiting the three rioters.
B. The plague will get the three rioters because there is a graveyard near the grove.
C. The man is directing the three rioters toward their own deaths.
D. The three rioters will be victorious over Death because they are not afraid of him.

_____ 8. The moral of "The Pardoner's Tale" is
A. Friends should never be trusted.
B. Greed is the source of evil.
C. A promise is a promise.
D. Old men are unreliable.

_____ 9. Which of the following best describes the three rioters in "The Pardoner's Tale"?
A. prating, kindly, old
B. hoary, arrogant, insincere
C. earnest, brave, handsome
D. prating, arrogant, greedy

_____ 10. For what reason does the Pardoner usually tell "The Pardoner's Tale"?
A. He is convinced that greed is evil and has himself given all his money away to the poor.
B. He uses it as an exemplum in a sermon designed to get listeners to part with their money.
C. He is a poor man who tells the story in storytelling contests in the hopes of earning enough money to pay for his travels.
D. all of the above

_____ 11. How do two of the rioters decide to increase their share of the gold?
A. poison the other rioter upon his return
B. stab the other rioter upon his return
C. turn the third rioter in to the priest
D. find the original owner of the gold and rob him for more

_____ 12. Who is the real traitor in "The Pardoner's Tale"?
A. the three rioters
B. Death
C. the old man
D. the plague

Vocabulary and Grammar

____ 13. Which word has the same meaning as *tarry*?
A. hesitate
B. hurry
C. refuse
D. chatter

____ 14. Somebody whose face shows *pallor* is _____.
A. flushed
B. blue with cold
C. pale
D. sunburned

____ 15. In "The Pardoner's Tale," when the murderer *sauntered* back to his friends, he _____?
A. ran quickly
B. walked slowly
C. walked heavily
D. tiptoed

____ 16. The word most nearly opposite in meaning to *hoary* is _____.
A. contemporary
B. honest
C. senior
D. young

Essay

17. What is the moral message that the allegory of "The Pardoner's Tale" conveys? In a brief essay, state the moral message of the tale. Then use information from "The Pardoner's Tale" to show how several details work together to help build the message.

18. In a brief essay, compare and contrast the Pardoner to the tale he tells in "The Pardoner's Tale." What kind of person is he? Consider the kind of person he is and the reason that he generally tells this kind of tale.

19. Who is the old man in "The Pardoner's Tale"? Is he a spy for Death? Is he an innocent bystander? Is he Death itself? Write an essay in which you assert your position. Use examples from the text to support your position.

20. **Thinking About the Essential Question: Do writers influence social trends or just reflect them?** Many of Chaucer's characters reflect the social issues of his time. How does the Pardoner reflect the condition of the Catholic Church and society's attitudes toward death? In an essay, describe the Pardoner's job and how it reflects society's attitudes toward the Church and toward Death. Use examples from "The Pardoner's Tale" to support your ideas.

Vocabulary Warm-up Word Lists

Study these words from the selection. Then, complete the activities.

Word List A

bottled [BAHT uhld] *v.* (with *up*) held in; restrained; contained
   The mourner kept her grief and sadness <u>bottled</u> up.

crone [KROHN] *n.* an ugly old woman; hag
   Fairy tales often feature a <u>crone</u> who later becomes a beautiful maiden.

extort [ek STOHRT] *v.* obtain by using violence or threats
   Blackmailers <u>extort</u> money by threatening to reveal damaging secrets.

forlorn [fohr LOHRN] *adj.* abandoned or forsaken; sad and lonely
   The stray dog looked hungry and <u>forlorn</u> when the children found her.

matrons [MAY truhns] *n.* married women or widows; mature women
   The <u>matrons</u> in the garden club have exchanged advice for years.

purged [PERJD] *v.* removed; cleansed; to have gotten rid of
   The exterminator <u>purged</u> the house of unwanted insects.

reprove [ri PROOV] *v.* admonish; find fault with; rebuke
   The coach had to <u>reprove</u> his players for not following the game plan.

void [VOYD] *adj.* empty; containing no matter
   The manager discovered that the safe was mysteriously <u>void</u> of cash.

Word List B

ceaselessly [SEES lis lee] *adv.* without stopping; continuously
   The crew bailed water <u>ceaselessly</u> to make sure the ship would float.

defiance [di FY uhns] *n.* open resistance to an opposing force or authority
   The tennis player wore black clothing in <u>defiance</u> of the rules.

disperses [di SPERS ez] *v.* drives off; scatters; distributes widely
   The scent of this candle <u>disperses</u> mosquitoes, so we will not be bitten.

enquire [en KWYR] *v.* to seek information by asking a question
   Some people do not realize that it is rude to <u>enquire</u> about personal matters.

incentive [in SEN tiv] *n.* something that encourages you to do something
   A raise in pay is often enough <u>incentive</u> for most employees to work harder.

maim [MAYM] *v.* injure; impair; mutilate
   Even a minor automobile accident can <u>maim</u> occupants for life.

saddle [SAD uhl] *v.* load down; burden
   The manager thought it best to <u>saddle</u> new employees with extra work.

temporal [TEM puh ruhl] *adj.* lasting for only a time; not eternal; worldly
   The monk's meditations did not focus on <u>temporal</u> matters, such as money.

"The Wife of Bath's Tale" *from* **The Canterbury Tales** by Geoffrey Chaucer
Vocabulary Warm-up Exercises

Exercise A *Fill in each blank in the paragraph with the appropriate word from Word List A. Use each word only once.*

Grooming was important to people in the Middle Ages. They bathed openly in lakes and rivers without fear that someone might [1] _____ them for being inde-cent. Hot baths were popular, but because woodcutters had [2] _____ the forests of trees and the landscape became [3] _____ of firewood, the cost of heating water became too great for most people. However, people did not keep their dismay about this lack of hygiene [4] _____ up. They spoke about it openly and used perfumes to mask body odors. To avoid looking like a [5] _____ as they aged, wealthy [6] _____ painted their faces with cosmetics and sun-bleached their hair. Those who could not keep up appear-ances were often avoided and became desperately [7] _____. An easy way to [8] _____ money from them was to sell miracle elixirs promising the appearance of youth.

Exercise B *Answer each question in a complete sentence using a word from Word List B that means the same as underlined word or group of words.*

1. How might you provide <u>motivation</u> for someone who's discouraged?
   _____

2. When would you <u>ask for information</u> about someone's health?
   _____

3. How were the deer able to <u>mutilate</u> the apple trees?
   _____

4. Why did the chef <u>burden</u> himself by adding so many specials to the menu?
   _____

5. What <u>scatters</u> the seeds from the wildflowers?
   _____

6. Is it safe to drive <u>without stopping</u> for more than five hours?
   _____

7. Do artists expect the value of their works to be eternal or to <u>last only for a time</u>?
   _____

8. What situation might make someone show <u>resistance to authority</u>?
   _____

"The Wife of Bath's Tale" *from* The Canterbury Tales by Geoffrey Chaucer
Reading Warm-up A

Read the following passage. Pay special attention to the underlined words. Then, read it again, and complete the activities. Use a separate sheet of paper for your written answers.

It was not unusual for widows in fifteenth-century England to wed again after the deaths of their husbands. Matrons in the lower classes often took new vows only weeks or months after burying their spouses. Some writers wanted to reprove widows for remarrying. However, the reasons for remarriage were compelling and strictly practical. It was difficult for a woman to raise a family, manage assets, and maintain her reputation on her own.

Instead of being forlorn, having no one to turn to, some widows used their chance of remarriage to find a man who could increase their fortunes. This was not frowned upon since medieval marriage was mostly seen as an economic arrangement, not the fulfillment of romantic love.

Of course, the survival of a family depended upon good alliances, and matrimonial partners were usually chosen for social or political reasons. If a husband and wife were fond of each other, that was considered fortunate. In many cases, these marriages were not void of the kind of love and affection one might find today. However, these were not requirements for a successful marriage. Because there were no illusions about this type of arrangement, spouses did not keep hostile feelings bottled up. As a result, sometimes the relationships were challenging, oppressive, and violent.

Girls were raised primarily to be wives, but they had little say about whom they would marry. Sometimes a groom's family would extort an extravagant dowry from the bride's parents. If a woman didn't want to marry, she could join a convent, but this required considerable wealth. To a degree, individual desires and preferences were purged from the minds of young girls. No young woman wanted to end up a lonely, unmarried crone, so she deferred to her parents' choice.

1. Underline the sentence that explains why matrons often took new vows quickly. Explain what *matrons* are.

2. Underline the words that tell what some writers wanted to reprove widows for. Then, tell what *reprove* means.

3. Underline the words that suggest what forlorn means. Then, describe something that might make a person *forlorn*.

4. Explain what marriages in the Middle Ages were not void of. Then, give a synonym for *void*.

5. Underline the words that tell why spouses did not keep negative feelings bottled up. Then give a synonym for "*bottled* up."

6. Circle the words that tell what a groom's family might extort. Then, explain what *extort* means.

7. Rewrite the sentence using a synonym for purged. Then, tell what *purged* means.

8. Circle the words that tell what a young woman did so she would not end up a lonely, unmarried crone. Then, describe a *crone*.

"The Wife of Bath's Tale" *from* **The Canterbury Tales** by Geoffrey Chaucer
Reading Warm-up B

Read the following passage. Pay special attention to the underlined words. Then, read it again, and complete the activities. Use a separate sheet of paper for your written answers.

The medieval knight began training at the age of eight, which was when he was sent to a nearby castle to become a page. Although the household would saddle him with considerable domestic duties, the boy was expected to master wrestling, horsemanship, and fighting with both spear and sword. A page in training practiced ceaselessly by attacking a dummy with a shield, which was hung on a wooden pole. When the page hit the shield with his weapon, the device could easily spin around and maim him unless he moved away quickly. Pages also learned to read, write, sing, dance, and behave properly in the king's court.

At the age of fifteen or sixteen, the page advanced to the rank of squire. Then, it was his job to enquire about a specific knight's needs, and once he found out what they were, attend to them. A squire's responsibilities included dressing the knight, serving his meals, caring for his horse, and cleaning his armor and weapons. He also followed the knight to tournaments and assisted him in battle.

When a squire reached the age of twenty, he could become a knight by proving himself worthy by valor in combat, by defiance of a foe, or by a charge that disperses enemy combatants. Sometimes the squire was named a knight before an actual battle took place in order to provide him with incentive and courage.

When a lord agreed to knight a squire, a formal dubbing ceremony took place, which was witnessed by nobility, family, and friends. The evening before, the squire typically turned his thoughts away from temporal matters in order to fast and pray for the purification of his soul. The next day, he would be summoned before the lord of the castle who would tap him lightly on each shoulder with his sword and proclaim him a knight.

1. Circle the words that tell what the household would saddle the boy with. Name something that someone might *saddle* another person with.

2. Rewrite the sentence, using a synonym for ceaselessly.

3. Circle the words that tell what could maim the page. Then explain what *maim* means.

4. Underline the phrase that is a clue to meaning of enquire. Describe a situation where you might need to *enquire* about a person's needs.

5. Rewrite the sentence, using a synonym for defiance.

6. Circle the words that tell what a charge disperses. Then, name a force that *disperses* people and property.

7. Underline the phrase that tells what incentive a squire was given. Explain why a squire would need *incentive* before going into battle.

8. Rewrite the sentence, using a synonym for temporal.

"The Wife of Bath's Tale" *from* The Canterbury Tales by Geoffrey Chaucer
Literary Analysis: Frame/Setting

A **frame** is a story in which one or more other stories unfolds. The frame usually introduces a set of characters in a particular situation that prompts one or more of these characters to tell a **story-within-the-story.** Chaucer begins The *Canterbury Tales* with a Prologue that provides a frame. In the frame, Chaucer introduces the characters who will tell their own stories. The **setting** of the frame story provides the characters with the opportunity to tell their stories. Each of the characters who tells his or her own story then provides an additional setting—the time and place where the character's story takes place. As the narrator's voice changes between stories, so does the setting.

A. DIRECTIONS: *On the lines provided, answer these questions about the frame of* The Canterbury Tales *and its relationship to "The Wife of Bath's Tale."*

1. What is the main frame of *The Canterbury Tales*?

_____

2. What setting does Chaucer supply in the frame to explain his story collection?

_____

3. How does the frame and its setting make reading the different stories more interesting?

_____

_____

4. In addition to the main story about the knight, what other story does the Wife of Bath tell in part in "The Wife of Bath's Tale"? What settings does she describe?

_____

_____

5. Consider the characterization of the Wife of Bath in the general Prologue to *The Canterbury Tales.* How does the story she tells suit her personality and background?

_____

_____

B. DIRECTIONS: *What setting would you use in a frame that would bring together a group of contemporary storytellers? Jot down your ideas for a modern frame on the lines below.*

_____

_____

_____

_____

_____

Name _____ Date _____

Reading Strategy: Use Context Clues

You can often figure out the meaning of an unfamiliar word if you examine its **context,** or surroundings, for clues to its meaning. The following list shows common types of context clues and examples in which they appear. In the examples, the possibly unfamiliar words are underlined, and the context clues are in italics.

- **Synonym or Definition:** a word or words that mean the same as the unfamiliar word

  She dined in a bistro, *a small French restaurant.*

- **Antonym or Contrast:** a word or words that mean the opposite of the unfamiliar word or tell you what the unfamiliar word is not

  The race will *begin* at 6 o'clock and terminate three hours later.

- **Explanation:** words that give more information about an unfamiliar word

  Ocelots are *like leopards, only smaller.*

- **Example:** a word or words that illustrate the unfamiliar word, or a word or words that tell what the unfamiliar word illustrates

  Rodents include *rats, mice, and squirrels.*

- **Sentence Role:** hints about the word's meaning based on its use in a sentence. For example, in this sentence, you can tell that a *bistro* is a noun and that it is not abstract, since it can be entered.

  Example: The couple entered the bistro.

DIRECTIONS: *Answer these questions about words in "The Wife of Bath's Tale."*

1. What synonym in line 72 helps you know the meaning of *jollity?* _____

2. What two examples in lines 78–80 help clarify the meaning of *flattery?* _____
   _____

3. In lines 82–84, what does the contrast suggest that *reprove* means? _____
   _____

4. What nearby synonym helps clarify the meaning of *maim* in line 278? _____

5. From the explanation in lines 303–304, what do you think *churl* means? _____
   _____

"The Wife of Bath's Tale" *from* **The Canterbury Tales** by Geoffrey Chaucer
Vocabulary Builder

Word List

bequeath   contemptuous   esteemed   implored   prowess   rebuke   relates

A. DIRECTIONS: *Use your knowledge of the words in the Word List to decide whether each statement below is true or false. Then, on the line before the statement, write* T *if it is true and* F *if it is false.*

_____ 1. Someone who skates with *prowess* often falls flat on her face.

_____ 2. A smile is a *contemptuous* expression.

_____ 3. A storyteller *relates* a story.

_____ 4. People sometimes *bequeath* property to their heirs.

_____ 5. Most people enjoy having someone *rebuke* them.

_____ 6. If someone *implored* you to leave, they would not want you to move.

_____ 7. People often stand up when an *esteemed* figure enters the room.

B. WORD STUDY: *The italicized words in these lines from "The Wife of Bath's Tale" each can have more than one meaning. Use the context to determine which of the two possible meanings applies to the lines from the selection, and circle that meaning. Then, on the line provided, write a sentence illustrating the other meaning of the word.*

1. Ovid *relates* that under his long hair / The unhappy Midas grew a splendid pair / Of ass's ears.

   Possible Meanings: shows a connection   narrates

   _____

2. He begged her not to tell a living creature / That he possessed so horrible a *feature*:

   Possible Meanings: any part of the face   a special newspaper or magazine story

   _____

3. There wasn't a living creature to be seen / Save on old woman sitting on the *green*

   Possible Meanings: a color blending yellow and blue   an expanse of grass or plants

   _____

4. It was such torture that his wife looked *foul*.

   Possible Meanings: disgusting   hit out of bounds

   _____

"The Wife of Bath's Tale" *from* **The Canterbury Tales** by Geoffrey Chaucer

Integrated Language Skills: Support for Writing

Use the chart to organize the information for your response to criticism. Paraphrase the critic's interpretation, explain your reaction to the critic's interpretation, and provide support for your reaction, using details and examples from the text. Record any new ideas that you develop from your work.

Critic's Interpretation:		
My Reaction:		
Supporting Detail:	**Supporting Detail:**	**Supporting Detail:**
New Ideas About Original Text:		

On a separate page, draft your response to criticism. Make sure that you clearly state your opinion of the critic's interpretation, include supporting details for your opinion, and provide additional insight into the original text.

Unit 1 Resources: From Legend to History
121

Name _____ Date _____

"The Wife of Bath's Tale" *from* The Canterbury Tales by Geoffrey Chaucer
Grammar and Style: Correlative Conjunctions

Correlative conjunctions are paired conjunctions that connect two words or groups of words of equal significance.

Correlative Conjunctions				
either . . . or	neither . . . nor	both . . . and	whether . . . or	not only . . . but also

EXAMPLES

We will **either** read "The Wife of Bath's Tale" **or** "The Pardoner's Tale."
Neither Jamal **nor** Freida will be in class today.
The class wants to read **both** Chaucer **and** Bede.
We will decide **whether** we should go out **or** stay home.
The story provides **not only** entertainment **but also** social commentary.

Be careful not to confuse *either* and *neither* when they are used alone. In such a case, the word is used as either an adjective or a pronoun.

EXAMPLES

Neither of us could make it to the show. (pronoun)   **Neither** one will fit. (adjective)
Either works for this job. (pronoun)   **Either** shirt will be fine. (adjective)

DIRECTIONS: *Use correlative conjunctions to combine the sentence pairs.*

1. The knight would die. The knight would go on a quest.

   _____

   _____

2. The knight did not want to die. He did not want to marry an old woman.

   _____

   _____

3. The knight had to decide to marry the old woman. He had to decide to die.

   _____

   _____

4. The knight got to live. The knight had a beautiful wife.

   _____

   _____

"The Wife of Bath's Tale" *from* **The Canterbury Tales** by Geoffrey Chaucer
Enrichment: King Midas

The Wife of Bath tells only part of the famous legend of King Midas. These legends are based on an actual king who ruled the kingdom of Phrygia in Anatolia, or Asia Minor, the Asian part of today's nation of Turkey. In ancient times, much of Asia Minor was part of Greek civilization. The real King Midas lived from about 740 to 696 B.C. According to the Greek historian Herodotus, he was a wealthy king who married a Greek princess and built wonderful gardens. He successfully battled the Assyrians, signing a peace treaty with Assyrian ruler Sargon II in 709 B.C. However, in 696 B.C., fierce horse-riding nomads known as the Cimmerians invaded and destroyed his kingdom.

The legends of Midas often paint him as much more foolish than the real King Midas was. According to one famous legend, Midas rescues Silenus, good friend of Dionysius, the god of wine. To thank him, Dionysius offers to grant any wish Midas chooses. Midas, going against the advice of Dionysius, wishes that everything he touches turns to gold. He walks throughout his palace and turns everything to gold. When he grows hungry, however, all the foods and liquids he touches also turn to gold, and he is unable to eat or drink.

The Wife of Bath tells part of another legend of King Midas. In this legend, Midas serves as a judge between the god Apollo and the satyr Marsyas and rules in Marsyas' favor. Apollo is so furious that he gives Midas a pair of donkey's ears. In many versions of the legend, it is Midas' barber, not his wife, who cannot keep the secret of the ears and whispers it into a hole in the meadow, where he is overheard.

A. DIRECTIONS: *Answer these questions based on the material you have just read about Midas.*

1. What event do you think might have led to the death of the real King Midas?

   _____

2. What lesson about greed does the first legend of Midas teach?

   _____

3. What lesson about magic or fate does the first legend of Midas also teach?

   _____

4. How does the legend involving Apollo stress the idea that Midas was foolish?

   _____

5. Why does it make sense that Midas' barber knows the secret of his ears?

   _____

B. DIRECTIONS: *Today, when a businessperson is praised for having a "Midas touch," what do you think the expression means? Write your answer on the lines below.*

   _____

   _____

"The Wife of Bath's Tale" *from* **The Canterbury Tales** by Geoffrey Chaucer
Open-Book Test

Short Answer *Write your response to the questions in this section on the lines provided.*

1. The setting of the story about the knight in "The Wife of Bath's Tale" is different from the setting of *The Canterbury Tales*. Where is each story set?

_____

_____

_____

2. In *The Canterbury Tales*, the Wife of Bath describes the disappearance of the elves. Why does she do this?

_____

_____

_____

3. In *The Canterbury Tales*, what is the Wife of Bath's opinion of holy friars? How do you know?

_____

_____

_____

4. In *The Canterbury Tales*, the Wife of Bath tells the story of Midas. What point is she making with this story?

_____

_____

_____

5. In "The Wife of Bath's Tale" from *The Canterbury Tales*, the queen gives the knight a chance to save his life. Why does she do this?

_____

_____

_____

6. In "The Wife of Bath's Tale" from *The Canterbury Tales*, the old woman insists the knight marry her, and he replies, "Alas that any of my race and station / Should ever make so foul a misalliance!" What does the word *misalliance* mean, and how do you know?

_____

_____

_____

7. According to "The Wife of Bath's Tale" from *The Canterbury Tales*, near the end of the story the knight correctly answers the queen's question. Why does the old woman suddenly leap up and claim her reward in front of the queen?

_____

_____

_____

8. Use the context of each italicized word to figure out the meaning of the word. Write the meaning in the chart.

Quotation	Meaning
The queen then *bade* the knight to tell them all / What thing it was that women wanted most.	
you spoke of *gentle* birth, / Such as descends from ancient wealth and worth.	
You are no gentleman, though duke or earl. / Vice and bad manners are what make a *churl*.	

9. In "The Wife of Bath's Tale" from *The Canterbury Tales*, when the knight is returning to the castle, he sees young maidens dancing in the woods. When he rides up, he finds only the old woman. What can you infer about the woman from these events?

_____

_____

_____

10. In "The Wife of Bath's Tale" from *The Canterbury Tales*, why does the old woman *rebuke* her husband? Focus on the meaning of *rebuke* in your response.

_____

_____

_____

Essay

Write an extended response to the question of your choice or to the question or questions your teacher assigns you.

11. In an esssay, explain why the old woman in "The Wife of Bath's Tale" from *The Canterbury Tales* first presents herself to the knight as old and ugly, rather than as young and beautiful. Why does she later transform herself into a young and beautiful woman? Explain the possible reasons for this change, based on your reading of the tale.

12. In an essay, describe the setting of "The Wife of Bath's Tale" from *The Canterbury Tales* and explain how the setting affects the plot. Then explain how the plot would be different if the setting were changed. Give at least two examples from the tale to support your ideas.

13. In the Prologue of *The Canterbury Tales,* the narrator gives some background about the Wife of Bath, mentioning her five husbands "Apart from other company in youth." In an essay, explain how his description is consistent with the story she tells in "The Wife of Bath's Tale." How is the Wife of Bath's own past reflected in the story she tells? In what ways is her own life similar to and different from the old woman's experience in the story? Give reasons and examples to support your ideas.

14. **Thinking About the Essential Question: Do writers influence social trends or just reflect them?** After *The Canterbury Tales* was written, the Wife of Bath became a recognizable social type, found in many literary works. What characteristics does she represent as a woman? What social ideas, both positive and negative, do she and her tale reflect? Use details from "The Wife of Bath's Tale" to support your ideas.

Oral Response

15. Go back to questions 2, 3, 6, or to the question your teacher assigns to you. Take a few minutes to expand your answer and prepare an oral response. Find additional details in "The Wife of Bath's Tale" from *The Canterbury Tales* that will support your points. If necessary, make notes to guide your response.

Name _____ Date _____

"The Wife of Bath's Tale" *from* The Canterbury Tales by Geoffrey Chaucer
Selection Test A

Critical Reading *Identify the letter of the choice that best answers the question.*

_____ 1. According to "The Wife of Bath's Tale," why was the knight condemned to die?
   A. He insulted the queen.
   B. He was a coward.
   C. He attacked a maiden.
   D. He disobeyed the king's order.

_____ 2. What does the word *reprove* mean in these lines from "The Wife of Bath's Tale"?
   Some say the things we most desire are these:
   Freedom to do exactly as we please,
   With no one to reprove our faults and lies,
   Rather to have one call us good and wise.

   A. scold
   B. congratulate
   C. allow
   D. encourage

_____ 3. What is the main setting of the story about the knight in "The Wife of Bath's Tale"?
   A. England in the time of King Arthur
   B. the court of a great queen
   C. an unknown country in the distant past
   D. a mythical kingdom at an unknown time

_____ 4. According to "The Wife of Bath's Tale," in the story of Midas, his wife tells her secret to the water. What is the point of this story?
   A. Women should not go near water.
   B. Women cannot keep secrets to themselves.
   C. Women enjoy telling secrets to others.
   D. Women can be trusted to keep secrets.

_____ 5. In "The Wife of Bath's Tale," the knight decides to return to the queen and meet his fate even before he meets the old woman. Why?
   A. He thinks he knows the answer.
   B. He gave his word he would return.
   C. He thinks she will forgive him.
   D. She will find him wherever he runs.

____ **6.** According to "The Wife of Bath's Tale," why does the knight agree to marry the old woman?

    A. He thinks the queen will not have him killed if he is married.

    B. She deceives him with magic, making him think she is beautiful.

    C. She promises him that she knows the secret to what all women want.

    D. He believes she will turn into a young woman when he marries her.

____ **7.** In "The Wife of Bath's Tale," the old woman insists the knight marry her as her reward. What does the word *misalliance* mean in his reply?

    "My love?" said he. "By Heaven, my damnation! / Alas that any of my race and station / Should ever make so foul a misalliance!" / Yet in the end his pleading and defiance / All went for nothing, he was forced to wed.

    A. a missed chance   **C.** an incorrect guess

    B. perfect wedding   **D.** a bad marriage

____ **8.** According to "The Wife of Bath's Tale," near the end of the story, the knight correctly answers the queen's question. Why does the old woman suddenly leap up and claim her reward in front of the queen?

    A. The knight will not be able back out on his promise.

    B. She wants the queen to perform the wedding ceremony.

    C. She wants the queen to know the knight had her help.

    D. The queen will reward her for her excellent wisdom.

____ **9.** In "The Wife of Bath's Tale," after the knight and the old woman are married, the old woman gives him two choices. What are they?

    A. He can have an old and faithful wife or a young and faithful wife.

    B. He can have a young and faithful wife or an old and rich wife.

    C. He can have an old and faithful wife or a young wife who is unfaithful.

    D. He can have an old and faithful wife, or he can have his freedom.

____ **10.** In the final scene of the story in "The Wife of Bath's Tale," the ugly old woman transforms herself into a beautiful young wife. How do you know she might be a fairy?

    A. Only fairies have the power to transform themselves.

    B. The Wife of Bath suggests the existence of fairies when she frames the tale.

    C. The old woman is so wise she must be something more than human.

    D. The queen would not have allowed the knight to marry her as a human.

Unit 1 Resources: From Legend to History
128

___ **11.** What is the moral of "The Wife of Bath's Tale"?

    A. Men should never let women gain the upper hand.

    B. Women make wiser decisions than men in all matters.

    C. The best judges are women because they are compassionate.

    D. It is best for husbands and wives when women rule the marriage.

Vocabulary and Grammar

___ **12.** Which vocabulary word best completes this sentence?

    The knight _____ every woman he met to tell him what women most desired.

    A. esteemed   **C.** rebuked

    B. bequeathed   **D.** implored

___ **13.** Which sentence <u>incorrectly</u> uses the italicized vocabulary word?

    A. The Wife of Bath *relates* the story of Midas.

    B. Everyone *esteemed* the queen for her wisdom.

    C. The successful knight showed great *misalliance* in battle.

    D. The *contemptuous* knight turned away from his wife.

___ **14.** What are the correlative conjunctions in this sentence?

    Either the knight must learn what women most desire or he will die.

    A. either, or   **C.** will die

    B. must learn   **D.** learn, die

Essay

15. In the Prologue of *The Canterbury Tales*, the narrator gives some background about the Wife of Bath. He describes her as follows: "She'd had five husbands, all at the church door, / Apart from other company in youth; / No need just now to speak of that, forsooth." In an essay, explain how his description is consistent with the story she tells in "The Wife of Bath's Tale." Do you think the theme is one she would have a strong opinion about? Why? Give reasons and examples from the text to support your ideas.

16. In an essay, explain why the old woman first presents herself to the knight as old and ugly, rather than as young and beautiful. Why does she later transform herself into a young and beautiful woman? Explain the possible reasons for this change, based on your reading of the "The Wife of Bath's Tale."

17. **Thinking About the Essential Question: Do writers influence social trends or just reflect them?** After *The Canterbury Tales* was written, the Wife of Bath became a recognizable social type, found in many literary works. What characteristics does she represent as a woman? Use details from "The Wife of Bath's Tale" to support your ideas.

Name _____ Date _____

"The Wife of Bath's Tale" *from* **The Canterbury Tales** by Geoffrey Chaucer
Selection Test B

Critical Reading *Identify the letter of the choice that best completes the statement or answers the question.*

_____ 1. What is the Wife of Bath's purpose in telling about the disappearance of the elves in "The Wife of Bath's Tale"?
   A. to introduce King Arthur and the queen
   B. to get her listeners' attention as she starts her tale
   C. to foreshadow the later transformation of the old woman
   D. to explain why the knight's behavior was so shocking

_____ 2. What is the Wife of Bath's opinion of holy friars, according to "The Wife of Bath's Tale"?
   A. They are holy men who help all who ask.
   B. They are a danger to women.
   C. They are worse than the elves.
   D. They are as useless as the elves.

_____ 3. Why does the queen ask the king not to kill the knight in "The Wife of Bath's Tale"?
   A. She thinks justice will be better served if he learns a lesson.
   B. She thinks a woman should pass sentence on him.
   C. She wants to make an example of him for other men.
   D. She wants to avoid the loss of another of King Arthur's knights.

_____ 4. According to "The Wife of Bath's Tale," why does the queen give the knight a chance to save his life?
   A. She thinks it is more important to teach him a lesson than to kill him.
   B. She knows that he is good at heart and will never rape another woman.
   C. She thinks killing is too severe a punishment for such a common crime.
   D. She believes that the knight will be loyal to her forever if she saves him.

_____ 5. What question does the queen ask the knight in "The Wife of Bath's Tale"?
   A. Why do men and women not agree on their roles?
   B. What do all women desire above everything?
   C. What kind of husband do most women want?
   D. What must a man do to earn a woman's love?

_____ 6. In "The Wife of Bath's Tale," what does the knight do after hearing the queen's question and leaving her presence?
   A. He searches all over and asks every woman he finds for the answer.
   B. He leaves the kingdom and tries to find a safe place to hide.
   C. He goes to prison because he could not answer the question.
   D. He searches for the old woman to get her advice.

_____ 7. What is the main idea of the story of Midas in "The Wife of Bath's Tale"?
   A. Women do not want ugly men.
   B. Women cannot keep a secret.
   C. Some men look like animals.
   D. Every man has some horrible secret.

_____ 8. Based on the context of "The Wife of Bath's Tale," what is the meaning of the word *extort* in these lines?

"'I will concede you this: you are to go / A twelvemonth and a day to seek and learn / Sufficient answer, then you shall return. / I shall take gages from you to extort / Surrender of your body to the court.'"

A. to enjoy
B. to offer up freely
C. to obtain by threat
D. to prevent

_____ 9. What question does the old woman ask the knight after they are married in "The Wife of Bath's Tale"?
A. Do you want me to be young and poor or old and wealthy?
B. Why do men want young, wealthy wives instead of older wives?
C. Do you want me to be young and faithless or old and faithful?
D. Do you want me to be young and rule our marriage or old and obedient?

_____ 10. In "The Wife of Bath's Tale," while the knight is returning to the castle, he sees young maidens dancing in the woods. When he rides up, he finds only the old woman. What can you infer about the woman from these events?
A. She is blind and did not see him coming or she would have escaped.
B. She is an elf or fairy, and she has transformed herself into an old woman.
C. She was too old and unable to slip away with the younger ladies.
D. She was sent by the queen to meet him in order to help him find the answer.

_____ 11. Based on the context of this sentence from "The Wife of Bath's Tale," what is the meaning of the word *anguish*?

Great was the anguish churning in his head / When he and she were piloted to bed; / He wallowed back and forth in desperate style. / His ancient wife lay smiling all the while. . . .

A. pleasure
B. nervousness
C. eagerness
D. torment

_____ 12. Based on the context, what is the meaning of the word *churl* in this sentence from "The Wife of Bath's Tale"?

You are no gentleman, though duke or earl. / Vice and bad manners are what make a churl.

A. a humorless person
B. dangerous and wicked person
C. a rude and mean person
D. a wealthy person

Vocabulary and Grammar

____ 13. Which vocabulary word best completes this sentence?

The knight _____ the old woman to tell him how he could save his life.

A. esteemed   C. implored
B. bequeathed   D. related

____ 14. Which of these vocabulary words is used <u>incorrectly</u>?

A. The old woman gave a *contemptuous* snort when the knight said she was not well-born.
B. The queen *implored* her husband to give the knight's fate into her hands.
C. The old woman *bequeathed* the knight the knowledge he desired.
D. The knight *rebuked* his wife for her help and relied on her judgment in all things.

____ 15. Which sentence uses the italicized vocabulary word <u>incorrectly</u>?

A. The Wife of Bath *relates* a story of a knight and an old woman.
B. The knight *bequeathed* the old woman to tell him what all women want.
C. The knight showed *prowess* in battle but uncertainty in dealing with women.
D. The knight was *contemptuous* of his wife at first.

____ 16. Which sentence uses correlative conjunctions?

A. Either the knight must find the answer or he will die.
B. The queen asks the knight what women desire, but he does not know.
C. The old woman gives the knight the answer, and he is grateful.
D. The knight is not sure if he wants his wife to be young or old.

____ 17. Which vocabulary word best completes this sentence?

The knight _____ the old woman for being poor.

A. implores   C. rebukes
B. bequeaths   D. relates

Essay

18. In an essay, describe the setting of "The Wife of Bath's Tale" and explain how its setting affects the plot. Then explain how the plot would be different if the setting were changed. Give at least two examples from "The Wife of Bath's Tale" to support your ideas.

19. Based on "The Wife of Bath's Tale," is the Wife of Bath a modern women? How well would she fit in twenty-first century America? Do her views of the role of women in society match those of most women today? How would today's men regard her views? In an essay, explore these questions. Give at least two examples from "The Wife of Bath's Tale" to support your opinions.

20. **Thinking About the Essential Question: Do writers influence social trends or just reflect them?** After *The Canterbury Tales* was written, the Wife of Bath became a recognizable social type, found in many literary works. What characteristics does she represent as a woman? What social ideas, both positive and negative, do she and her tale reflect? Use details from "The Wife of Bath's Tale" to support your ideas.

from **The Canterbury Tales** by Geoffrey Chaucer
from the **Decameron** by Boccaccio
Literary Analysis: Comparing Frame Stories

A **frame** is a story in which one or more other stories unfolds. The frame usually introduces a set of characters in a particular situation that prompts one or more of these characters to tell a story within a story. Many writers of frame stories use the technique to bring together tales from a variety of sources. Frame stories can make fantastic stories easier for readers to accept because the frame is realistic. They can make the act of storytelling seem more natural while capturing the quality of the oral tradition.

When you compare frame stories, you have to look at a variety of levels of comparison. You need to examine the actual frames of the works and make comparisons between elements of the two. Then you need to look at the stories within the frame to make comparisons.

DIRECTIONS: *Use the following chart to organize your ideas for comparing the frames of* The Canterbury Tales *and the* Decameron.

The Canterbury Tales	*Decameron*
Main frame:	Main frame:
Premise for storytelling:	Premise for storytelling:
Effect of premise:	Effect of premise:

from **The Canterbury Tales** by Geoffrey Chaucer
from the **Decameron** by Boccaccio
Vocabulary Builder

Word List

courtly   deference   despondent   frugally   impertinence   affably

A. DIRECTIONS: *Write the word from the Word List that best completes each sentence.*

1. The child was reprimanded for his _____ when he shouted back at his mother.

2. The page was expected to show _____ to the king.

3. Luis's grandmother spent her money _____, as she feared the steady depletion of her retirement fund.

4. The Arthurian legend of the knight and a queen was a _____ romance.

5. The young girl looked _____ when her glass menagerie fell to the floor and shattesed into a thousand pieces.

6. As I complained of this season's long, bitte winte, my friend responded _____ that the approaching summer would seem all the more sweet.

B. DIRECTIONS: *On each line, write the letter of the word or phrase that is most nearly opposite in meaning to the Word List word.*

___ 1. affably
   A. calmly
   B. regularly
   C. wittily
   D. nastily

___ 2. frugally
   A. weakly
   B. wastefully
   C. shrewdly
   D. loudly

___ 3. despondent
   A. inattentive
   B. frustrated
   C. relaxed
   D. joyful

___ 4. impertinence
   A. freedom
   B. patience
   C. respect
   D. affection

___ 5. deference
   A. disrespect
   B. closeness
   C. eagerness
   D. vigor

Name _____ Date _____

from **The Canterbury Tales** by Geoffrey Chaucer
from **The Decameron** by Boccaccio

Integrated Language Skills: Support for Writing to Compare Literary Works

Use the following chart to organize your ideas for writing a comparison of themes.

Boccaccio—"Federico's Falcon"	Chaucer—"The Wife of Bath's Tale"
Plot Summary:	Plot Summary:
Main Characters:	Main Characters:
Characters' Actions and Beliefs:	Characters' Actions and Beliefs:
Theme:	Theme:

Consider these questions as you prepare your essay:

What is the theme of each story?
How does each author present this theme?

On a separate page, use information from your chart and answers to your questions to help you organize ideas as you draft your essay. Make sure you clearly state each theme and your major points of comparison.

from **The Decameron** by Giovanni Boccaccio
Selection Test

MULTIPLE CHOICE

Critical Reading *Identify the letter of the choice that best completes the statement or answers the question.*

____ 1. What is the setting of the frame story in *The Decameron*?
  A. England in the 1400s
  B. France in the 1300s
  C. Italy in the 1300s
  D. Italy in the 1500s

____ 2. The person telling the story in the selection from *The Decameron* is
  A. the queen
  B. Frederigo
  C. Dioneo
  D. Filomena

____ 3. In *The Decameron*, why does Monna Giovanna hesitate to ask Frederigo for his falcon?
  A. She is afraid that having the falcon will not help her son.
  B. She is afraid that Frederigo will refuse her request.
  C. She does not want to anger Frederigo with her request.
  D. She does not want to take away Frederigo's last pleasure.

____ 4. In *The Decameron*, what does Frederigo's choice to serve the falcon to Monna Giovanna show about him?
  A. He is ignorant about ladies' wishes.
  B. He is very stingy.
  C. He is devoted and generous.
  D. He is very foolish.

____ 5. What is ironic about Frederigo's actions in *The Decameron*?
  A. By losing his money, he makes it impossible for Monna Giovanna to love him.
  B. By moving to the country, he loses the opportunity to win Monna Giovanna's love.
  C. By serving the falcon, he deprives his beloved of the one thing she wants.
  D. By keeping the falcon, he causes the death of Monna Giovanna's son.

____ 6. In *The Decameron*, why does Monna Giovanna decide to marry Frederigo?

    A. She has lost all her money and needs a husband.

    B. She admires his actions and his kindness.

    C. She has promised her dying son to marry Frederigo.

    D. She has fallen deeply in love with Frederigo.

____ 7. The frame story of *The Decameron* is different from that of *The Canterbury Tales* in that

    A. it is set in the 1300s.

    B. It features people thrown together by chance.

    C. it sets up a situation for storytelling.

    D. It features people of a single social class.

____ 8. Which of the following identifies an important similarity between "The Pardoner's Tale" and Frederigo's story in *The Decameron*?

    A. Both are about a murder.

    B. Both take place during the plague.

    C. Both feature the death of a child.

    D. Both are about men in love.

____ 9. Which of the following is an accurate statement of the theme of both "The Wife of Bath's Tale" and "Frederigo's Falcon"?

    A. Older people make the most devoted lovers.

    B. People of different social classes should not marry.

    C. Generosity of spirit can be rewarded by love.

    D. Disease can strike down anyone at any time.

____ 10. What purpose do the storytellers in both *The Decameron* and *The Canterbury Tales* have for telling their tales?

    A. They want to pass the time.

    B. They are competing for a prize.

    C. They are writing a book.

    D. They are acting on a dare.

Vocabulary Warm-up Word Lists

Study these words the selections. Then, complete the activities.

Word List A

slumbering [SLUHM ber ing] *v.* sleeping; dozing
    The child was <u>slumbering</u> during the entire concert, in spite of the loud music.

fused [FYOOZD] *v.* mixed together; united together to become inseparable
    The electrician <u>fused</u> the separate strands of wire together.

marvel [MAHR vuhl] *v.* to become filled with astonishment and wonder; be in awe
    We <u>marvel</u> at the tricks performed by a skilled magician.

swooned [SWOOND] *v.* fainted; collapsed
    The starstruck fan <u>swooned</u> when she finally shook hands with her idol.

puny [PYOO nee] *adj.* of inferior size, strength, or significance; weak
    The tomatoes in the garden looked <u>puny</u> and needed water and fertilizer.

almighty [AWL my tee] *adj.* great; extreme; all-powerful
    Most religions teach that their god is <u>almighty</u>.

hermit [HUR mit] *n.* person living alone away from society; a recluse
    Sometimes a medieval monk would leave his monastery to live as a <u>hermit</u>.

accorded [uh KORD id] *v.* granted; given what is due or appropriate
    The audience <u>accorded</u> the star respect and stood when he entered.

Word List B

wilful [WIL fuhl] *adj.* (also willful) deliberate; said or done on purpose; obstinate
    The soldier was court-martialed for <u>wilful</u> disregard of orders.

condescended [kahn di SEND id] *v.* agreed to lower oneself; deigned; stooped
    Because he was broke, the law student <u>condescended</u> to deliver pizzas.

barren [BAR ren] *adj.* not producing offspring or vegetation; infertile; empty
    The <u>barren</u> landscape didn't have any trees, shrubs, or grasses.

groveling [GRAHV el ing] *v.* cringing; totally submissive
    Once the criminal was found guilty, he stopped being arrogant and started <u>groveling</u>.

authorized [AW thuh ryzd] *v.* granted authority or power to; gave permission for
    The city agencies <u>authorized</u> the construction of a new bridge.

sans [SAHNZ] *prep.* (from the French) without
    The immigrant came to America <u>sans</u> baggage, money, or relatives.

arrogance [AHR e genz] *n.* overbearing pride; haughtiness
    Although he was a superior tennis player, <u>arrogance</u> made him unpopular with his team.

dismayed [dis MAYD] *v.* caused to lose enthusiasm; upset and disillusioned
    The actress was <u>dismayed</u> when she did not get called back for the next audition.

from Sir Gawain and the Green Knight, translated by Marie Borroff
from Morte d'Arthur by Sir Thomas Mallory
Vocabulary Warm-up Exercises

Exercise A *Fill in each blank in the paragraph with the appropriate word from Word List A.*
Use each word only once.

People in the Dark Ages were very superstitious. They believed that while naughty chil-

dren were [1] _____ fairies could steal them out of their beds. Although

legends [2] _____ fairies some magical powers, they were by no means

[3] _____. People would [4] _____ at natural wonders,

such as icicles, spider webs, and dewdrops, convinced that fairies made them. Fairies

were physically [5] _____, but used their small size to travel unnoticed.

They also developed spells as a means of self-protection. Anyone who came in contact

with a fairy promptly [6] _____. When the person awoke, he or she would

believe that seeing the fairy had been just a dream. Artists' drawings show fairies as tiny

people with dragonfly wings [7] _____ on their backs. Of course, no one

ever really saw fairies, not even a [8] _____ living alone in the forest.

Exercise B *Revise each sentence so that the word from Word List B is used correctly.*

Example: The king was <u>groveling</u> before his subjects.
The subjects were <u>groveling</u> before their king.

1. The <u>barren</u> tree produced baskets of fruit.
   _____

2. The child who loved sweets drank her tea <u>sans</u> sugar.
   _____

3. The reporter displayed his <u>arrogance</u> by apologizing profusely for his mistakes.
   _____

4. Visitors were <u>authorized</u> to enter the restricted area of the power plant.
   _____

5. Paul was <u>dismayed</u> to hear he had won the lottery.
   _____

6. The car accident was not caused by the driver's <u>wilful</u> running of a red light.
   _____

7. The unknown sculptor <u>condescended</u> to teach a class at our local art studio.
   _____

from Sir Gawain and the Green Knight, translated by Marie Borroff
from Morte d'Arthur by Sir Thomas Mallory

Reading Warm-up A

Read the following passage. Pay special attention to the underlined words. Then, read it again, and complete the activities. Use a separate sheet of paper for your written answers.

When "courtly love" emerged during the 1100s, it consisted of a code of noble behavior called chivalry that <u>fused</u> loyalty, honor, self-sacrifice, and defense of the weak. It was made popular through tales of brave knights, and maidens who <u>swooned</u> when battles were fought in their name. Ideal love for one pure woman was supposed to inspire a knight to magnificent deeds. It was also expected to make the knight's beloved <u>marvel</u> at his attempts to be worthy of her. Because of her virtue, the lady was put on a pedestal. For the first time, the woman was considered superior to her male suitor.

This attitude was a dramatic change in the way noble women were viewed. Although they received more respect, being adored didn't give women more freedom, and they still had little choice when it came to a mate. Romantic love rarely led to a marriage, since matrimonial decisions were <u>accorded</u> to the parents of the bride and groom. Often wedding plans were made while the future husband and wife were still <u>slumbering</u> in their cradles.

The social classes and assets of both families had to be taken into account when marriages were arranged. A wealthy father would never promise his daughter to a <u>hermit</u>, or expect her to marry someone whose prospects were <u>puny</u>. It was understood that a man who married the daughter of a wealthy merchant would receive a generous dowry. Finances, not love, continued to determine most marriages. Money was still <u>almighty</u>, in spite of the poets, and the longing for true love that they created.

1. Circle the part of the sentence that tells what chivalry <u>fused</u> together to create a code of behavior. Then, give an antonym for *fused*.

2. Circle the words that explain when maidens <u>swooned</u>. Then, give a synonym for *swooned*.

3. Circle the words that tell who was expected to <u>marvel</u> at a knight's attempts to be worthy. Then, rewrite the sentence using a synonym for *marvel*.

4. Circle the word that says what was <u>accorded</u> to parents. Define *accorded*.

5. Circle the words that tell who was <u>slumbering</u>. Describe *slumbering*.

6. Circle the part of the sentence that tells who would never promise his daughter to a <u>hermit</u>. Where might you find a *hermit*?

7. Underline the words that say what a father wouldn't expect his daughter to do if a groom's prospects were <u>puny</u>. What would you consider a *puny* sum?

8. Circle the word that tells what was <u>almighty</u>. Explain what *almighty* means.

Name _____   Date _____

from Sir Gawain and the Green Knight, translated by Marie Borroff
from Morte d'Arthur by Sir Thomas Mallory

Reading Warm-up B

Read the following passage. Pay special attention to the underlined words. Then, read it again, and complete the activities. Use a separate sheet of paper for your written answers.

It was Greg's first day interning at Round Table Industries, a major conglomeration, and his initiation was about to begin. Judy, the receptionist, ushered him to his barren cubicle that was sans a chair, and contained little more than a phone and a computer.

"This will be your desk," she announced. "Mr. Bernhardt will orient you shortly." Greg mustered his courage and asked about obtaining a chair. "I'll look into it, if I get a chance," she said, and turned sharply away, "but you'll be occupied on your feet running errands and copying papers."

Greg wasn't dismayed even though he knew he had just been condescended to, so he set about making his cubicle more personal with a trophy from his high school swimming team, a comical mouse pad, and a photo of his girlfriend. Then, he heard a gruff voice from behind him.

"Well, Gary, we've got a big day ahead, so I'll show you what you'll need to know."

Greg ignored the fact that Mr. Bernhardt had called him by the wrong name. "This is the coffee machine," Mr. Bernhardt continued, "and the copier is by the supply room, but don't try to access either of those until you're authorized. Judy can arrange it, if she'll get off the phone to talk to you. And get yourself a chair, kid."

Greg was astonished that Mr. Bernhardt would tolerate Judy's display of arrogance and wilful rudeness. He brewed a pot of coffee, deciding he might get help without groveling if he brought Judy a cup. He strode confidently to her desk and introduced himself.

"If you're here about a chair, you'll have to be patient," she snapped, sipping the coffee. "Take a seat."

Seizing the opportunity, Greg replied, "Thanks, I'll take this one." He snatched the chair nearest her desk, and dragged it triumphantly to his cubicle.

1. Underline the words that show that Greg's workspace is barren. Write a sentence using a synonym of *barren.*

2. Circle the words that tell what Greg's cubical is sans. In a sentence, describe a place you think is *sans* the proper equipment.

3. Underline the words that show how Greg is not dismayed. Give an antonym for *dismayed.*

4. Circle who had been condescended to. What kind of person wouldn't appreciate being *condescended* to?

5. Underline the words that tell what is not authorized. Name a job or activity you might need to be *authorized* to do.

6. Circle the name and job of the person displaying arrogance. What is a synonym for *arrogance.*

7. Circle the name of the person who seems to tolerate Judy's wilful rudeness. Rewrite the sentence using a synonym for *wilful.*

8. Underline the words that describe what Greg thinks he should do instead of groveling. What might a person who is *groveling* do in this situation?

from **Sir Gawain and the Green Knight,** translated by Marie Borroff
from **Morte d'Arthur** by Sir Thomas Malory
Literary Analysis: Medieval Romance

Medieval romances were the popular adventure stories of the Middle Ages. Originally cast in verse, they were later sometimes told in prose. In England, the best known of the medieval romances are based on the legends of King Arthur and his knights. **Legends** are anonymous traditional stories about the past. They may be based in fact but are always embellished with descriptions of heroic figures and memorable deeds, quests and conquests, or tests of strength and character.

DIRECTIONS: *Following is a series of characteristics of medieval romances, which are often based on legends. On the lines below each characteristic, cite at least two details from* Sir Gawain and the Green Knight *and* Morte d'Arthur *that illustrate the characteristic.*

1. Medieval romances convey a sense of the supernatural.

   Sir Gawain and the Green Knight: _____

   _____

   Morte d'Arthur: _____

   _____

   _____

2. Medieval romances give a glamorous portrayal of castle life.

   Sir Gawain and the Green Knight: _____

   _____

   Morte d'Arthur: _____

   _____

3. Chivalric ideals—bravery, honor, courtesy, fairness to enemies, respect for women—guide the characters.

   Sir Gawain and the Green Knight: _____

   _____

   Morte d'Arthur: _____

   _____

   _____

4. Medieval romances are imbued with adventure.

   Sir Gawain and the Green Knight: _____

   _____

   Morte d'Arthur: _____

   _____

   _____

Name _____ Date _____

from **Sir Gawain and the Green Knight,** translated by Marie Borroff
from **Morte d'Arthur** by Sir Thomas Malory
Reading Strategy: Main Idea

The **main idea** of a passage is its key point or message. When you read a passage, you need to make sure you understand the point the author is making. To do so, you need to determine which information is the most important. **Summarizing** is one way to check your understanding of what you have read. A summary briefly states the main idea and key details in your own words. A summary is always much shorter than the original, but it must reflect the original accurately. Look at this example from *Morte d'Arthur.*

Passage	Main Idea and Key Events	Summary
King Arthur smote Sir Mordred under the shield, with a thrust of his spear, throughout the body more than a fathom. And when Sir Mordred felt that he had his death's wound, he thrust himself with the might that he had up to the burr of King Arthur's spear, and right so he smote his father King Arthur with his sword holden in both his hands, upon the side of the head, that the sword pierced the helmet and the casing of the brain.	King Arthur speared Sir Mordred. Sir Mordred felt that he was dying from the wound, but he forced himself to hit King Arthur in the head.	Sir Mordred and King Arthur fought a terrible battle. Sir Mordred was killed and King Arthur was wounded in the head.

DIRECTIONS: *Use this graphic organizer to summarize this excerpt.*

Passage	Main Idea and Key Events	Summary
. . . Sir Lucan departed, for he was grievously wounded in many places. And so as he walked he saw and harkened by the moonlight how that pillagers and robbers were come into the field to pill and to rob many a full noble knight of brooches and bracelets and of many a good ring and many a rich jewel. And who that were not dead all out there they slew them for their harness and their riches. When Sir Lucan understood this work, he came to the King as soon as he might and told him all what he had heard and seen.		

from **Sir Gawain and the Green Knight,** translated by Marie Borroff

from **Morte d'Arthur** by Sir Thomas Malory

Vocabulary Builder

Word List

adjure   adroitly   entreated   interred   largesse   peril

A. DIRECTIONS: *Each excerpt below is from one of the poems. Choose the word from the Word List that best matches the meaning of the italicized word or phrase.*

1. First I ask and *appeal* to you, how you are called
   That you tell me true. . . . _____

2. Sir Mordred did his devoir that day and put himself in great *danger.* _____

3. . . . Withdrew the ax *skillfully* before it did damage. _____

4. . . . and there they *pleaded with* Sir Mordred . . . _____

5. . . . contrary both to *noble spirit* and loyalty belonging to the knights . . .
   _____

6. "What man is there here *buried* that you pray so fast for?" _____

B. WORD STUDY: *The word root -droit- means "right." In the following sentences, decide whether the italicized word is used properly. If it is, write "correct." If it is not, rewrite the sentence using the correct form of a word with the root -droit-.*

1. Because of his *adroitness* with a football, Charley was unable to make the football team.
   _____

2. Amber was very *adroit* at gymnastics, so she knew she would never go to the Olympics.
   _____

3. Marla is no longer *maladroit* in her movements now that she takes ballet lessons.
   _____

4. Tad prides himself on his *maladroitness,* having never broken a leg in all his years as a skier.
   _____

from **Sir Gawain and the Green Knight,** translated by Marie Borroff
from **Morte d'Arthur** by Sir Thomas Malory
Integrated Language Skills: Support for Writing

Use the graphic organizers below to help you think of ideas. Choose an event or a situation that Sir Gawain would react to that could become an interior monologue.

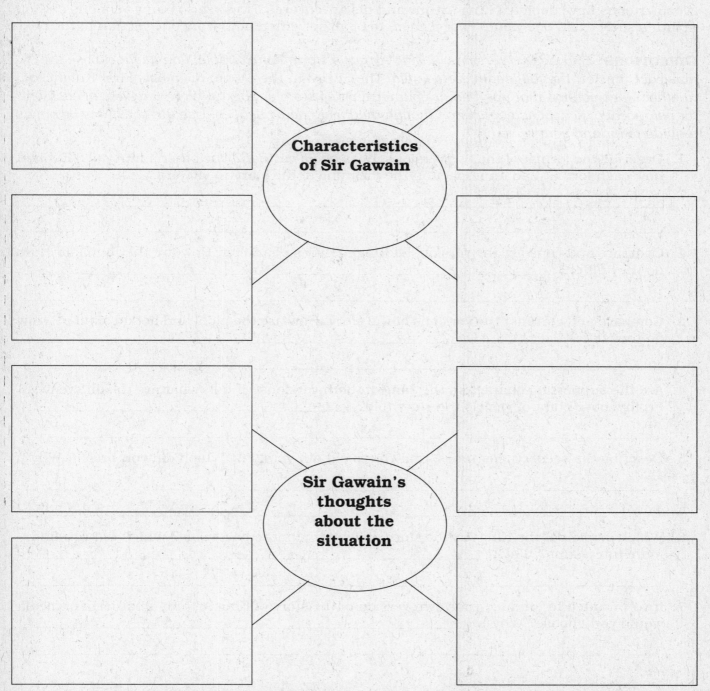

Use a separate page to draft Sir Gawain's interior monologue. Write in the first person as though you are Gawain, talking to himself.

Name _____ Date _____

from **Sir Gawain and the Green Knight,** translated by Marie Borroff
from **Morte d'Arthur** by Sir Thomas Malory
Enrichment: Film Depictions of King Arthur

The story of King Arthur has been told many times over the years. Musicals, movies, and even cartoons have depicted King Arthur and his adventures. Because so many versions of King Arthur's story exist, one would expect there to be major differences from one version to the next.

DIRECTIONS: *Choose two versions of King Arthur's story. For example, you might choose the musical* Camelot, *the full-length cartoon film* The Sword in the Stone, *the movie* First Knight, *or another video version that you find at your local video store or library. Write a review of each one for your local or school newspaper as though they were new releases. Use the questions below as a guide to writing your reviews.*

1. Describe the format of the two versions. (Was one a cartoon? The other a musical?) Explain how each format had an impact on the meaning of the story to viewers.

   _____

   _____

2. Compare and contrast the versions of King Arthur's character. How are they similar? How do they differ? _____

   _____

3. Compare and contrast the versions of the story. How are the plots and action similar? How do they differ? _____

   _____

4. Are the supporting characters the same in both versions? If not, what are the differences? From whose point of view is the story told? _____

   _____

5. Describe the scenery, costumes, and voices of both versions. Which did you prefer? Why?

   _____

   _____

6. Which version of the King Arthur story did you find more believable? Which did you find more interesting? Why? _____

   _____

7. If you wanted to produce your own version of the story of King Arthur, what form of media would you choose? Why? _____

   _____

from Sir Gawain and the Green Knight Translated by Marie Borroff and
from Morte d'Arthur by Sir Thomas Malory
Open-Book Test

Short Answer *Write your response to the questions in this section on the lines provided.*

1. What does King Arthur do when he first meets the Green Knight in *Sir Gawain and the Green Knight*? Describe his attitude and behavior.

   _____

   _____

   _____

2. Most medieval romances share certain plot elements. Which elements are missing from the excerpt from *Sir Gawain and the Green Knight*?

   _____

   _____

   _____

3. How would you summarize the first section of *Sir Gawain and the Green Knight* (to line 27)?

   _____

   _____

   _____

   _____

4. In *Sir Gawain and the Green Knight*, Sir Gawain apologizes to the Green Knight in the final scene. Why does he do so?

   _____

   _____

   _____

5. What extraordinary event occurs in *Morte d'Arthur*? Explain.

   _____

   _____

   _____

6. How would you summarize the battle between King Arthur and Sir Mordred in *Morte d'Arthur*?

   _____

   _____

   _____

   _____

7. What events in *Sir Gawain and the Green Knight* and *Morte d'Arthur* deviate from the ideals of chivalry? Explain.

_____

_____

_____

_____

8. In the chart below, write an example of each principle of knightly behavior from *Sir Gawain and the Green Knight* and *Morte d'Arthur*.

Principle	Example from *Sir Gawain and the Green Knight*	Example from *Morte d'Arthur*
Honoring promises		
Courage		
Honoring one's lord or king		

9. What central theme can you find in both *Sir Gawain and the Green Knight* and *Morte d'Arthur*?

_____

_____

_____

10. In *Sir Gawain and the Green Knight,* Sir Gawain *feigned* courage. Why did he do this? Focus on the meaning of *feigned* in your response.

_____

_____

_____

Essay

Write an extended response to the question of your choice or to the question or questions your teacher assigns you.

11. Medieval romances often blend realistic and unusual or magical details. In an essay, describe how these elements are used in *Sir Gawain and the Green Knight* and *Morte d'Arthur.* Give at least one example of a realistic and a magical detail from each tale. Then explain how the details affect the tales and their meaning.

12. *Sir Gawain and the Green Knight* and *Morte d'Arthur* were written by two different people. Do you think the portrait of King Arthur is consistent in these two stories? Write an essay in which you analyze the character of King Arthur as he is portrayed in the tales. Cite examples from the texts to back up your observations. Then compare the two versions King Arthur.

13. *Sir Gawain and the Green Knight* and *Morte d'Arthur* are two of the best-known chivalric romances of the Middle Ages. Write an essay in which you explain, first, what chivalry is, and second, how its ideals and code of conduct are represented in the poems. Refer not only to the characters and conduct of Gawain and Arthur but also to those of other characters. Note the conflicts that arise over chivalric values and how the romances resolve those conflicts.

14. **Thinking About the Essential Question: Do writers gain more by accepting or by rejecting tradition?** Both *Sir Gawain and the Green Knight* and *Morte d'Arthur* include very traditional versions of the chivalric knight, but in both the chivalric tradition is broken to some extent. In an essay, describe how Gawain and Bedivere both exemplify tradition and break with it. Explain what their break with tradition adds to the readers' understanding of the characters.

Oral Response

15. Go back to questions 3, 4, 7, or to the question your teacher assigns to you. Take a few minutes to expand your answer and prepare an oral response. Find additional details in *Sir Gawain and the Green Knight* and *Morte d'Arthur* that will support your points. If necessary, make notes to guide your response.

from Sir Gawain and the Green Knight, translated by Marie Borroff
from Morte d'Arthur by Sir Thomas Malory
Selection Test A

Critical Reading *Identify the letter of the choice that best answers the question.*

____ 1. What detail should be part of a summary of the first half of *Sir Gawain and the Green Knight*?
A. The Green Knight visits King Arthur's court during a New Year's Eve feast.
B. The Green Knight leaps lightly from his horse to the ground.
C. Sir Gawain keeps the braided girdle given him by the lord's wife.
D. The Green Knight coughs to clear his throat before speaking to King Arthur's knights.

____ 2. What extraordinary event happens in *Sir Gawain and the Green Knight*?
A. The Green Knight only scratches Sir Gawain when he swings the ax.
B. The Green Knight rides his horse into King Arthur's hall.
C. The Green Knight picks up his severed head and rides away.
D. Sir Gawain discovers the Green Knight was his host of the night before.

____ 3. In *Sir Gawain and the Green Knight,* who first accepts the Green Knight's challenge?
A. Sir Gawain
B. Sir Bedivere
C. Sir Lancelot
D. King Arthur

____ 4. Which character would be absent from a summary of *Sir Gawain and the Green Knight*?
A. the wife of the lord of the castle near Green Chapel
B. Queen Guenevere
C. King Arthur
D. the lord of the castle near Green Chapel

____ 5. In *Sir Gawain and the Green Knight,* why does Sir Gawain apologize to the Green Knight in the final scene?
A. Sir Gawain is ashamed that he kept the girdle that the Green Knight's wife gave him.
B. Sir Gawain feels uncomfortable for thinking the Green Knight meant to kill him.
C. Sir Gawain did not keep his part of the bargain made the year before on New Year's Eve.
D. Sir Gawain flinched during the moment when the Green Knight swung the ax.

____ 6. Which of these elements of the medieval romance are missing from *Sir Gawain and the Green Knight*?

    A. adventures and excitement   **C.** knights and kings

    B. damsels in distress   **D.** tests of courage

____ 7. In *Morte d'Arthur*, what does Sir Gawain tell King Arthur in a dream?

    A. Mordred will pretend to agree to peace and then attack.

    B. Sir Lancelot is coming to join Mordred in fighting King Arthur.

    C. King Arthur should not trust Sir Bedivere with his sword.

    D. King Arthur will be killed if he fights Mordred the next day.

____ 8. In *Morte d'Arthur*, why does Sir Gawain want King Arthur to delay the war with Mordred for a month?

    A. to recover from his wounds

    B. to gather a larger, stronger army

    C. to give Lancelot time to come to his aid

    D. to allow Mordred's hate to die down

____ 9. What extraordinary event occurs in *Morte d'Arthur*?

    A. the accidental way in which the battle begins

    B. the catching of the sword by a hand in the lake

    C. Sir Bedivere's decision to stay with the hermit

    D. the battle between King Arthur and Mordred

____ 10. In *Morte d'Arthur*, what causes Sir Bedivere to disobey King Arthur's command to throw the sword in the lake?

    A. greed   **C.** fear

    B. loyalty   **D.** pride

____ 11. In *Morte d'Arthur*, when King Arthur is dying, women come to pick him up in a barge. How do they treat him?

    A. as though he deserves respect

    B. as though he is contagious

    C. as though he is an enemy

    D. as though he is very powerful

___ 12. At the end of *Morte d'Arthur*, the narrator says he is not sure what happened to King Arthur. Some say he was buried by a hermit who was once the bishop of Canterbury. What do other people say happened to him?

    A. He stayed with the hermit until he died.

    B. He went to France to find Sir Lancelot.

    C. He did not die but will live again.

    D. He was buried in the lake near his sword.

Vocabulary and Grammar

___ 13. Which sentence uses the italicized vocabulary word correctly?

    A. Sir Gawain *entreated* courage, although he did not feel it.

    B. King Arthur drew his sword and *adroitly* fought Mordred's army.

    C. Sir Gawain faced the *largesse* of the Green Knight's challenge.

    D. The Green Knight *interred* Arthur's knights to accept his challenge.

___ 14. Which vocabulary word best describes what the hermit did for King Arthur?

    A. interred, or buried

    B. imperiled, or endangered

    C. adjured, or requested

    D. entreated, or pleaded

___ 15. Which word is the closest in meaning to *largesse*?

    A. heaviness   C. gentility

    B. tallness   D. generosity

Essay

16. Medieval romances often blend realistic and unusual or magical details. In an essay, describe how these elements are used in *Sir Gawain and the Green Knight* and *Morte d'Arthur*. Give at least one example of a realistic and a magical detail from each tale. Tell how these details affect the tales and your reaction to them. Do they increase your enjoyment? Do they add a different meaning? How would the tales be different if they lacked the unusual or magical elements? Be sure to use details from the tales to support your response.

17. King Arthur appears in both *Sir Gawain and the Green Knight* and *Morte d'Arthur*. In an essay, compare the character of King Arthur in these two medieval romances. How is his character in the two stories alike? How is his character different? Give at least two examples from the texts to support your comparison.

18. **Thinking About the Essential Question: Do writers gain more by accepting or by rejecting tradition?** Both *Sir Gawain and the Green Knight* and *Morte d'Arthur* include very traditional versions of the chivalric knight. In an essay, describe how Gawain and Bedivere both exemplify traditional types of knights.

from Sir Gawain and the Green Knight, translated by Marie Borroff
from Morte d'Arthur by Sir Thomas Malory
Selection Test B

Critical Reading *Identify the letter of the choice that best completes the statement or answers the question.*

_____ 1. Which statement would you include in a summary of the first section of *Sir Gawain and the Green Knight?*
   A. The Green Knight has a beard.
   B. The Green Knight arrives at King Arthur's court in the middle of a New Year's Eve feast.
   C. Sir Gawain flinches when the Green Knight swings his ax.
   D. King Arthur is amazed by the Green Knight but he does not show it.

_____ 2. Which of the following events from *Sir Gawain and the Green Knight* conveys a sense of the supernatural?
   A. The Green Knight challenges King Arthur's knights.
   B. Sir Gawain arrives at the Green Castle and finds it hideous.
   C. The Green Knight does not die from Sir Gawain's blow.
   D. The Green Knight only scratches Sir Gawain with his ax.

_____ 3. Which of the following primary plot elements that are characteristic of medieval romances is missing from the excerpt from *Sir Gawain and the Green Knight?*
   A. castle life
   B. adventure
   C. chivalry
   D. a damsel in distress

_____ 4. In *Sir Gawain and the Green Knight,* why does Sir Gawain volunteer to fight the Green Knight?
   A. He wants to protect the honor of his king and fellow knights.
   B. He wants to settle an old dispute he has with the Green Knight.
   C. He wants to protect the queen.
   D. He wants to prove that the Green Knight is not real.

_____ 5. Which of the following events in *Sir Gawain and the Green Knight* represents a deviation from the ideals of chivalry?
   A. King Arthur accepts the Green Knight's challenge.
   B. Sir Gawain keeps the magic girdle.
   C. Sir Gawain takes the Green Knight's ax.
   D. The Green Knight reminds Sir Gawain of his promise.

_____ 6. Which could you leave out of a summary of *Sir Gawain and the Green Knight?*
   A. King Arthur
   B. the lady of the castle near the Green Chapel
   C. the lord of the castle near the Green Chapel
   D. Guenevere

____ 7. Sir Gawain's internal conflict in *Sir Gawain and the Green Knight* involves his guilt over
  A. accepting the lady's gift.
  B. disappointing King Arthur.
  C. violating the chivalric code.
  D. accepting the knight's challenge.

____ 8. Which saying best paraphrases what the Green Knight says to Sir Gawain at the end of *Sir Gawain and the Green Knight?*
  A. Live by the sword and die by the sword.
  B. Admit your mistakes and move on.
  C. A leopard never changes his spots.
  D. The best is yet to come.

____ 9. The central theme of *Morte d'Arthur* involves the
  A. consequences of greed.
  B. nobility of war.
  C. principles of chivalry.
  D. perils of battle.

____ 10. Which of the following parts of *Morte d'Arthur* involves an element of the supernatural?
  A. King Arthur's campaign against Sir Lancelot
  B. the death of Sir Lucan the Butler
  C. Sir Bedivere's decision to stay with the hermit
  D. the catching of King Arthur's sword

____ 11. The battle between King Arthur and Sir Mordred in *Morte d'Arthur* is similar to other legends of the Middle Ages because
  A. it is historically accurate.
  B. is not realistic.
  C. its heroes fight nobly.
  D. it presents death solely in an idealized, spiritual manner.

____ 12. In *Morte d'Arthur,* which personal characteristic motivates Sir Bedivere to disobey King Arthur's order to throw the king's sword into the lake?
  A. evil
  B. ambition
  C. common sense
  D. greed

____ 13. Which statement would you *not* include in a summary of *Morte d'Arthur?*
  A. King Arthur has a dream in which he is warned to delay his battle with Mordred.
  B. Sir Bedivere reluctantly throws King Arthur's sword into the lake.
  C. Both King Arthur and Mordred tell their men to charge if they see a sword drawn.
  D. The hermit who buries King Arthur was once the Bishop of Canterbury.

Vocabulary and Grammar

_____ 14. In *Sir Gawain and the Green Knight,* Sir Gawain fought adroitly. *Adroitly* means.
   A. fiercely
   B. gracefully
   C. courageously
   D. slowly

_____ 15. Sir Gawain entreated King Arthur to let him face the Green Knight. *Entreated* means _____.
   A. feared
   B. ordered
   C. begged
   D. demanded

_____ 16. Which word is closest in meaning to *adjure*?
   A. demand
   B. request
   C. shout
   D. judge

_____ 17. Which is the most appropriate word to describe what the hermit did to King Arthur in *Morte d'Arthur*?
   A. rejected
   B. emancipated
   C. instructed
   D. interred

_____ 18. Which word is most nearly opposite in meaning to *largesse*?
   A. generosity
   B. reliability
   C. stinginess
   D. eagerness

Essay

19. *Sir Gawain and the Green Knight* and *Morte d'Arthur* were written by two different people. Do you think the portrait of King Arthur is consistent in these two stories? Write an essay in which you analyze the character of King Arthur as he is portrayed in these two stories. Cite examples from the texts to back up your observations. Then compare the two Arthurs.

20. *Sir Gawain and the Green Knight* and *Morte d'Arthur* are two of the best-known chivalric romances of the Middle Ages. Write an essay in which you explain, first, what chivalry is and, second, how its ideals and code of conduct are represented in the poems. Refer not only to the character and conduct of Gawain and Arthur, but also to the character and conduct of other characters. Make note of the impulses and interests that chivalry conflicts within these romances, and the ways that the romance resolves these conflicts.

21. **Thinking About the Essential Question: Do writers gain more by accepting or by rejecting tradition?** Both *Sir Gawain and the Green Knight* and *Morte d'Arthur* include very traditional versions of the chivalric knight, but in both, the chivalric tradition is broken to some extent. In an essay, describe how Gawain and Bedivere both exemplify tradition and break with it. Explain what their break with tradition adds to the readers' understanding of the characters.

Unit 1 Resources: From Legend to History
155

Name _____ Date _____

Letters of Margaret Paston by Margaret Paston
"Twa Corbies" Anonymous
"Lord Randall" Anonymous
"Get Up and Bar the Door" Anonymous
"Barbara Allan" Anonymous
Evaluate Author's Perspective

An **author's perspective** is his or her way of seeing things. Many factors contribute to an author's perspective. Gender, ethnicity, and other elements of an author's background inform his or her perspective. Also, the time period, including the politics and beliefs of the time, affects the perspective. Finally, on a more personal note, the belief systems, opinions, and social positions of the author solidify his or her perspective. You can even learn more about anonymous authors by examining the perspectives they present in their writing.

When you read a primary source or any other text, you should consider the author's perspective as you read. Identify elements of his or her perspective. Then you can evaluate how the perspective affects the literary work.

DIRECTIONS: *Use the following chart to identify elements of and evaluate author's perspective. The first element has been completed for you.*

Letters of Margaret Paston		
Element of Perspective	Description	Evaluation: How It Affects the Work
Gender	Female	Shows the limitations of women's rights during the time period
Time period		
Beliefs and opinions		
Social position		
Ethnicity		

On a separate page, draw a chart like this one for the four ballads. Evaluate the perspectives the authors present.

Letters of Margaret Paston by Margaret Paston
"Twa Corbies" Anonymous
"Lord Randall" Anonymous
"Get Up and Bar the Door" Anonymous
"Barbara Allan" Anonymous
Vocabulary Builder

Word List

alderman   assault   asunder   certify   ransacked   remnant   succor

A. DIRECTIONS: *On each line, write the word from the Word List that has the same meaning as the italicized word or phrase in the sentence.*

1. Two thieves broke into a house and *pillaged* every room in search of valuables.
   _____

2. The *official* voted against a proposal to raise parking meter rates in her district.
   _____

3. The only *remainder* of the delicious meal was a spoonful of mashed potatoes.
   _____

4. The pirates planned to *violently attack* the trade ship and steal any cargo on board.
   _____

5. Nurse Florence Nightingale offered *aid* to wounded soldiers during the Crimean War.
   _____

6. The explosives expert recommended using dynamite to blow the boulder *into pieces*.
   _____

7. Only an anthropologist will be able to *verify* whether the artifact is authentic.
   _____

B. WORD STUDY: *Many words in the English language have Anglo-Saxon roots. Look up each of these words and identify their language of origin and their original meaning.*

1. **ransack:** _____
   _____

2. **Tuesday:** _____
   _____

3. **before:** _____
   _____

Primary Sources Letters of Margaret Paston, "Twa Corbies," "Lord Randall," Get Up and Bar the Door," "Barbara Allan" by Anonymous

Selection Test

MULTIPLE CHOICE

Critical Reading *Identify the letter of the choice that best completes the statement or answers the question.*

_____ 1. These primary sources tell about
   A. love affairs.   C. ballad form.
   B. medieval life   D. the effects of death.

_____ 2. In the letter to John Paston dated 17 October 1465, the reader indirectly learns about
   A. government in the middle ages.   C. results of gossip in the
   B. the relationship between   community.
      Margaret and her son.   D. life in medieval London.

_____ 3. What element of medieval attitudes and life are described in the letter dated 27 October 1465?
   A. the cruelty of landowners in   C. the power struggle between
      regards to their tenants   husband and wife over tenants
   B. the difficulty of conducting a   D. the fight for land rights and the
      long-distance marriage   brutality used to acquire them

_____ 4. What does the continuous discussion of the fight for land rights say about the importance of landownership at the time?
   A. Without owning land, no one would consider you.
   B. Landownership guaranteed a person a say in government.
   C. Landownership was closely linked to status and security.
   D. Owning land was stressful and not worth the fight.

_____ 5. How do the accounts in these letters as primary sources differ from a secondary source, such as contemporary history book account?
   A. The letters provide a firsthand perspective of events, not a removed explanation.
   B. A history book provides more insight into particular events than the letters.
   C. The primary sources allow for a more objective view than a history book.
   D. A history book requires readers to draw conclusions, but the letters directly state information.

_____ 6. In "Twa Corbies," what medieval attitude toward life and death does the author present?
   A. critical and serious   C. accepting
   B. darkly humorous   D. vengeful and angry

___ 7. In "Lord Randall," the comparison between love and poison
   A. expresses the time's exaggerated sense of love's power.
   B. warns of the pitfalls of chivalry and romance.
   C. emphasizes the realistic view of love and death.
   D. mirrors the importance of a mother-son relationship.

___ 8. What do the ladies' actions in "Twa Corbies" and "Lord Randall" indicate about the medieval perspective of women?
   A. Women are highly respected and loved.
   B. Women are viewed as untrustworthy and dangerous.
   C. Women are unwitting victims of chivalry and romance.
   D. Women are considered unnecessary and uneducated.

___ 9. How do the events in "Barbara Allan" echo the medieval ideas presented in "Lord Randall"?
   A. The events in "Barbara Allan" equate love sickness with death in the same way "Lord Randall" does.
   B. "Lord Randall" and "Barbara Allan" express thoughts about the fleeting nature of life.
   C. "Barbara Allan" and "Lord Randall" investigate the importance of romance, chivalry, and revenge.
   D. Barbara Allan's death mirrors the death of Lord Randall, both having been poisoned by love.

___ 10. How is the perspective of medieval life presented in "Get Up and Bar the Door" different from those presented in the other ballads?
   A. This ballad expresses a more romantic view of life and love than the other ballads.
   B. This ballad lacks the same sense of humor in addressing medieval attitudes as the other ballads have.
   C. This ballad presents a humorous and exaggerated look at married life, not a romanticized view of love.
   D. This ballad tells more about medieval relationships than the other ballads do.

Narration: Autobiographical Narrative

Prewriting: Choosing Your Topic

Complete the chart below by listing names and descriptions of memorable people, places, and events in your life.

People	*Places*	*Events*

Drafting: Shaping Your Writing

Complete the following graphic organizer to help your essay start strong and stay organized.

Introduction

Description of the main character:	Description of opening dialogue:	Description of the setting:

↕

Background Information

↕

Main Incident

↕

Interesting Closing

Name _____ Date _____

Writing Workshop—Unit 1

Autobiographical Narrative: Integrating Grammar Skills

Even though you may be moving back and forth in time in your narrative, do not change tenses unnecessarily.

Incorrect: It *was* midnight when the vote tally *is* finally complete.

Correct: It *was* midnight when the vote tally *was* finally complete.

Identifying Incorrect Tense Changes

A. DIRECTIONS: *Underline the verbs in the following sentences. On the line, write whether the verb tenses used are* correct *or* incorrect.

____ 1. I walked up to the microphone and deliver my speech.

____ 2. She is the person who inspires me most in my daily life.

____ 3. We worked hard and made the banquet a big success.

____ 4. When the storm finally ended, we venture cautiously outside.

____ 5. I enjoy working with children because their outlook on life was so fascinating.

Fixing Incorrect Tense Changes

B. DIRECTIONS: *Rewrite the following sentences, correcting any unnecessary changes in verb tenses. If there are no errors in the sentence, write* correct.

1. The summer I went to baseball camp, I never dream I would learn so much.

_____

2. When I am learning a new skill, I needed hours of practice to finally master it.

_____

3. In the past, I believed that family members were not as important as friends. Today, I know that my relatives are an important resource.

_____

_____

4. Today, when I see little kids on the playground, I remembered how important my earliest friendships were to me when I was a kid.

_____

_____

5. Sometimes I think that my Uncle Steve has played the biggest part in making me the person I am today.

_____

_____

Unit 1 Resources: From Legend to History
© Pearson Education, Inc. All rights reserved.
161

Name _____ Date _____

Evaluating a Persuasive Speech

Choose a persuasive speech to evaluate. Use this form to identify the type of proposition the speech makes and to give examples of the speaker's use of persuasive techniques.

Speaker: _____

Title of speech	_____
Media type	_____
Intended audience	_____
Purpose	_____
Proposition	State the proposition: _____ _____ (Circle) fact value problem policy

Persuasive techniques (examples)	Appeals to ethos (credibility): _____
	_____
	Appeals to pathos (emotion): _____
	
	_____
	Appeals to logos (fact and logic): _____
	   –facts _____
	
	_____
	    –analogies _____
	
	_____
	    –syllogisms _____
	
	_____

Persuasive languages (examples)	Rhetorical questions _____ _____ Parallel structure _____ _____ Figurative language _____ _____
Negative Persuasive techniques	Logical fallacies: _____ _____ _____ _____

In your opinion, does this speaker argue persuasively and ethically? Why or why not?

_____

_____

Unit 1 Vocabulary Workshop
Using a Dictionary and Other Resources

A **dictionary** provides the denotation, the literal meaning, of words as well as their etymologies, or origins. A **thesaurus** identifies synonyms, words with the same or similar meanings.

A. DIRECTIONS: *For each item below, use a dictionary to find the etymology.*

Example: **kin** Middle English *kyn* < Old English *cynn*, related to Old Norse *kyn* < Indo-European base *gen-*, to produce

1. shield _____

_____

2. destiny _____

_____

3. fame _____

_____

4. hero _____

_____

5. dragon _____

_____

6. sword _____

_____

B. DIRECTIONS: *Use a thesaurus to find at least three synonyms for each item listed above. Write a sentence using one synonym.*

Example: **kin** Synonyms: family, relation, clan
The whole *clan* gathered to celebrate the wedding.

1. **shield**   Synonyms: _____

_____

2. **destiny**   Synonyms: _____

_____

3. **fame**   Synonyms: _____

_____

4. **hero**   Synonyms: _____

_____

5. **dragon**   Synonyms: _____

_____

6. **sword**   Synonyms: _____

_____

Essential Questions Workshop—Unit 1

In their poems, epics, and nonfiction works, the writers in Unit One express ideas that relate to the three Essential Questions framing this book. Review the literature in the unit. Then, for each Essential Question, choose an author and at least one passage from his or her writing that expresses an idea related to the question. Use this chart to complete your work.

Essential Question	Author/Selection	Literary Passage
What is the relationship between place and literature?		
How does literature shape or reflect society?		
What is the relationship of the writer to tradition?		

Unit 1: From Legend to History
Benchmark Test 2

MULTIPLE CHOICE

Literary Analysis and Reading Skills *Answer the following questions.*

1. What is a frame in a literary work?
   A. a story within a story
   B. a type of setting
   C. the important elements of a story
   D. the theme of a story

2. Which is always true of a frame story?
   A. It includes characters who stand for ideas or qualities.
   B. It involves the adventures of gods and goddesses.
   C. It ridicules the faults of individuals or groups.
   D. It includes any number of different narratives.

3. Which of the following is true of the setting of a frame story?
   A. The time and place of its action may not match the settings of the tales it comprises.
   B. The setting specifies a time but rarely mentions a particular place.
   C. The time and place of its action always match the settings of the tales it comprises.
   D. It is always a crucial element of the plot or central conflict.

4. Which of these is an element of most medieval romances?
   A. knights   B. crimes   C. mysteries   D. satire

5. Which of these are the basis of many medieval romances?
   A. novels   B. poems   C. legends   D. fables

6. What are legends?
   A. stories that present an idealized view of rural life
   B. traditional stories that take place in the past
   C. stories that depict the downfall of the main character
   D. romantic stories that place a premium on emotion

7. Which of the following statements is true of legends?
   A. They are usually allegories.
   B. They are always written in the first person.
   C. They ridicule or criticize institutions or social conventions.
   D. They may have been inspired by real events and real people.

8. Which of the following is most likely to be the subject of a social commentary?
   A. weather patterns in various parts of the country
   B. the treatment of children in the workplace
   C. updates on the lives of celebrities
   D. highlights of sporting events

9. Which of these is a definition of archetypal narrative elements?
   A. patterns in literature found around the world
   B. descriptive or figurative language used in literature
   C. characters and details unique to a particular geographic area
   D. narrative techniques that present thoughts as if coming from a character's mind

10. Archetypal elements do which of the following?
    A. present cultural idiosyncrasies
    B. help create word pictures for the reader
    C. make stories easier to remember and retell
    D. capture the thoughts and feelings of characters

11. Which of the following can most influence the mood of a literary work?
    A. point of view
    B. characterization
    C. setting
    D. symbolism

12. Which would most likely be the best source for verifying the following statement?

    The rate of obesity in the United States is highest among children who watched 4 or more hours of TV a day and lowest among children who watched 1 hour or less a day.

    A. your private physician
    B. an encyclopedia article on obesity
    C. the Web site for the Centers for Disease Control and Prevention
    D. an article in a fitness magazine by a doctor promoting a weight-loss product

13. What is the following sentence mainly about?

    Contrary to the ancients' belief that the phenomena we now call supernovas—exploding large stars—were appearances of new stars, scientists now know, thanks to specialized computers and powerful telescopes, that these events mark the death of old stars.

    A. Supernovas are dying stars.
    B. Scientists now are using modern tools.
    C. Ancient people, like modern people, noticed supernovas.
    D. Ancient people thought they had discovered new stars.

Read this passage. Then, answer the questions that follow.

     In a summer season when soft was the sun,
     I clothed myself in a cloak as I shepherd were,
     Habit like a hermit's unholy in works,
     And went wide in the world wonders to hear.
 5   But on a May morning on Malvern hills,
     A marvel befell me of fairy, methought.
     I was weary with wandering and went me to rest
     Under a broad bank by a brook's side,
     And as I lay and leaned over and looked into the waters
10   I fell into a sleep for it sounded so merry.

     from *The Vision Concerning Piers Plowman* by William Langland

Unit 1 Resources: From Legend to History

14. How does the poet reveal the narrator's character in this selection?

    A. through social commentary

    B. through archetypal narrative elements

    C. through direct characterization

    D. through indirect characterization

15. What does the narrator suggest about himself in this selection?

    A. He is a farmer.

    B. He is a seeker of knowledge.

    C. He leads a hermit's life.

    D. He misses his home.

16. *The Vision Concerning Piers Plowman* is an allegorical narrative poem. Knowing this, what would you most likely expect to find in the poem?

    A. references to historical events

    B. both literal and symbolic meaning

    C. autobiographical elements

    D. vivid imagery

17. Which of these genres best describes an allegory such as *The Vision Concerning Piers Plowman*, which warns against the evils of worldly power?

    A. a satire   **B.** a legend   **C.** an exemplum   **D.** a sermon

Read this passage. Then, answer the questions that follow.

> Then began I to dream a marvellous dream,
> That I was in a wilderness wist I not where.
> As I looked to the east right into the sun,
> I saw a tower on a toft° worthily built;   °**toft** knoll; hillside.
> 5 A deep dale beneath a dungeon therein,
> With deep ditches and dark and dreadful of sight
> A fair field full of folk found I in between,
> Of all manner of men the rich and the poor,
> Working and wandering as the world asketh.
> 10 Some put them to plow and played little enough,
> At setting and sowing they sweated right hard
> And won that which wasters by gluttony destroy.

from *The Vision Concerning Piers Plowman* by William Langland

18. Reread lines 11–12 for clarification. What do they most likely mean?

    A. The rewards of hard work are sometimes wasted by greed.

    B. Hardworking people reap the most rewards for their effort.

    C. Some people misuse what they earn from their hard work.

    D. The greedy must work twice as hard as those who want little.

19. What is the most likely meaning of *wist* in line 2? Use context clues to determine your answer.

    A. were   **B.** found   **C.** wish   **D.** knew

20. Which of these is the best summary of the selection?
  A. The narrator sees rich and poor people helping to build a tall tower.
  B. The narrator observes poor people working to provide for the rich.
  C. The narrator dreams of various people at work in a strange setting.
  D. The narrator falls asleep in a dark and dreadful wilderness.

Read the following passage from a traditional Scottish ballad. Then, answer the questions that follow. Note that the Gadie is a branch of the river Don. Bennachie is a hill. Both are in Aberdeenshire, a region of Scotland.

       O gin I were whaur Gadie rins,
       Whaur Gadie rins, whaur Gadie rins,
       O gin I were whaur Gadie rins
       At the back o' Bennachie.
   5   Aince mair to hear the wild birds' sang,
       To wander birks an' braes amang
       Wi' friends and fav'rites left sae lang
       At the back o' Bennachie.
       O gin I were whaur Gadie rins,
  10   Whaur Gadie rins, whaur Gadie rins,
       O gin I were whaur Gadie rins
       At the Back o' Bennachie.

                from "Whaur Gadie Rins"

21. Which of these terms describes the language used in the selection?
  A. metaphor   **B.** slang   **C.** formal   **D.** dialect

22. Which of these phrases is closest to the meaning suggested by *aince mair* in line 5 of the selection?
  A. no more   **C.** I want
  B. we may   **D.** once more

Read this passage from a late-eighteenth-century work. Then, answer the questions that follow.

   It may fairly be questioned, whether government be not still more considerable in its incidental effects, than in those intended to be produced. Vice, for example, depends for its existence upon the existence of temptation. May not a good government strongly tend to extirpate,* and a bad one to increase the mass of temptation? Again, vice depends for its existence upon the existence of error. May not a good government by taking away all restraints upon the enquiring mind hasten, and a bad one by its patronage of error procrastinate the discovery and establishment of truth?

              from *Of the Importance of Political Institutions* by William Godwin
  *extirpate: remove.

23. What argument does the author make about the existence of temptation in society?

    A. Bad governments increase the temptation to engage in wrongdoing.

    B. When governments procrastinate, they lead citizens to criminal activities.

    C. A government must be strong enough to control the activities of all its citizens.

    D. The majority of people are tempted to do evil, regardless of the type of government.

Vocabulary

24. Based on your knowledge of the suffix *-tion*, choose the best meaning of *presumption* as it is used in the following sentence.

    Leslie regretted her presumption that she would pass the test without studying.

    A. someone who has expectations

    B. the act of assuming something will happen

    C. an expression of disappointment

    D. the state of being pleased

25. Based on your knowledge of the prefix *apo-*, choose the best meaning of *apostasy* as it is used in the following sentence,

    Because of the scandal, the senators feared the apostasy of members of their political party.

    A. expression of criticism

    B. takeover by force

    C. abandonment of a loyalty

    D. revelation of a secret

26. What is the meaning of *compound* as it is used in the following sentence?

    The family compound is located on fifty wooded acres in Albemarle County.

    A. a word formed from two words

    B. a fenced or walled-in area

    C. a chemical substance made from elements

    D. an agreeable settlement

27. Based on your knowledge of the root *-droit-*, choose the best definition of *adroitness* as it is used in the following sentence.

    Carson admired the adroitness with which his son repaired the computer.

    A. skill   B. speed   C. courage   D. generosity

Grammar

28. Which of the following sentences contains correlative conjunctions?

    A. Carlos wrote down the number, but he lost it.

    B. Our car is small, so we rented a van for the trip.

    C. My brother and I volunteered to work on the project.

    D. We should decide whether to stay or to go.

29. Which choice best combines these sentences using correlative conjunctions?

Sonia won a medal in the contest. She also received prize money in the contest.

    A. Sonia not only won a medal in the contest but also received prize money.

    B. Sonia won a medal in the contest, and she also received prize money.

    C. Sonia both won a medal and also received prize money in the contest.

    D. Sonia won a medal in the contest, and she received prize money too.

ESSAY

30. Read this selection from *Middlemarch*, by the nineteenth-century novelist George Eliot.

It was hardly a year since they had come to live at Tipton Grange with their uncle, a man nearly sixty, of acquiescent temper, miscellaneous opinions, and uncertain vote. He had travelled in his younger years, and was held in this part of the country to have contracted too rambling habit of mind. Mr. Brooke's conclusions were as difficult to predict as the weather: it was only safe to say that he would act with benevolent intentions, and that he would spend as little money as possible in carrying them out.

Now, read this line of criticism:

When describing characters, Eliot tended to focus too much on their personal habits and underlying thoughts, with the result being that readers barely had a chance to actually picture what the characters looked like and how they acted toward one another.

Based on your reading of the passage from *Middlemarch*, do you agree with this criticism? Write a well-organized response, and support it with examples from the selections.

31. Imagine that you are running for president of your school's student body and the results of the election will soon be announced. Write an interior monologue in which you describe your thoughts and feelings about the upcoming announcement. Write in the first person, using strong, vivid words to express your thoughts.

32. Imagine that you are planning to write an autobiographical narrative of an incident in your life, perhaps a funny one. Create a chart, diagram, or other visual representation relating to the narrative, and use it to plan the narrative. Show the main characters, setting, and sequence of events. Below the graphic organizer, write one sentence describing an insight that you gained from the incident.

Vocabulary in Context

Read the selection. Then, answer the questions that follow.

1. Crystal always felt it was her _____to be a musical-comedy star.
   A. destined
   B. predestined
   C. destiny
   D. deserted

2. Dr. Kumar was a_____expert in the field of child development.
   A. convicted
   B. associated
   C. apprehensive
   D. prominent

3. They couldn't tell, with any_____, what time the family would arrive.
   A. hermit
   B. disorders
   C. certainty
   D. virtues

4. After looking all over the fabric store, Amy finally found a_____of the cloth she wanted.
   A. specator
   B. blunder
   C. remnant
   D. substitute

5. After spending time in the dense jungle forest, he liked the_____beauty of the desert.
   A. stark
   B. realms
   C. favorable
   D. unjust

6. Ray's grandparents faced_____in the 1950s because of the color of their skin.
   A. participation
   B. reign
   C. discrimination
   D. congratulation

7. The Portugese were the _____ of the African country of Angola.
   A. colonies
   B. colonial
   C. colonized
   D. colonizers

8. In the night, Alweyn slipped quietly away so as not to wake those _____ in the castle.
   A. unprecedented
   B. namely
   C. whitewashed
   D. slumbering

9. When I realized I didn't have my sweater, Mom told me, "You should have thought of that _____."
   A. traditionally
   B. beforehand
   C. unjustly
   D. certifiably

10. The older map showed that the _____ between the two counties was not where they thought it was.
    A. ventilation
    B. veranda
    C. biographer
    D. boundary

11. During the basketball game, the referee called three _____ against the home team.
    A. penalties
    B. straits
    C. hilts
    D. barbarians

12. Jesse worried that the virus had _____ his files and made them unusable.
    A. banished
    B. ransacked
    C. authorized
    D. corrupted

13. Solving world hunger has a _____ appeal
    A. reverent
    B. classical
    C. universal
    D. barbarian

Unit 1 Resources: From Legend to History
172

14. When citing facts to back up your point, you must be very_____.
   A. corrupted
   B. specific
   C. deprived
   D. vibrant

15. In English class, we read about Helen of Troy as we studied Greek_____.
   A. publicity
   B. roman
   C. fathom
   D. mythology

16. My friend Eban wrote the music for the songs, and I wrote the_____.
   A. succession
   B. lyrics
   C. valor
   D. occurrences

17. In order to get your real estate license, the board needs to_____you.
   A. certain
   B. certificate
   C. certainly
   D. certify

18. I hope I'll be able to get_____aid to help pay for college.
   A. finances
   B. financial
   C. finally
   D. financially

19. The Colemans came home to mess and found that their apartment had been_____.
   A. specific
   B. deprived
   C. ransacked
   D. blissful

20. The family had moved every few months, and Kyle was tired of all the_____.
   A. upheaval
   B. immunity
   C. reverence
   D. estimation

Diagnostic Tests and Vocabulary in Context
Use and Interpretation

The Diagnostic Tests and Vocabulary in Context were developed to assist teachers in making the most appropriate assignment of *Prentice Hall Literature* program selections to students. The purpose of these assessments is to indicate the degree of difficulty that students are likely to have in reading/comprehending the selections presented in the *following* unit of instruction. Tests are provided at six separate times in each in each grade level—a *Diagnostic Test* (to be used prior to beginning the year's instruction) and a *Vocabulary in Context,* the final segment of the Benchmark Test appearing at the end of each of the first five units of instruction. Note that the tests are intended for use not as summative assessments for the prior unit, but as guidance for assigning literature selections in the upcoming unit of instruction.

The structure of all Diagnostic Tests and Vocabulary in Context in this series is the same. All test items are four-option, multiple-choice items. The format is established to assess a student's ability to construct sufficient meaning from the context sentence to choose the only provided word that fits both the semantics (meaning) and syntax (structure) of the context sentence. All words in the context sentences are chosen to be "below-level" words that students reading at this grade level should know. All answer choices fit *either* the meaning or structure of the context sentence, but only the correct choice fits *both* semantics and syntax. All answer choices—both correct answers and incorrect options—are key words chosen from specifically taught words that will occur in the subsequent unit of program instruction. This careful restriction of the assessed words permits a sound diagnosis of students' current reading achievement and prediction of the most appropriate level of readings to assign in the upcoming unit of instruction.

The assessment of vocabulary in context skill has consistently been shown in reading research studies to correlate very highly with "reading comprehension." This is not surprising as the format essentially assesses comprehension, albeit in sentence-length "chunks." Decades of research demonstrate that vocabulary assessment provides a strong, reliable prediction of comprehension achievement— the purpose of these tests. Further, because this format demands very little testing time, these diagnoses can be made efficiently, permitting teachers to move forward with critical instructional tasks rather than devoting excessive time to assessment.

It is important to stress that while the Diagnostic and Vocabulary in Context were carefully developed and will yield sound assignment decisions, they were designed to *reinforce*, not supplant, teacher judgment as to the most appropriate instructional placement for individual students. Teacher judgment should always prevail in making placement—or indeed other important instructional—decisions concerning students.

Diagnostic Tests and Vocabulary in Context
Branching Suggestions

These tests are designed to provide maximum flexibility for teachers. Your *Unit Resources* books contain the 40-question **Diagnostic Test** and 20-question **Vocabulary in Context** tests. At *PHLitOnline,* you can access the Diagnostic Test and complete 40-question Vocabulary in Context tests. Procedures for administering the tests are described below. Choose the procedure based on the time you wish to devote to the activity and your comfort with the assignment decisions relative to the individual students. Remember that your judgment of a student's reading level should always take precedence over the results of a single written test.

Feel free to use different procedures at different times of the year. For example, for early units, you may wish to be more confident in the assignments you make—thus, using the "two-stage" process below. Later, you may choose the quicker diagnosis, confirming the results with your observations of the students' performance built up throughout the year.

The **Diagnostic Test** is composed of a single 40-item assessment. Based on the results of this assessment, make the following assignment of students to the reading selections in Unit 1:

Diagnostic Test Score	Selection to Use
If the student's score is 0–25	more accessible
If the student's score is 26–40	more challenging

Outlined below are the three basic options for administering **Vocabulary in Context** and basing selection assignments on the results of these assessments.

1. For a one-stage, quicker diagnosis using the *20-item* test in the *Unit Resources:*

Vocabulary in Context Test Score	Selection to Use
If the student's score is 0–13	more accessible
If the student's score is 14–20	more challenging

2. If you wish to confirm your assignment decisions with a *two-stage* diagnosis:

Stage 1: Administer the 20-item test in the *Unit Resources*	
Vocabulary in Context Test Score	**Selection to Use**
If the student's score is 0–9	more accessible
If the student's score is 10–15	(Go to Stage 2.)
If the student's score is 16–20	more challenging

Stage 2: Administer items 21–40 from *PHLitOnline*	
Vocabulary in Context Test Score	**Selection to Use**
If the student's score is 0–12	more accessible
If the student's score is 13–20	more challenging

3. If you base your assignment decisions on the full 40-item **Vocabulary in Context** from *PHLitOnline:*

Vocabulary in Context Test Score	Selection to Use
If the student's score is 0–25	more accessible
If the student's score is 26–40	more challenging

Unit 1 Resources: From Legend to History

Grade 12—Benchmark Test 1
Interpretation Guide

Skill Objective	Test Items	Number Correct	Reading Kit
Literary Analysis			
Anglo-Saxon Lyrics	3, 5, 11, 12, 13, 14		pp. 14, 15
Elegy	4, 20		pp. 66, 67
Epic	1, 2		pp. 72, 73
Legend	8, 9, 10		pp. 122, 123
Historical Writing	6, 18		pp. 100, 101
Reading Strategy			
Paraphrase	7, 15		pp. 142, 143
Cultural and Historical Context	16, 17, 22, 23		pp. 44, 45
Using stylistic effects	19		pp. 230, 231
Using Maps	8, 9		pp. 228, 229
Vocabulary			
Latin Root: –sol-	24, 25		pp. 268, 269
Grammar			
Coordinating Conjunctions	26, 27		pp. 322, 323
Writing			
Editorial	29		pp. 350, 351
Job Application	30		pp. 354, 355
Business Memo	28		pp. 348, 349

Grade 12—Benchmark Test 2
Interpretation Guide

Skill Objective	Test Items	Number Correct	Reading Kit
Literary Analysis			
Characterization	14, 15		pp. 32, 33
Allegory	16, 17		pp. 2, 3
Plot Devices	1, 2		pp. 152, 153
Medieval Romances	4, 5		pp. 126, 127
Political and Social Commentary	8		pp. 162, 163
Archetype	9, 10		pp. 20, 21
Setting	3, 11		pp. 196, 197
Legend	6, 7		pp. 122, 123
Reading Strategy			
Evaluate Web Site credibility	12		pp. 86, 87
Reread for Clarification	18		pp. 188, 189
Context Clues	19		pp. 42, 43
Summarize	20		pp. 212, 213
Breaking Down and Analyzing Long Sentences	13, 23		pp. 26, 27
Dialect	21, 22		pp. 50, 51
Vocabulary			
Latin Suffix: -tion	24		pp. 288, 289
Greek Prefix: apo-	25		pp. 256, 257
Multiple-Meaning Words	26		pp. 294, 295
Word Root: -droit-	27		pp. 292, 293
Grammar			
Correlative Conjunctions	28, 29		pp. 322, 323
Writing			
Response to Criticism	30		n/a
Interior Monologue	31		pp. 367, 368
Autobiographical Narrative	32		n/a

ANSWERS

Diagnostic Test 1, p. 2

MULTIPLE CHOICE

1. ANS: B
2. ANS: D
3. ANS: C
4. ANS: C
5. ANS: A
6. ANS: C
7. ANS: D
8. ANS: D
9. ANS: B
10. ANS: D
11. ANS: A
12. ANS: D
13. ANS: C
14. ANS: B
15. ANS: D
16. ANS: B
17. ANS: D
18. ANS: B
19. ANS: C
20. ANS: A
21. ANS: D
22. ANS: A
23. ANS: B
24. ANS: C
25. ANS: C
26. ANS: A
27. ANS: A
28. ANS: D
29. ANS: B
30. ANS: A
31. ANS: C
32. ANS: D
33. ANS: A
34. ANS: D
35. ANS: B
36. ANS: C
37. ANS: C
38. ANS: D
39. ANS: A
40. ANS: B

Unit 1 Introduction

Names and Terms to Know, p. 5

A. 1. F; 2. E; 3. B; 4. G; 5. A; 6. C; 7. D

B. Sample Answers

1. The Celts originated in southern Europe and had priests called Druids. The Anglo-Saxons came from what is now Germany.
2. Alfred the Great encouraged a rebirth of learning and education.
3. In Magna Carta, the king promised not to tax land without first meeting with the barons.
4. The feudal system declined after the great plague called the Black Death, when a labor shortage increased the value of a peasant's work.

Focus Questions, p. 6

Sample Answers

1. Alfred earned the title "the Great" by resisting further Danish encroachments in Britain and by concluding a truce with the Danes in 886, whereby the Danes agreed to respect Saxon rule in the south. His attitude toward pre-Danish civilization in Britain was that it should be preserved, so he encouraged a revival of learning and education.
2. In his *History of the English Church and People*, Venerable Bede gave an account of England from the Roman invasion until his own time in the early eighth century. *The Anglo-Saxon Chronicles*, written in Old English, compiled a valuable group of journals that had been created in monasteries. In his *Canterbury Tales*, Chaucer presented a cross section of medieval English society by realistically characterizing the pilgrims from every walk of life. The medieval romances, especially tales about King Arthur, often blended fact with fiction.

"The Seafarer,"
translated by Burton Raffel
"The Wanderer,"
translated by Charles W. Kennedy
"The Wife's Lament,"
translated by Ann Standford

Vocabulary Warm-up Exercises, p. 8

A. 1. unfurl
2. billowing
3. strive
4. perched
5. whirled

6. scorch
7. smitten
8. terns

B. Sample Answers

1. Determined to spot the <u>fleeting</u> asteroid, the astronomer *constantly* watched the sky.
2. The <u>decrees</u> issued by the emperor were *never* ignored.
3. The *complaints* from readers' <u>tarnished</u> the magazine's reputation.
4. The director began to <u>brood</u> when his new film was a *flop*.
5. When the prince was *injured,* the church bells rang with <u>mournful</u> sounds.
6. Immigrants *often* experience feelings of <u>desolation</u> after leaving their homeland.
7. The school *held* the party, so the preparation was not for naught.

Reading Warm-up A, p. 9

Sample Answers

1. (map the world's oceans); *Strive* means "to exert much effort or energy."
2. The *swelling* sails on their longships also permitted voyages across the freezing Atlantic to Iceland and North America.
3. (the riches of the east); Someone *smitten* might daydream, write, or sing about the person or thing that fascinates him.
4. (on their canoes); *Perched* means "to stand, sit, or rest on an elevated place or position."
5. <u>hot</u>; A hot iron might *scorch* a shirt.
6. (their sails); It's common to see a flag *unfurl* as it is raised.
7. (hovered and whirled over their vessels); You might find terns near any seaport or along coastlines.
8. Something that *whirled* would spin rapidly, often changing direction.

Grammar and Style: Compound Predicates, p. 14

A. 1. Compound predicate: called me eagerly out, sent me over / The horizon; subject: soul
2. Compound predicate: ages and shrinks; subject: honor
3. Compound predicate: grieved each dawn / wondered where my lord my first on earth might be; subject: I
4. Compound predicate: took me, swept me back / and forth in sorrow and fear and pain, / showed me suffering; subject: sea
5. Compound predicate: ages and droops into death; subject: earth

B. Sample Answers

1. Hardship groaned and wrenched around my heart.
2. The weakest survives and eventually thrives.
3. Lonely and wretched I wailed and moaned my woe.
4. Ever I know and bemoan the dark of my exile.
5. I must far and near bear and lament the anger of my beloved.

Reading Warm-up B, p. 16

Sample Answers

1. (person was forced to leave his city or country for years); *Wretched* means "in a deplorable state of distress or misfortune."
2. Those left behind might brood because they wouldn't know whether their loved one was alive, hurt, starving, or in some other kind of distress.
3. (the entire family's reputation); To make matters worse, often the entire family's reputation was *ruined* by the conviction, and often their personal property was seized as well.
4. (loneliness); *Desolation* can mean feeling the grief of being abandoned.
5. lifetime; A snowflake that is brought inside is *fleeting.*
6. (announced); Sometimes a person's fate was announced by *orders from a government official.*
7. <u>further opposition</u>; When the cake burned, all her mixing and measuring came to *naught.*
8. The foghorn sounded *mournful; mournful* means sad.

Literary Analysis: Anglo-Saxon Lyrics, p. 17

1. But there ísn't a mán on eárth so próud,
   So bórn to greátness, so bóld with his yóuth,
   Grówn so bráve, or so gráced by Gód
   That he féels no féar as the sáils unfúrl.
2. two: greatness, brave
3. Those pówers have vánished, those pleásures are deád.
   The weákest survíves and the wórld contínues.
   Kept spínning by tóil. All glóry is tárnished.
4. wave-tumult
5. These poems are elegies because they lament people who have passed away. Each mourns the loss of a person, and the end of an era.

Reading Strategy: Connect to Historical Context, p. 18

Sample Answers

1. The life of a seafarer was always at risk. They were frequently far from home or in exile. All of these conditions can bring sorrow, fear, and pain.
2. Warriors were dependent upon their lords for protection and provisions. The loss of a master could bring great despair and financial insecurity.

3. Women had few rights and were subjected to whatever their fathers, masters, husbands, or lovers demanded.

Vocabulary Builder, p. 19

A. 1. sweetness; sample answer: The sweetness of the cake upset her stomach.
  2. brightness; sample answer: The brightness of the light gave me a headache.
  3. eagerness; sample answer: Ryan's eagerness was easy to see.
  4. helpfulness; sample answer: The teacher was impressed with Alan's helpfulness.

B. 1. F; 2. G; 3. D; 4. B; 5. H; 6. A; 7. I; 8. E; 9. C; 10. J

C. 1. D; 2. B; 3. B

Enrichment: Social Studies, p. 21

Sample Answer

Students should clearly draw and label the migration routes of the Angles, Saxons, and Jutes. The Angles came from southern Denmark and settled in the eastern half of England. The Saxons came from northern Germany and settled in southern England. The Jutes probably came from northern Denmark and northern Germany and settled in Kent and on the Isle of Wight.

Open-Book Test, p. 22

Short Answer

1. It is a kenning, a two-word renaming of a person, place, or thing.
   Difficulty: *Easy* **Objective:** *Literary Analysis*

2. He is passionate about the sea and curious about what he might discover.
   Difficulty: *Challenging* **Objective:** *Interpretation*

3. The theme is the sorrow of being homeless.
   Difficulty: *Easy* **Objective:** *Interpretation*

4. Knowing that exile was common at that time helps clarify why the Wanderer's fate is to be an exile.
   Difficulty: *Average* **Objective:** *Reading*

5. She assumes that her husband is now melancholy, as she is.
   Difficulty: *Average* **Objective:** *Interpretation*

6. It provides a break in the middle of the line where the speaker could pause for breath.
   Difficulty: *Challenging* **Objective:** *Literary Analysis*

7. caesura
   alliteration
   kenning
   Difficulty: *Average* **Objective:** *Literary Analysis*

8. It helps the reader understand why the theme of "exile," found in all three poems, was so common.
   Difficulty: *Average* **Objective:** *Reading*

9. They were cheerful, or happy, because they loved each other.
   Difficulty: *Easy* **Objective:** *Vocabulary*

10. The death of his lord and his resulting homelessness cause him terrible sorrow and are hard to bear.
    Difficulty: *Average* **Objective:** *Vocabulary*

Essay

11. Students should demonstrate an understanding of Anglo-Saxon culture and history. They may note that people sometimes went into exile or were separated from one another for long periods. Anglo-Saxon people lived in a warrior culture during a time when religious faith was becoming a vital part of daily life.
    Difficulty: *Easy* **Objective:** *Essay*

12. Students may respond that in each case, the poem's subject accepts his or her fate. Students may point out that in "The Seafarer," the sailor accepts that he will always follow the call of the sea. In "The Wanderer," the man accepts that his life with his lord and friends is over. In "The Wife's Lament," the wife accepts that her husband now hates her and has exiled her.
    Difficulty: *Average* **Objective:** *Essay*

13. Students may respond that the use of kennings provides interesting descriptions that are easy to remember and repeat. The caesura helps establish the rhythm, as well as providing a natural pause. Students should provide examples from the selections to illustrate these points.
    Difficulty: *Challenging* **Objective:** *Essay*

14. Students who choose "The Seafarer" may note that the speaker has lost his land home with its orchards, blooming towns, and spring fields. His exile on the "roaring sea" gives the poem both its sorrow and its sense of exploration and excitement. Students who choose "The Wanderer" may point out that the speaker has lost his home with his kinsmen in a battle. The sense of "rime-covered" walls and battlements fallen gives the poem its feeling of mournful loss. Students who choose "The Wife's Lament" may note that the speaker has lost her husband and home, now a "ruined hall." The description of the lost, destroyed home and happiness gives the poem its sense of despair.
    Difficulty: *Average* **Objective:** *Essay*

Oral Response

15. Oral responses should be clear, well organized, and well supported by appropriate examples from the selections.
    Difficulty: *Average* **Objective:** *Oral Presentation*

Selection Test A, p. 25

Critical Reading

1. **ANS:** C	**DIF:** Easy	**OBJ:** Literary Analysis
2. **ANS:** B	**DIF:** Easy	**OBJ:** Literary Analysis
3. **ANS:** A	**DIF:** Easy	**OBJ:** Comprehension
4. **ANS:** B	**DIF:** Easy	**OBJ:** Interpretation
5. **ANS:** D	**DIF:** Easy	**OBJ:** Reading Strategy
6. **ANS:** A	**DIF:** Easy	**OBJ:** Comprehension

7. ANS: C	DIF: Easy	OBJ: Interpretation
8. ANS: D	DIF: Easy	OBJ: Comprehension
9. ANS: D	DIF: Easy	OBJ: Literary Analysis
10. ANS: C	DIF: Easy	OBJ: Interpretation
11. ANS: B	DIF: Easy	OBJ: Reading Strategy

Vocabulary and Grammar

12. ANS: C	DIF: Easy	OBJ: Vocabulary
13. ANS: D	DIF: Easy	OBJ: Vocabulary
14. ANS: A	DIF: Easy	OBJ: Vocabulary

Essay

15. Students should demonstrate an understanding of Anglo-Saxon culture and history during the period when these poems were written and how this historic context helps them understand the poems. For example, they should know that people sometimes went into exile or were separated from one another for long periods of time. People of this period lived in a warrior-culture. It was also a period when religious faith was becoming a strong part of daily life. These elements enter into all three of the poems and provide insight into the feelings and thoughts of the speakers.
    Difficulty: *Easy*
    Objective: *Essay*

16. In the case of every poem, students should recognize that the speaker accepts his or her fate. Although the speakers continue to battle for life, they also believe they cannot change what fate has decided. For example, in "The Seafarer," the sailor accepts that the sea will always call him and that he will always follow the call. In "The Wanderer," the man accepts that his life with his ord and friends is over, and that he will never find such friends or a sense of belonging again. In "The Wife's Lament," the wife accepts that her husband now hates her and has exiled her, even though she did nothing to deserve this fate.
    Difficulty: *Easy*
    Objective: *Essay*

17. Students who choose "The Seafarer" may note that the speaker has lost his land home with its orchards, blooming towns, and spring fields. Students who choose "The Wanderer" may point out that the speaker has lost his home with his kinsmen in a battle. Students who choose "The Wife's Lament" may note that the speaker has lost her husband and home, now a "ruined hall."
    Difficulty: *Easy*
    Objective: *Essay*

Selection Test B, p. 28

Critical Reading

1. ANS: A	DIF: Easy	OBJ: Literary Analysis
2. ANS: D	DIF: Easy	OBJ: Comprehension
3. ANS: C	DIF: Average	OBJ: Reading Strategy

4. ANS: C	DIF: Easy	OBJ: Interpretation
5. ANS: B	DIF: Average	OBJ: Reading Strategy
6. ANS: D	DIF: Average	OBJ: Interpretation
7. ANS: D	DIF: Average	OBJ: Interpretation
8. ANS: B	DIF: Easy	OBJ: Literary Analysis
9. ANS: A	DIF: Average	OBJ: Comprehension
10. ANS: C	DIF: Challenging	OBJ: Literary Analysis
11. ANS: B	DIF: Challenging	OBJ: Comprehension
12. ANS: A	DIF: Challenging	OBJ: Reading Strategy
13. ANS: B	DIF: Challenging	OBJ: Interpretation
14. ANS: C	DIF: Average	OBJ: Literary Analysis

Vocabulary and Grammar

15. ANS: A	DIF: Average	OBJ: Vocabulary
16. ANS: A	DIF: Easy	OBJ: Vocabulary
17. ANS: D	DIF: Average	OBJ: Vocabulary
18. ANS: A	DIF: Average	OBJ: Vocabulary

Essay

19. Students may respond that in each case, the subject of the poem accepts what fate has dealt to him or her. In "The Seafarer," the sailor accepts that the sea will always call him and that he will always follow the call. In "The Wanderer," the man accepts that his life with his lord and friends is over, and that he will never find such friends or sense of belonging again. In "The Wife's Lament," the wife accepts that her husband now hates her and has exiled her, even though she did nothing to deserve this.
    Difficulty: *Average*
    Objective: *Essay*

20. Students may respond that the use of kennings provides interesting descriptions that are easy to remember and repeat. The caesura helps establish the rhythm, as well as providing a natural pause. Students should provide examples from the selections to illustrate these points.
    Difficulty: *Challenging*
    Objective: *Essay*

21. Students who choose "The Seafarer" may note that the speaker has lost his land home with its orchards, blooming towns, and spring fields. His exile on the "roaring sea" gives the poem both its elegiac sorrow and its sense of exploration and excitement. Students who choose "The Wanderer" may point out that the speaker has lost his home with his kinsmen in a battle. The sense of "rime-covered" walls and battlements fallen gives the poem its feeling of mournful loss. Students who choose "The Wife's Lament" may note that the speaker has lost her husband and home, now a "ruined hall." The description of the lost, destroyed home and happiness gives the poem its sense of despair.
    Difficulty: *Average*
    Objective: *Essay*

Unit 1 Resources: From Legend to History

from the Translator's Desk

Burton Raffel Introduces *Beowulf,* p. 31

1. A pair of powerful man-eating monsters and a fire-sprouting dragon drive the narrative.
2. He can swim for days on end; he can breathe a long time under water.
3. Beo means "bear"; Wulf means "wolf"; the fact that his name does not begin in the same way as his father's name is an exceptional break with tradition.
4. The poet does not introduce the hero at the beginning of the poem but features man-eating Grendel instead in order to create an atmosphere of darkness and terror. The poet then narrates Beowulf's exciting sea journey as the hero travels to help King Hrothgar.
5. She enters the scene to take revenge on behalf of her son.
6. Unlike a good king, the dragon never shares its treasures.
7. The poet repeatedly evokes "Almighty God"; the poem has an ethical framework, in which human beings are held to high moral standards; the poet paraphrases the creation story of Genesis; the story of Abel and Cain is explicitly mentioned; evil is punished; hell is cited as the home of evil. Most students will agree that the arguments are persuasive.

Burton Raffel

Listening and Viewing, p. 32

Sample answers and guidelines for evaluation:

Segment 1: When he translates, he makes himself into an author and attempts to recreate what the original author has written in today's time and place. Students may agree that the message is more important than the words used to convey it, while others might believe that the choice of words in poetry is equally important as their meaning.

Segment 2: Beowulf is an epic poem that includes the social and psychological issues that our ancestors experienced; it provides insight into what was important to them at that time period. Beowulf is also a very early example of the English language that shows us how much our language has evolved since that time.

Segment 3: He uses two computers: one that he types his translation on and one that has a dictionary of the original language of the text. He checks with reference books as he translates and figures out what the author was trying to do by dividing the poem into small sections and working on each section individually. Students may say that such a method helps to ensure accuracy as to the poet's meaning.

Segment 4: Translations represent the diversity of human experience carried from one place to another and enable us to understand and relate to what is happening in the world. Students may suggest that translated works, such as foreign poems, Old English texts, etc., could enable them to learn about what was culturally significant in another place and time.

from Beowulf, translated by Burton Raffel

Vocabulary Warm-up Exercises, p. 33

A.
1. mail
2. protector
3. swayed
4. boast
5. fleeing
6. truce
7. feud
8. inherited

B. Sample Answers
1. F; Once the visitors and guards left the museum, there was no one there, so it was deserted.
2. T; The chlorine became liquid or dissolved once it was added to the water.
3. F; If it were easy to see, they would not have groped their way out of the theater.
4. T; Traditionally, the groom does carry his bride over the threshold of their new home.
5. F; If they were silent, then the students would not have uttered a word.
6. F; The designer would not have looked for or sought brand-new furniture at antique stores.
7. F; The recruit's comrades would be close to his age and have about the same level of skill and experience that he had.

Reading Warm-up A, p. 35

Sample Answers
1. (from chain links woven together to form a metal fabric.) *Mail* offered defense because a sword could not cut through it.
2. The metal mesh allowed the warrior flexibility as lifted his weapon or shifted from side to side to avoid an enemy's blade. *Swayed* means "shifted from side to side."
3. Mail probably did serve as a *protector* from a bullet because it was not thick or strong enough to stop the bullet. A *protector* keeps people or things safe from harm.
4. (it indicated wealth and position); *Boast* means "to brag."
5. (his father); It was helpful if mail was *inherited* because mail was expensive and took a long time to make.
6. when a battle or feud ended; Sometimes a truce is reached because both sides wish to stop the killing and neither is strong enough to win.
7. (battle); A *feud* is a long, bitter quarrel. Unlike a war, it often involves two families.
8. Even when running away, they had an advantage. I have seen a rabbit *fleeing* a dog.

Reading Warm-up B, p. 36

Sample Answers

1. They *relished* the chance to explore the castle because it had been in a Hollywood movie. *Relished* means "found pleasure in."
2. (entered, crossing); A *threshold* might be covered with a wooden board or marked by a welcome mat.
3. with no one around; I like to go to the beach when it is deserted.
4. (They were overwhelmed by the amount of history that had taken place in that one stronghold.); *Uttered* means "spoke aloud."
5. The boys *groped* their way up the staircase because it was dark, narrow and difficult to climb. *Groped* means "felt around uncertainly."
6. The soldiers' *comrades* were each other. People on sports teams feel like *comrades*.
7. (found); I would have *sought* the dungeon.
8. (all the images of grandeur in their heads); *Dissolved* means "melted".

Literary Analysis: The Epic, p. 37

Sample Answers

1. Descriptions of Grendel as "mankind's enemy" and Hrothgar's "glorious throne protected by God" make these characters larger than life. Grendel is portrayed as a force of evil in a Christian context in that he can't know the love of God.
2. Beowulf uses elevated, formal language to present himself and his heroic deeds. Herot and Hrothgar, too, come across as grander and larger than life. The recognition of a duty to help others reflects Christian values.
3. Beowulf addresses Hrothgar in elevated language. His desire to conquer on his own reflects a cultural value of self-reliance. He recognizes that Grendel represents evil, and so implies that he is on the side of good.

Reading Strategy: Paraphrase, p. 38

Student passages will differ, but all columns should be filled in order to paraphrase the passage.

Vocabulary Builder, p. 39

Sample Answers

A. 1. *Disconsolate* means depressed and dejected, because there was no comfort they could find for the loss of their companions to Grendel.
2. *Consoled* means relieved or lessened the grief from loss.
3. *Inconsolably* means unable to be comforted.
4. A *consolation* tournament is meant to "comfort" players who have lost in the main contest.

B. 1. large and imposing; 2. disgusting; 3. cleanse; purify; 4. twisting and turning; 5. comfort; relief; 6. amends; making up for wrongs

Grammar and Style: Appositives and Appositive Phrases, p. 40

A. 1. underline *and*; connects independent clauses.
2. underline *but*; connects independent clauses.
3. underline *and*; connects adjectives; underline *for*; connects independent clauses.}

Enrichment: Film Portrayals of Monsters, p. 42

Sample Answers

Characteristics of the contemporary movie monsters should be compared and contrasted with those of Grendel.

Open-Book Test, p. 43

Short Answer

1. He is larger than life and is remembered in tales from long ago.
   Difficulty: *Easy*   **Objective:** *Literary Analysis*
2. He means that the monster thinks very quickly.
   Difficulty: *Easy*   **Objective:** *Reading*
3. He refuses to use weapons because Grendel uses none.
   Difficulty: *Average*   **Objective:** *Literary Analysis*
4. The gift means that Beowulf is making Wiglaf the ruler of Geatland, because the necklace is the symbol of his leadership.
   Difficulty: *Easy*   **Objective:** *Interpretation*
5. He is saying that the warriors are trying to kill Grendel.
   Difficulty: *Average*   **Objective:** *Reading*
6. The overlapping circles should show that both men are great warriors, have royal blood, inherited wealth, are brave, loyal, and honorable, are leaders, and believe in God and fate. Differences may include that Beowulf is older and is a greater lord than Wiglaf.
   Difficulty: *Average*   **Objective:** *Interpretation*
7. The watchman sees Beowulf as confident, honest, and great and observes that he carries noble weapons. These things make him seem larger than life, strong, and self-confident.
   Difficulty: *Challenging*   **Objective:** *Literary Analysis*
8. It is ironic because most of the Geats deserted him in battle.
   Difficulty: *Challenging*   **Objective:** *Interpretation*
9. Belief in God could provide comfort and relief for the characters in *Beowulf*.
   Difficulty: *Easy*   **Objective:** *Vocabulary*
10. He wants to cleanse all evil from the hall by killing Grendel.
    Difficulty: *Average*   **Objective:** *Vocabulary*

Essay

11. Students may say that some of the themes of *Beowulf*, such as the fight between good and evil, the glory of generous rulers who try to help their people, and the importance of loyalty and courage, are still important.

Others may say that the emphasis on physical strength and violence should not be part of today's world. They may feel that the battle between good and evil is too simple an idea for today's complex world.

Difficulty: *Easy* **Objective:** *Essay*

12. Students should use reasons, examples, and quotations to show the Danes' acceptance of fate. They may say that Beowulf believed he was destined to fight the monster and accepted the outcome as predetermined.

Difficulty: *Average* **Objective:** *Essay*

13. Students should mention such virtues as bravery, fairness, responsibility, concern for others, piety, ambition, loyalty, and intelligence. They should point to places in the text where Beowulf exhibits the virtues they choose.

Difficulty: *Challenging* **Objective:** *Essay*

14. Some students may feel that Beowulf's heroism is so extreme that the author must have meant his character to be a lesson on how a hero should behave. Others may feel that Beowulf's character reflects the type of legendary hero popular in traditional tales of the time.

Difficulty: *Average* **Objective:** *Essay*

Oral Response

15. Oral responses should be clear, well organized, and well supported by appropriate examples from the selections.

Difficulty: *Average* **Objective:** *Oral Presentation*

Selection Test A, p. 46

Critical Reading

1. ANS: C	DIF: Easy	OBJ: Literary Analysis
2. ANS: B	DIF: Easy	OBJ: Reading Strategy
3. ANS: A	DIF: Easy	OBJ: Comprehension
4. ANS: D	DIF: Easy	OBJ: Interpretation
5. ANS: B	DIF: Easy	OBJ: Comprehension
6. ANS: A	DIF: Easy	OBJ: Comprehension
7. ANS: C	DIF: Easy	OBJ: Interpretation
8. ANS: A	DIF: Easy	OBJ: Comprehension
9. ANS: C	DIF: Easy	OBJ: Interpretation
10. ANS: B	DIF: Easy	OBJ: Literary Analysis
11. ANS: D	DIF: Easy	OBJ: Reading Strategy
12. ANS: A	DIF: Easy	OBJ: Interpretation

Vocabulary and Grammar

13. ANS: C	DIF: Easy	OBJ: Vocabulary
14. ANS: D	DIF: Easy	OBJ: Vocabulary
15. ANS: C	DIF: Easy	OBJ: Grammar

Essay

16. In their essays, students may say that some of the themes of *Beowulf*—such as the fight between good and evil, the glory of generous rulers who try to do good for others, the importance of loyalty and bravery—are still

important today. Others may say that the emphasis on the forces of good conquering evil by physical strength and violence should not be part of today's world. They may feel that the battle of good and evil is too simple an idea for today's complicated world.

Difficulty: *Easy*

Objective: *Essay*

17. Students should realize that one of Beowulf's main goals in all his battles is to earn fame and glory. They may observe that he is a great boaster about his accomplishments. They should also note that when he dies, he asks that a tower be built overlooking the sea to remind people of his greatness and his glory.

Difficulty: *Easy*

Objective: *Essay*

18. Students should point out that the author portrays Beowulf as strong, courageous, and courteous, all heroic qualities. They may also note that his heroism is extreme and may have been intended as a lesson for readers on how a hero should behave.

Difficulty: *Easy*

Objective: *Essay*

Selection Test B, p. 49

Critical Reading

1. ANS: C	DIF: Average	OBJ: Literary Analysis
2. ANS: B	DIF: Easy	OBJ: Comprehension
3. ANS: D	DIF: Average	OBJ: Literary Analysis
4. ANS: A	DIF: Easy	OBJ: Interpretation
5. ANS: B	DIF: Average	OBJ: Interpretation
6. ANS: D	DIF: Average	OBJ: Interpretation
7. ANS: A	DIF: Easy	OBJ: Reading Strategy
8. ANS: D	DIF: Average	OBJ: Comprehension
9. ANS: D	DIF: Easy	OBJ: Comprehension
10. ANS: B	DIF: Easy	OBJ: Interpretation
11. ANS: D	DIF: Challenging	OBJ: Interpretation
12. ANS: A	DIF: Average	OBJ: Literary Analysis
13. ANS: C	DIF: Easy	OBJ: Reading Strategy

Vocabulary and Grammar

14. ANS: A	DIF: Average	OBJ: Vocabulary
15. ANS: B	DIF: Average	OBJ: Grammar
16. ANS: C	DIF: Challenging	OBJ: Grammar
17. ANS: A	DIF: Challenging	OBJ: Vocabulary

Essay

18. Students should realize that one of Beowulf's main goals is to win glory by killing Grendel. His deeds have given him a reputation for heroism and support from his people to help the Danes. When he goes into the lake to fight Grendel's mother, the bystanders fear he has lost his life—and fame: here, death equals defeat equals loss of

glory. Even when old, Beowulf wants to seek fame by fighting the dragon. He doesn't wish to die at the end, but when he sees that it is inevitable, he asks his warriors to build a tower that will keep his name alive in memory.

Difficulty: *Average*

Objective: *Essay*

19. Students may mention such virtues as bravery (*e.g.,* He faces death at the hands of three monsters fearlessly.); fairness (He fights Grendel bare-handed.); responsibility (He feels it's his duty to help the Danes.); concern for others (He saves the communities the monsters ravage.); piety (He thanks God for his victories.); ambition (He wants to earn fame by his deeds.); loyalty (He's good to his subjects.); and intelligence (He plans how he will battle Grendel and the dragon.).

Difficulty: *Challenging*

Objective: *Essay*

20. Some students may feel that Beowulf's heroism is so extreme that the author must have meant his character to be a lesson to readers or listeners on how a hero should behave. Others may feel that Beowulf's character reflects the type of legendary hero popular in traditional tales of the time.

Difficulty: *Average*

Objective: *Essay*

from **A History of the English Church and People** by Bede

Vocabulary Warm-up Exercises, p. 53

A. 1. extracted
2. amber
3. lingers
4. climate
5. breadth
6. horizon
7. twilight
8. fortified

B. Sample Answers
1. (boundary); The farmer put "No Hunting" signs along the boundary of his property to keep hunters away from his crops.
2. (migrated); American pioneers used covered wagons as they *migrated* west.
3. (immunity); Some criminals are given *immunity* from prosecution.
4. (abounding); If you do not water a garden regularly, it is unlikely to be *abounding* with flowers.
5. (corrupted); A judge who takes a bribe or pay-off has been *corrupted*.
6. (consequently); If you witness a car accident you are *consequently* required by law to be available to tell police what you saw.
7. (pasturage); Livestock could not thrive without *pasturage*.

Reading Warm-up A, p. 54

Sample Answers

1. (jewelry); *Amber* is a hard, yellow or orange material that comes from fossils.
2. a lot of information about Stonehenge; Jason extracted the loose tea leaves from the hot tea in the pot.
3. place, strengthened against attack; The opposite of *fortified* is unprotected and vulnerable.
4. (the sun); The *horizon* is the line where the earth and sky appear to meet.
5. dim light; *Twilight* occurs after the sun has set, during the time before dark when there is still a small amount of light in the sky.
6. (The mystery of Stonehenge); has not yet been solved
7. (seven feet); A synonym for *breadth* is width.
8. (rainy); The word 'weather' could be substituted for the word *climate* in this sentence.

Reading Warm-up B, p. 55

Sample Answers

1. (Britain); Experts believe that people of the Stone Age *moved to and settled in* Britain by crossing a land bridge that joined the island to the rest of Europe.
2. Access to the island was available to outsiders only by sea; Every copy of the book I need is checked out of the library. *Consequently*, I will look at the library catalog to see if the book is available at another branch.
3. the developing culture of the new inhabitants; *Unspoiled* and *unstained* are two words that mean the opposite of *corrupted* as it is used in this passage.
4. (crops); *Abounding* means "plentiful."
5. (livestock) (grazed); Livestock still needs grass and hay to eat, so the uses for pasturage have not changed, but it may be cared for differently now, with fertilizers – or not, if it is located on an organic farm.
6. (hot); *Scalding* liquid is nearly boiling, so it would be hot enough to help wash away flesh sticking to the skins.
7. (safe); *protection*
8. border; The Romans constructed a gigantic wall, called Hadrian's Wall, to mark the boundary.

Literary Analysis: Historical Writing, p. 56

Sample Answers

1. The wording suggests that this story has been handed down orally. Because of its importance to the British, care was probably taken to transmit the story accurately from generation to generation.
2. Again, the wording suggests an oral tradition. The accuracy of the details is not strictly ascertainable.
3. Because this information relates to royal history, it is probable that it was recorded in court records. Its accuracy is most likely trustworthy, as the lineage should be traceable.

4. This wording suggests an oral interpretation of the events. The speaker determines that the English got away because their enemies ran aground.

5. This passage suggests that the records of the deaths came from an official source such as church or court records. This information could be verified.

Reading Strategy: Break Down Sentences, p. 57

A. 1. Bede includes information and description in this paragraph.

2. He provides factual information and also presents a positively biased view toward the resources of England.

3. His quotation provides a sense of his reliability and knowledge. The catalogues underscore his bias towards England's bounty.

B. Student responses will differ depending upon which sentences they choose to break down.

Vocabulary Builder, p. 58

A. Sample Answers

1. barricade—Barricade the gate or the draft animals will get out!

2. masquerade—The dancers were wearing costumes at the masquerade ball.

3. ambuscade—The king had not suspected an ambuscade.

4. promenade—The riders had their horses promenade through the town square.

B. 1. Innumerable; 2. immunity; 3. promontories; 4. cultivated; 5. migrated

C. 1. C; 2. C; 3. A; 4. D

Grammar and Style: Compound Sentences, p. 59

A. 1. (not a compound sentence)

2. They were nearly twice as long as the others; some had sixty oars, some more.

3. The Danes went out with three ships against them, and three stood higher up the river's mouth, beached on dry land; the men from them had gone inland.

4. (not a compound sentence)

5. Alfred died, who was town reeve at Bath; and in the same year the peace was fastened at Tiddingford, just as King Edward advised, both with the East Anglians and the Northumbrians.

B. Sample Answers

1. Ireland is broader than Britain, and its climate is superior.

2. There are no reptiles; no snake can exist there.

3. The island abounds with milk and honey, and there is no lack of vines, fish, and birds; deer and goats are widely hunted.

4. In these latitudes the sun does not remain long below the horizon; consequently, both summer days and winter nights are long.

5. Britain is rich in grain and timber; it has good pasturage, and vines are cultivated.

Enrichment: Career as a Historian, p. 60

Sample Answers

A. Print materials: books, newspapers, old diaries/journals, historical documents

Film/Video: old movies, still photos of past events, television documentaries

Audio Recordings: musical recordings from different periods, recordings of historical speeches

Other: Internet, historical societies, artifacts

B. Students may note that with so many sources available there are bound to be contradictions within the material that require decisions. Sometimes two respected historical references contradict each other about dates, the spelling of names, and many other details. It is often a time-consuming process to verify facts, at times requiring an almost arbitrary decision on the part of the researcher. In Bede's time there were few experts on hand to disagree with a historian's findings, let alone to write their own versions. Students may also respond that there are legal and ethical issues involved with writing—issues such as plagiarism, libel, etc. In Bede's time these problems were not as great, if in fact they existed at all.

Open-Book Test, p. 61

Short Answer

1. He wanted to record the history of Britain. He includes facts and details about the country and its people.
   Difficulty: *Easy* **Objective:** *Literary Analysis*

2. He sometimes accepted unlikely stories as true.
   Difficulty: *Easy* **Objective:** *Literary Analysis*

3. By saying "by the grace of God," he reveals that he is on the side of the English.
   Difficulty: *Easy* **Objective:** *Reading*

4. Records from a monastic library would probably have given him the most reliable information because the church kept the most official records.
   Difficulty: *Average* **Objective:** *Interpretation*

5. The reader can infer that Bede believed in the teachings of the English Church.
   Difficulty: *Challenging* **Objective:** *Interpretation*

6. Under Reuda, the Scots migrated to Britain
   Ireland is larger than Britain
   Ireland's natural resources include honey, fish, birds, deer, and goats
   Ireland has a superior climate
   Reptiles die when they breathe Irish air
   Almost everything in Ireland is immune to poison
   Difficulty: *Average* **Objective:** *Interpretation*

7. The large amount of factual specific information shows that Bede was careful and precise about researching his subject.

   Difficulty: *Average*   **Objective:** *Reading*

8. Bede would not have been present to hear a direct quote from the Scots; those who preserved the history might have been biased.

   Difficulty: *Challenging*   **Objective:** *Literary Analysis*

9. There are too many to count.

   Difficulty: *Easy*   **Objective:** *Vocabulary*

10. It is unlikely, because there is no single group of people who are unaffected by poison.

    Difficulty: *Average*   **Objective:** *Vocabulary*

Essay

11. Students should recognize that Bede's history may not be entirely accurate because he had limited resources, and some of his sources would have been unreliable. Other sources may have been incomplete. They should note that he probably had to rely on common folk knowledge and observations.

    Difficulty: *Easy*   **Objective:** *Essay*

12. Students may suggest resources from areas like transportation, communications, technology, and science. Examples from the text should accompany their opinions. For example, historians could use carbon-dating techniques to date objects. They could also take advantage of modern cars, trains, and airplanes to travel with ease to the places they wanted to investigate.

    Difficulty: *Average*   **Objective:** *Essay*

13. Students may discuss Bede's attention to British geography, the history of Britain, and the folktales of the Irish.

    Difficulty: *Challenging*   **Objective:** *Essay*

14. Students may suggest that the text gives details about Britain in Anglo-Saxon times. They should also point out that we learn about the lack of resources for historical research and the reliance of writers on folk knowledge and observation from the text itself.

    Difficulty: *Average*   **Objective:** *Essay*

Oral Response

15. Oral responses should be clear, well organized, and well supported by appropriate examples from the selections.

    Difficulty: *Average*   **Objective:** *Oral Presentation*

Selection Test A, p. 64

Critical Reading

1. ANS: D	DIF: Easy	OBJ: Reading	
2. ANS: A	DIF: Easy	OBJ: Comprehension	
3. ANS: B	DIF: Easy	OBJ: Literary Analysis	
4. ANS: C	DIF: Easy	OBJ: Comprehension	
5. ANS: A	DIF: Easy	OBJ: Literary Analysis	

6. ANS: B	DIF: Easy	OBJ: Reading Strategy	
7. ANS: C	DIF: Easy	OBJ: Reading Strategy	
8. ANS: D	DIF: Easy	OBJ: Comprehension	
9. ANS: B	DIF: Easy	OBJ: Interpretation	
10. ANS: D	DIF: Easy	OBJ: Interpretation	

Vocabulary and Grammar

11. ANS: B	DIF: Easy	OBJ: Vocabulary	
12. ANS: A	DIF: Easy	OBJ: Vocabulary	
13. ANS: C	DIF: Easy	OBJ: Vocabulary	

Essay

14. Students may note that Bede describes the geography, climate, and natural resources, adds quotations, includes instructive details, and uses a friendly, informative tone.

    Difficulty: *Easy*

    Objective: *Essay*

15. Students should recognize that Bede's history may not be entirely accurate because he had limited sources of information. Moreover, some of the sources, such as the oral tales, would have been unreliable. Other sources of information would have been incomplete, so he would have had difficulty knowing exactly who ruled when or where or for how long. For many things, he had to rely on common folk knowledge, such as for his information on the snakes in Ireland. His observations would have been one of his most reliable sources of information.

    Difficulty: *Easy*

    Objective: *Essay*

16. Students may suggest that the text gives details about Britain in Anglo-Saxon times. They should give details about the land and people from the text.

    Difficulty: *Easy*

    Objective: *Essay*

Selection Test B, p. 67

Critical Reading

1. ANS: B	DIF: Easy	OBJ: Interpretation	
2. ANS: C	DIF: Average	OBJ: Interpretation	
3. ANS: A	DIF: Challenging	OBJ: Comprehension	
4. ANS: C	DIF: Easy	OBJ: Comprehension	
5. ANS: D	DIF: Average	OBJ: Literary Analysis	
6. ANS: C	DIF: Average	OBJ: Interpretation	
7. ANS: A	DIF: Challenging	OBJ: Interpretation	
8. ANS: A	DIF: Average	OBJ: Interpretation	
9. ANS: B	DIF: Easy	OBJ: Literary Analysis	
10. ANS: B	DIF: Easy	OBJ: Reading Strategy	
11. ANS: C	DIF: Challenging	OBJ: Reading Strategy	
12. ANS: D	DIF: Average	OBJ: Literary Analysis	

Vocabulary and Grammar

13. ANS: D   DIF: Challenging   OBJ: Vocabulary
14. ANS: D   DIF: Average   OBJ: Vocabulary
15. ANS: C   DIF: Easy   OBJ: Vocabulary

Essay

16. Students may suggest that historical literature can provide a guide by which we may learn from the mistakes of the past. They may cite documents such as the Declaration of Independence and the Constitution and important speeches by leaders such as Abraham Lincoln and Martin Luther King, Jr.

    Difficulty: *Easy*

    Objective: *Essay*

17. Students may respond that depending on oral tradition could lead to inaccuracies; reasons for this could be faulty memory on the part of the storyteller, a tendency to change the truth to make it more interesting or its characters more heroic, and so on. They may also say that ancient manuscripts, no matter how carefully preserved, can be destroyed over time by such factors as weather, poor handling, and so on.

    Difficulty: *Average*

    Objective: *Essay*

18. Students may suggest that the text gives details about Britain in Anglo-Saxon times. They should also point out that we learn about the lack of resources for historical research and the reliance of writers on folk knowledge and observation from the text itself.

    Difficulty: *Average*

    Objective: *Essay*

Benchmark Test 1, p. 70

MULTIPLE CHOICE

1. ANS: B
2. ANS: C
3. ANS: A
4. ANS: D
5. ANS: C
6. ANS: B
7. ANS: C
8. ANS: C
9. ANS: D
10. ANS: A
11. ANS: A
12. ANS: C
13. ANS: B
14. ANS: D
15. ANS: A
16. ANS: D
17. ANS: C
18. ANS: B
19. ANS: A
20. ANS: B
21. ANS: C
22. ANS: C
23. ANS: A
24. ANS: D
25. ANS: B
26. ANS: C
27. ANS: B

ESSAY

28. Students should show an understanding of business memos and early Anglo-Saxon times. They should write about a plausible product or service or a plausible practice relating to the sale of a product or the provision of a service. They might write a memo about selling a particular farm crop, doing ship repairs, or drumming up business for poetry recitals in mead-halls.

29. Students should choose a custom or practice that was widespread in Anglo-Saxon times—warfare or invasion, for example. They should state their position clearly and provide sufficient facts, reasons, and/or examples that support it and demonstrate their understanding of early Anglo-Saxon life.

30. Students should show an understanding of both job-application forms and legendary or epic heroes. They should adapt typically requested information as appropriate—for example, to cover education, they might ask, "Under what warrior or warriors did you train?" For references, they might ask, "Who is your lord or king?"

The Prologue from *The Canterbury Tales*
by Geoffrey Chaucer

Vocabulary Warm-up Exercises, p. 77

A.
1. prudent
2. distinguished
3. adversity
4. devout
5. repented
6. pilgrimages
7. courteous
8. dispense

B. Sample Answers

1. Because Will was <u>diligent</u>, his parents *never had to nag* him to finish his homework.
2. The gymnast's natural <u>agility</u> *helped her become* a finalist in the state competition.
3. The manager fired any worker who was *not* consistently <u>prompt</u>.

4. The teammates *agreed* on a captain, choosing Lauren <u>unanimously</u>.

5. The college offered <u>sundry</u> courses in science, *with biology one of many choices.*

6. The operator will <u>dispatch</u> the messenger to *deliver an urgent package.*

7. The <u>dainty</u> statuette was *tiny and delicately* made.

Reading Warm-up A, p. 78

Sample Answers

1. (slow, difficult); By studying hard, you can overcome the adversity that results from poverty and neglect.

2. <u>well-known and excellent in their field</u>; Someone who is distinguished is highly regarded in his field. For example, Thurgood Marshall was a distinguished Supreme Court justice.

3. <u>the advice of other travelers</u>; Pilgrimages are long journeys to an important place, such as a holy shrine.

4. <u>treat a fellow traveler rudely</u>; A courteous person is polite and considerate of other's needs and feelings.

5. (hoping to find protection in numbers); *Prudent* means "careful and thoughtful"—someone who is prudent would not take risks.

6. (valued performing religious acts); A *devout* person takes extra care observing and respecting religious traditions.

7. <u>wishing to cleanse themselves of remorse</u>; *Repented* means "felt regret and decided to reform."

8. (granting); distribute

Reading Warm-up B, p. 79

Sample Answers

1. <u>putting great effort and care into his work</u>; *Diligent* means "being very careful and thorough."

2. <u>in law, religion, and matters of state</u>; *Miscellaneous* is a synonym for *sundry.*

3. (ease and speed); The *agility* of the gymnast was astounding.

4. (with hardly any delay); Because I like my job, I am always *prompt,* arriving before anyone else.

5. <u>refusing the dainty, delicately beautiful luxuries he had previously enjoyed</u>; *Frugal* means "thrifty."

6. (delicately beautiful); The miniature cakes were dainty and delicious.

7. (their differences); *Unanimously* means "with everyone agreeing."

8. (the king's anger); *Dispatch* means "send to a destination on specific business."

Geoffrey Chaucer: Biography, p. 80

A. Sample Answers

I. Geoffrey Chaucer (1343?–1400)

A. The Poet's Beginnings

1. Worked as a page for Lionel of Antwerp

2. Served in the English Army in France in 1359

3. Married Philippa Pan in 1366

B. The Poet Matures

1. Began writing in his twenties

2. First major work is *The Book of the Duchess*

3. Wrote *Troilus and Criseyde*

C. *The Canterbury Tales*

1. Were written in Chaucer's later life

2. Encompasses all of medieval society

D. The Father of English Poetry

1. Was respected during his time and is studied now

2. Buried in Westminster Abbey

B. Sample Answers

1. *It was my first major work and I wanted to do justice to the great Blanche of Lancaster in the eyes of her husband.*

2. *Fighting in the English Army in France was quite memorable, especially being captured.*

3. *Living in France improved my language skills so I was able to go on to translate French poetry.*

4. *I spent so much time with different classes of people that I wanted to capture a vision of my society through the voice of that society.*

Literary Analysis: Characterization, p. 81

1. Circled item(s) (direct characterization) should include the following: "she was known as Madam Eglantyne"

(indirect characterization:) Her way of smiling very simple and coy. / Her greatest oath was only "By St. Loy!"; well she sang a service, with a fine / Intoning through her nose, as was most seemly; she spoke daintily in French, extremely, / After the school of Stratford-atte-Bowe; French in the Paris style she did not know; At meat her manners were well taught withal/No morsel from her lips did she let fall,/Nor dipped her fingers in the sauce too deep;/But she could carry a morsel up and keep/The smallest drop from falling on her breast.

Sample answer: The Nun is the kind of person who tries to act like a well-mannered and delicate lady but is actually rather vain, affected, and lower-class.

2. Circled item(s) (direct characterization) should include the following: "Wary and wise"; "Discreet he was"; "of noted excellence"

(indirect characterization:) who paid his calls; for clients at St. Paul's; a man to reverence, / Or so he seemed, his sayings were so wise.

Sample answer: The Sergeant at the Law seems to be a man who boasts of his own discretion and accomplishments and feels himself wise enough to make remarks for the benefit of others—all of which suggests that he may be more "wary, wise, and discreet" in his own opinion than he actually is.

3. Circled item(s) (direct characterization) should include the following: "worthy woman"; "somewhat deaf"; "Her

hose were of the finest scarlet red/And gartered tight; her shoes were soft and new."

(indirect characterization:) In making cloth she showed so great a bent / She bettered those of Ypres and of Ghent. / In all the parish not a dame dared stir / Towards the altar steps in front of her. / And if indeed they did, so wrath was she / As to be quite put out of charity. / Her kerchiefs were of finely woven ground; / I dared have sworn they weighed a good ten pound, / The ones she wore on Sunday on her head.

Sample answer: This woman appears to be a vain, materialistic, competitive, show-off type of person.

4. Circled item(s) (direct characterization) should include the following: "a chap of sixteen stone./A great stout fellow big in brawn and bone"; "Broad, knotty and short-shouldered"

(indirect characterization:) he could go / And win the ram at any wrestling show: he would boast / He could heave any door off hinge and post, / Or take a run and break it with his head.

Sample answer: The Miller is the kind of person who relies on his brute strength, is proud of his physique and abilities, and isn't very smart.

Reading Strategy: Analyze Difficult Sentences, p. 83

1. He knew the taverns well and every innkeeper and barmaid.
2. He didn't know the lepers, beggars, and slum-and-gutter dwellers as well because they weren't his class of people and nothing good could come to him from knowing them.
3. If the enemy vessel sank, leaving him prisoners, he "sent them home."
4. He did this by making them walk the plank.
5. The Cook stood alone.
6. He stood alone for cooking flavorful chicken.
7. This is about the Doctor.
8. He can talk about medicine and surgery better than anyone else alive.
9. He watches his patient's favorable star and, using his knowledge of astronomy and his own Natural Magic, knows which hours and planetary degrees would be the luckiest for making charms and magic effigies.
10. He sings an Offertory.
11. He knows he'll have to preach and use his speaking skills to win silver from the crowd.
12. He wants to do the best job he can to win the most silver he can.

Vocabulary Builder, p. 84

A. Nouns: contribution, congregation, recreation, navigation, decoration

1. decoration
2. recreation
3. contribution

4. navigation

B. 1. sanguine
2. absolution
3. avouches
4. garnished
5. solicitous
6. prevarication
7. commission

Enrichment: Career as a Travel Agent, p. 86

Sample Answers

Student responses should reflect the type of tour they select. Possible ideas: a historical tour, a theme-based excursion such as a mystery to be solved, or an art and architecture trip. Arrangements should be based on some research (fares, weather, food, and lodging).

Open-Book Test, p. 87

Short Answer

1. His theme is the great variety of human nature, and he reveals it through his descriptions of the many types of people on the pilgrimage.
   Difficulty: *Easy*   **Objective:** *Interpretation*
2. He is scornful of her, as he shows when he describes how she spends her time and how she accepts gifts.
   Difficulty: *Average*   **Objective:** *Interpretation*
3. Whatever money he borrowed from his friends he spent on studies and books and then prayed earnestly for his friends as a way of giving them thanks.
   Difficulty: *Average*   **Objective:** *Reading*
4. It tells you that the Cook has a sore on his knee that might be dirty and might contaminate the food he makes.
   Difficulty: *Challenging*   **Objective:** *Literary Analysis*
5. She is proud and demanding; nobody dares walk in front of her.
   Difficulty: *Easy*   **Objective:** *Reading*
6. He accentuates both the virtues of the Plowman and the foolishness and unlawfulness of the Miller.
   Difficulty: *Challenging*   **Objective:** *Interpretation*
7. He is very judgmental. He passes judgment on every one of the pilgrims on the trip.
   Difficulty: *Easy*   **Objective:** *Literary Analysis*
8. Knight; brave, distinguished; upper class
   Merchant; well-dressed, self-important; middle class
   Plowman; honest, hard-working; lower class
   Difficulty: *Average*   **Objective:** *Literary Analysis*
9. He is cheerful. He loved to eat and drink and lived for pleasure.
   Difficulty: *Easy*   **Objective:** *Vocabulary*
10. He shows care and concern for his father by standing by to carve meat for him.
    Difficulty: *Average*   **Objective:** *Vocabulary*

Essay

11. Students should support their conclusions about the nature of the character they have chosen to write about with details of appearance, behavior, and speech as well as any direct statement Chaucer's narrator makes about the nature of that individual's personality.

    Difficulty: *Easy*   **Objective:** *Essay*

12. Students should realize that Chaucer has a fairly cynical attitude toward the church and its practitioners. He views most of them as corrupt and as given to sinful behavior as the people for whom they supposedly set an example. Students might point to the characterizations of the Nun, the Monk, the Friar, the Summer, and/or the Pardoner.

    Difficulty: *Average*   **Objective:** *Essay*

13. Students may discuss Chaucer's use of wit, allusion, irony, and innuendo to create his complex characters. He presents the qualities, frailties, values, and motivations of the pilgrims, several of which students should illustrate in their essays.

    Difficulty: *Challenging*   **Objective:** *Essay*

14. Students should point out that the Knight values military skill and follows the code of chivalry, showing honor, wisdom, and humility, which were characteristics of the perfect knight of the time. They may note that by creating such a perfect knight as a character, Chaucer might influence readers to expect such perfection from knights.

    Difficulty: *Average*   **Objective:** *Essay*

Oral Response

15. Oral responses should be clear, well organized, and well supported by appropriate examples from the selections.

    Difficulty: *Average*   **Objective:** *Oral Presentation*

Selection Test A, p. 90

Critical Reading

1. ANS: B	DIF: Easy	OBJ: Literary Analysis
2. ANS: B	DIF: Easy	OBJ: Reading Strategy
3. ANS: D	DIF: Easy	OBJ: Comprehension
4. ANS: B	DIF: Easy	OBJ: Interpretation
5. ANS: C	DIF: Easy	OBJ: Reading Strategy
6. ANS: A	DIF: Easy	OBJ: Comprehension
7. ANS: D	DIF: Easy	OBJ: Literary Analysis
8. ANS: D	DIF: Easy	OBJ: Comprehension
9. ANS: A	DIF: Easy	OBJ: Interpretation
10. ANS: A	DIF: Easy	OBJ: Literary Analysis
11. ANS: A	DIF: Easy	OBJ: Comprehension
12. ANS: C	DIF: Easy	OBJ: Interpretation

Vocabulary

13. ANS: C	DIF: Easy	OBJ: Vocabulary
14. ANS: B	DIF: Easy	OBJ: Vocabulary

Essay

15. Students should describe one of the characters presented in the Prologue and should clearly state what the person is like. They should describe the character's personality and talk about his or her virtues and flaws. They should conclude by telling whether they would like to travel with the character. Students should support their responses with details from the text.

    Difficulty: *Easy*

    Objective: *Essay*

16. Students should understand that the pilgrims have agreed to travel together to Canterbury. The Host suggests that they make their journey more enjoyable by telling two stories each on the way to Canterbury and two on the way back. The travelers agree that the Host should be in charge of their travel and of the stories they tell. They approve of him because he is a pleasant and wise man who is capable of leading them. They agree that the person who tells the best story will be rewarded with a supper paid for by all the other travelers.

    Difficulty: *Easy*

    Objective: *Essay*

17. Students should point out that the knight values military skill and follows the code of chivalry, showing honor, wisdom, and humility, which were characteristics of the perfect knight of the time.

    Difficulty: *Easy*

    Objective: *Essay*

Selection Test B, p. 93

Critical Reading

1. ANS: B	DIF: Easy	OBJ: Literary Analysis
2. ANS: D	DIF: Average	OBJ: Literary Analysis
3. ANS: B	DIF: Challenging	OBJ: Literary Analysis
4. ANS: A	DIF: Average	OBJ: Comprehension
5. ANS: D	DIF: Easy	OBJ: Reading Strategy
6. ANS: D	DIF: Challenging	OBJ: Interpretation
7. ANS: D	DIF: Challenging	OBJ: Interpretation
8. ANS: C	DIF: Average	OBJ: Reading Strategy
9. ANS: A	DIF: Average	OBJ: Literary Analysis
10. ANS: D	DIF: Average	OBJ: Reading Strategy
11. ANS: C	DIF: Average	OBJ: Literary Analysis
12. ANS: D	DIF: Challenging	OBJ: Interpretation
13. ANS: C	DIF: Average	OBJ: Interpretation

Vocabulary

14. ANS: C	DIF: Average	OBJ: Vocabulary
15. ANS: C	DIF: Easy	OBJ: Vocabulary
16. ANS: D	DIF: Challenging	OBJ: Vocabulary

Essay

17. Students should support their conclusions about the nature of the character they have chosen to write about with details of appearance, behavior, and speech as well as any direct statement Chaucer's narrator makes about the nature of that individual's personality.

Difficulty: *Easy*

Objective: *Essay*

18. Students should realize that Chaucer has a fairly cynical attitude toward the church and religious practitioners, viewing most of them as corrupt and as given to self-serving and so-called "sinful" behavior as the people for whom they supposedly set an example. To illustrate this, students might point to his characterizations of the Nun, the Monk, the Friar, the Summoner, and/or the Pardoner—and, in particular, what these characters say about how they spend their time and what they're willing to overlook or pardon in exchange for gifts.

Difficulty: *Average*

Objective: *Essay*

19. Students should point out that the knight values military skill and follows the code of chivalry, showing honor, wisdom, and humility, which were characteristics of the perfect knight of the time. They may note that by creating such a perfect knight as a character, Chaucer might influence readers to expect such perfection from knights.

Difficulty: *Average*

Objective: *Essay*

"The Pardoner's Tale" from *The Canterbury Tales* by Geoffrey Chaucer

Vocabulary Warm-up Exercises, p. 97

A. 1. pulpit
2. congregation
3. dignity
4. sermon
5. vice
6. wary
7. discourse
8. vanity

B. Sample Answers

1. The superhero's secret powers enabled him to overcome any *adversary*. (enemy)
2. The spy chose to *betray* his country, and he revealed government secrets to the enemy. (let down)
3. People visit a doctor when they need medical *counsel*. (advice)
4. If you *cultivate* a child's interest in reading when the child is young, he or she will become a lifelong reader. (nurture)
5. The advertisement might *deceive* customers because it does not explain that some of the parts they need are sold separately. (mislead)

6. The girl pretended to care about her cat, but her *hypocrisy* showed when she repeatedly forgot to feed the animal. (insincerity)
7. Certain magazines are known for gossip and for stories *slandering* celebrities. (spreading lies about)

Reading Warm-up A, p. 98

Sample Answers

1. (self-respect); To live with *dignity*, a person should take pride in the way he or she looks, speak with respect to others, and walk away if others try to insult him or her.
2. this weekly speech; A medieval *sermon* might have been about obeying the king or about the reasons to go on a pilgrimage.
3. (at the front of the church); A *pulpit* is a raised platform that a speaker stands on or desk that a speaker stands behind.
4. every member of; Tithing was a system in which every member of the *group of worshipers* was expected to give a tithe, or one-tenth of their earnings, to support the church.
5. complaining too freely; People in the modern United States are not too *wary* about complaining about taxes, since they know they have a right to freedom of speech.
6. (virtue); A *vice* is a bad or immoral habit, such as laziness or cheating.
7. excessive pride; Checking your looks in a mirror ten times a day is a sign of *vanity*.
8. (explaining); Simple people, such as medieval farmers, probably would not have the patience or the education to follow a complicated *discourse*, but they would find a play entertaining.

Reading Warm-up B, p. 99

Sample Answers

1. (advice); A modern person might go to a lawyer or a doctor for *counsel*.
2. taking care; A doctor needs to be *prudent* in treating illness because someone's life may depend on what he or she does, so he or she should proceed with caution.
3. (con artists); (swindlers); A synonym for *deceive* is *fool*.
4. (promising a cure he could not deliver); The patient would rely on the apothecary's diagnosis and advice, so if the apothecary lied about the chance of a cure, he would *betray* the patient's trust.
5. that they worked only out of a sense of duty; (Apothecaries did charge for their services)
6. watering and tending ; You can *cultivate* beautiful flowers in a planter on your fire escape if you choose the right type of plants.
7. (to harm); *Adversary* means "enemy" or "opponent."
8. (his reputation); To defend himself against *slandering* remarks, an apothecary could demand a public apology from the patient, or the apothecary could tell everyone he met stories about his successes with patients.

Literary Analysis: Allegory, p. 100

A. 1. greed, gambling, drinking, and/or disloyalty
2. old age or wisdom
3. Death
4. temptation, greed, or false idols
5. disloyalty or betrayal of friendship
6. Love of money is the root of all evil.

B. Responses will vary, but students should show an understanding of allegories and include details that point to the moral message they wish to convey.

Reading Strategy: Reread for Clarification, p. 101

1. Death
2. He is so old and wretched that not even Death will take his life.
3. People who saw them would think they were robbers, so they must bring the money back in darkness.
4. No, he is merely thinking about them and greedily yearning for them.
5. One would pretend to wrestle playfully with him and turn the game into an attack, while the other would knife him in the back with his dagger.

Vocabulary Builder, p. 102

A. 1. captain; the chief officer of a ship or airplane
2. capsize; to turn over or sink headfirst
3. capacity; maximum amount or highest limit
4. apologize; to acknowledge wrong-doing or offense
5. apothegm; a saying or maxim

B. 1. tarry; 2. apothecary; 3. prating; 4. pallor; 5. hoary

Enrichment: Plague, p. 104

1. Bubonic plague attacks the lymph nodes, septicemic plague attacks the bloodstream, and pneumonic plague attacks the lungs.
2. No; only when it becomes pneumonic plague can it be spread by breathing.
3. Because people lived in crowded quarters and had poor ventilation, pneumonic plague would have spread easily. In addition, lack of pest control and generally poor sanitation meant that people came into contact with infected body fluids and body parts of dead rodents as well as deceased human victims.
4. They probably felt frightened, since plague had struck fairly recently and threatened to strike again.
5. fatalism; the idea that death is all around and inescapable.

Open-Book Test, p. 105

Short Answer

1. The deeper, symbolic meaning of the tale the Pardoner tells is that greed is the root of all evil.
   Difficulty: *Easy*   **Objective:** *Literary Analysis*

2. The story takes place during an outbreak of the plague, as the lines refer to the plague that has "killed a thousand."
   Difficulty: *Easy*   **Objective:** *Reading*

3. He most closely resembles the three rioters, because he is greedy himself.
   Difficulty: *Easy*   **Objective:** *Interpretation*

4. They represent greed, because they each want all the money, and treachery, because they are each willing to kill the others for the money.
   Difficulty: *Average*   **Objective:** *Literary Analysis*

5. He is directing the three rioters toward their own deaths.
   Difficulty: *Challenging*   **Objective:** *Reading*

6. Each rioter later plots to kill the others to get a larger share of the gold.
   Difficulty: *Challenging*   **Objective:** *Interpretation*

7. They speak of how they want the gold
   Each plots to kill the others
   They treat the old man badly
   Difficulty: *Average*   **Objective:** *Interpretation*

8. He uses it as an exemplum, or example, in a sermon designed to get listeners to part with their money.
   Difficulty: *Challenging*   **Objective:** *Literary Analysis*

9. He is probably quite old, as *hoary* means gray or white with age.
   Difficulty: *Easy*   **Objective:** *Vocabulary*

10. He makes and sells medicines, and today would be called a pharmacist.
    Difficulty: *Average*   **Objective:** *Vocabulary*

Essay

11. Students may say that the old man and the rioters are very much alike. All are deceptive and try to trick each other. Many students will conclude that the rioters are less trustworthy because they were friends who pledged to help one another and quickly turned on one another out of greed.
    Difficulty: *Easy*   **Objective:** *Essay*

12. Students should recognize that the message is "Greed is the root of all evil," and that the three rioters die because they greedily try to kill one another to get a larger share of gold. Students may explore the symbolic meanings of characters like Death and may recognize that the rioters also represent disloyalty and treachery.
    Difficulty: *Average*   **Objective:** *Essay*

13. Students' opinions about the old man may vary, although most will recognize him as either an ally of Death's or Death itself. They should use examples from the text to show how the old man ultimately pointed the three rioters to their deaths.
    Difficulty: *Challenging*   **Objective:** *Essay*

14. Students should point out that the Pardoner's job is to sell documents that officially pardon sins. They may note that his job—to get poor people to pay money for the forgiveness of their sins—reflects the corruption of the Church at that time. The Pardoner's use of Death as a character reflects society's familiarity with death and the fact that death—particularly in a time of plague—was ever-present.

Difficulty: *Average*   **Objective:** *Essay*

Oral Response

15. Oral responses should be clear, well organized, and well supported by appropriate examples from the selections.

Difficulty: *Average*   **Objective:** *Oral Presentation*

job. The rioters, on the other hand, kill one another to get a greater share of the money. Many students will conclude that the rioters are less trustworthy because they were friends who trusted one another and quickly turned on one another out of greed.

Difficulty: *Easy*

Objective: *Essay*

18. Students should point out that the Pardoner's job is to sell documents that officially pardon sins. They may note that his job—to get poor people to pay money for the forgiveness of their sins—reflects the corruption of the Church at that time.

Difficulty: *Easy*

Objective: *Essay*

Selection Test A, p. 108

Critical Reading

1. **ANS:** D	**DIF:** Easy	**OBJ:** Comprehension
2. **ANS:** C	**DIF:** Easy	**OBJ:** Literary Analysis
3. **ANS:** B	**DIF:** Easy	**OBJ:** Reading Strategy
4. **ANS:** B	**DIF:** Easy	**OBJ:** Interpretation
5. **ANS:** C	**DIF:** Easy	**OBJ:** Reading Strategy
6. **ANS:** A	**DIF:** Easy	**OBJ:** Comprehension
7. **ANS:** D	**DIF:** Easy	**OBJ:** Literary Analysis
8. **ANS:** D	**DIF:** Easy	**OBJ:** Comprehension
9. **ANS:** A	**DIF:** Easy	**OBJ:** Comprehension
10. **ANS:** A	**DIF:** Easy	**OBJ:** Comprehension
11. **ANS:** C	**DIF:** Easy	**OBJ:** Interpretation
12. **ANS:** B	**DIF:** Easy	**OBJ:** Interpretation

Vocabulary and Grammar

13. **ANS:** D	**DIF:** Easy	**OBJ:** Vocabulary
14. **ANS:** A	**DIF:** Easy	**OBJ:** Vocabulary
15. **ANS:** C	**DIF:** Easy	**OBJ:** Vocabulary

Essay

16. Students should include that the Pardoner's job is to preach to his congregation about sin and to get them to ask for a pardon. The Pardoner can offer parishioners a pardon, which means their sins are forgiven, but he only offers the pardon if they pay him a fee. By teaching a lesson about how the love of money is the root of all evil, he reminds his listeners about the evil things they have done for money. To get forgiveness, they pay him their ill-gotten money to receive a pardon.

Difficulty: *Easy*

Objective: *Essay*

17. Students may say that the old man and the rioters are very much alike. All are deceptive. The old man tricks the rioters by sending them to the tree. The rioters trick one another. The old man gets the rioters killed because they threaten him and because he is Death and it is his

Selection Test B, p. 111

Critical Reading

1. **ANS:** B	**DIF:** Average	**OBJ:** Comprehension
2. **ANS:** D	**DIF:** Average	**OBJ:** Interpretation
3. **ANS:** C	**DIF:** Average	**OBJ:** Literary Analysis
4. **ANS:** D	**DIF:** Challenging	**OBJ:** Reading Strategy
5. **ANS:** A	**DIF:** Average	**OBJ:** Interpretation
6. **ANS:** A	**DIF:** Average	**OBJ:** Interpretation
7. **ANS:** C	**DIF:** Challenging	**OBJ:** Reading Strategy
8. **ANS:** B	**DIF:** Average	**OBJ:** Interpretation
9. **ANS:** D	**DIF:** Easy	**OBJ:** Interpretation
10. **ANS:** B	**DIF:** Average	**OBJ:** Literary Analysis
11. **ANS:** B	**DIF:** Average	**OBJ:** Reading Strategy
12. **ANS:** A	**DIF:** Challenging	**OBJ:** Reading Strategy

Vocabulary and Grammar

13. **ANS:** B	**DIF:** Average	**OBJ:** Vocabulary
14. **ANS:** C	**DIF:** Average	**OBJ:** Vocabulary
15. **ANS:** B	**DIF:** Challenging	**OBJ:** Vocabulary
16. **ANS:** D	**DIF:** Average	**OBJ:** Vocabulary

Essay

17. Students should recognize that the message is "Love of money is the root of all evil" and that the three rioters die because they greedily try to kill one another to get a larger share of gold. Students may explore the symbolic meanings of characters like Death and may recognize that the rioters themselves represent not merely greed but also disloyalty and treachery.

Difficulty: *Average*

Objective: *Essay*

18. Students should recognize that the Pardoner is actually greedy and tries to trick his listeners into making donations by stressing the idea that "Greed is the root of all evil." Most students are likely to feel that the Pardoner is a hypocrite for telling such a story.

Difficulty: *Average*

Objective: *Essay*

Unit 1 Resources: From Legend to History

19. Students may have varying opinions about the old man in the story, although most will recognize him as either an ally of Death's, or Death itself. They should use examples from the text to show how the old man ultimately pointed the three rioters to their deaths. Students also may make the argument that since Death was everywhere, the rioters could not avoid it.

Difficulty: *Challenging*

Objective: *Essay*

20. Students should point out that the Pardoner's job is to sell documents that officially pardon sins. They may note that his job—to get poor people to pay money for the forgiveness of their sins—reflects the corruption of the Church at that time. The Pardoner's use of Death as a character reflects society's familiarity with death and the fact that death—particularly in a time of plague—was ever-present.

Difficulty: *Average*

Objective: *Essay*

"The Wife of Bath's Tale" *from* The Canterbury Tales by Geoffrey Chaucer

Vocabulary Warm-up Exercises, p. 115

A. 1. reprove
2. purged
3. void
4. bottled
5. crone
6. matrons
7. forlorn
8. extort

B. Sample Answers

1. Compliments can provide <u>incentive</u> for someone who is discouraged.
2. You could <u>enquire</u> about someone's health if they had been ill.
3. The deer were able to <u>maim</u> the apple trees because the broken fence allowed them to feast on the leaves.
4. The chef wanted to show off his talent, so he chose to <u>saddle</u> himself with many specials.
5. The wind <u>disperses</u> the seeds from the wildflowers.
6. It probably is not safe or smart to drive <u>ceaselessly</u> for more than five hours.
7. Most artists probably expect the value of their works to be eternal, not <u>temporal</u>.
8. Being treated unfairly might make someone show <u>defiance</u>.

Reading Warm-up A, p. 116

Sample Answers

1. <u>It was difficult for a woman to raise a family, manage assets, and maintain her reputation on her own</u>;

Matrons are mature women who are either married or widowed.

2. <u>for re-marrying</u>; *Reprove* means "to find fault with."
3. <u>having no one to turn to</u>; Being excluded from a party might make someone feel *forlorn*.
4. Marriages in the Middle Ages were not void of love and affection; *Empty* is a synonym for *void*.
5. <u>Because there were no illusions about this type of arrangement</u>; *Contained* means the same as "bottled up."
6. (an extravagant dowry); *Extort* means "to gain by intimidation."
7. To a degree, individual desires and preferences were *removed* from the minds of young girls; *Purged* means "removed or rid of something."
8. (deferred to her parents' choice); A *crone* is an ugly, old woman.

Reading Warm-up B, p. 117

Sample Answers

1. (considerable domestic duties); Someone might *saddle* you with unpleasant chores.
2. A page in training practiced *endlessly* by attacking a dummy with a shield, which was hung on a wooden pole.
3. (the shield); *Maim* means "injure and disfigure."
4. <u>found out</u>; After an illness or some kind of disruptive event, such as a fire or a funeral, you might *enquire*, or ask, if a person needs anything.
5. When he was twenty, a squire could become a knight himself after proving himself worthy by valor in combat, by *bold resistance* to a foe, or by a charge that disperses enemy combatants.
6. (enemy combatants); A strong wind can scatter a range a things from leaves and umbrellas to shingles and signs.
7. <u>the squire was named a knight</u>; Because medieval battles were fierce and often fatal, a squire would need motivation to face the enemy and the possibility of death.
8. The evening before, the squire typically turned away from worldly matters in order to fast and pray for the purification of his soul.

Literary Analysis: Frame, p. 118

A. 1. the General Prologue
2. To entertain one another on the pilgrimage to Canterbury, the pilgrims will each tell one story going and one story coming, and the innkeeper will give a prize to the one who tells the best story.
3. It makes the reader wonder who will win the storytelling contest. Also, the characterization of the storytellers in the General Prologue makes the reader curious about the kind of stories they will tell.
4. She tells part of the story of King Midas.

5. She is a lusty, much-married woman, so she tells a story about love and marriage. She is also a woman who likes to have the upper hand, so she tells a story of a woman who gains the upper hand in her marriage.

B. Students' responses will vary.

Reading Strategy: Use Context Clues, p. 119

1. pleasure; 2. dance attendance, make a fuss;
3. criticize; 4. hurt; 5. someone low born or someone who behaves badly

Vocabulary Builder, p. 120

Using Multiple-Meaning Words

A. 1. narrates; 2. any part of the face; 3. an expanse of grass or plants; 4. disgusting

Using the Word List

B. 1. F; 2. F; 3. T; 4. T; 5. F; 6. F; 7. F; 8. T

Grammar and Style: Correlative Conjunctions, p. 122

Sample Answers

1. The knight would either die or go on a quest.
2. The knight neither wanted to die nor to marry the old woman.
3. The knight had to decide whether to marry the old woman or to die.
4. The knight not only got to live but also had a beautiful wife.

Enrichment: King Midas, p. 123

A. 1. the invasion and destruction of his kingdom (which happened in the same year)
2. Greed can lead to disaster.
3. Be careful what you wish for.
4. Donkey's ears are a common sign of foolishness.
5. Since the barber cuts Midas's hair, he would see Midas's ears.

B. A "Midas touch" is the ability to make money in every venture; such a businessman or woman is someone for whom everything he or she touches "turns to gold."

Open-Book Test, p. 124

Short Answer

1. *The Canterbury Tales* is set on a pilgrimage to Canterbury in the late 1300s. "The Wife of Bath's Tale" is set in long-ago England in the time of King Arthur.
   Difficulty: *Easy*   **Objective:** *Literary Analysis*
2. She wants to foreshadow the later transformation of the old woman.
   Difficulty: *Challenging*   **Objective:** *Literary Analysis*
3. She thinks they are a danger to women, saying they will "do no more than take your virtue."
   Difficulty: *Average*   **Objective:** *Interpretation*
4. She is saying that women cannot keep a secret.
   Difficulty: *Average*   **Objective:** *Literary Analysis*

5. She believes it is more important to teach him a lesson than to kill him.
   Difficulty: *Challenging*   **Objective:** *Interpretation*
6. It means a bad marriage. He refers to his race and station and calls the marriage "foul," so it is clear he feels that such a marriage would not be suitable for him.
   Difficulty: *Easy*   **Objective:** *Reading*
7. She wants to be sure that the knight will not be able to go back on his promise.
   Difficulty: *Easy*   **Objective:** *Interpretation*
8. begged, asked
   noble
   rude, mean person
   Difficulty: *Average*   **Objective:** *Reading*
9. She is an elf or fairy, and she has transformed herself into an old woman.
   Difficulty: *Challenging*   **Objective:** *Interpretation*
10. She scolds him because he criticized her for being old and poor.
    Difficulty: *Average*   **Objective:** *Vocabulary*

Essay

11. Students should understand that the woman's appearance as old and ugly is a test for the knight. She wants him to learn what women desire and to be willing to give it to his wife. At that point, she changes into a young, beautiful woman, rewarding him for learning his lesson.
    Difficulty: *Easy*   **Objective:** *Essay*
12. Students should note that the tale is set in the time of King Arthur, a time when elves still existed and knights were chivalrous. The protagonist is a knight who acts dishonorably but honors his promise. The setting in this time of magic also makes the transformation of the old woman more believable. Students may feel that if the setting were changed, it would require a change in characters, since true courtly knights and elves were part of the Arthurian legend.
    Difficulty: *Average*   **Objective:** *Essay*
13. Students should state that the Wife of Bath's tale is consistent with the background given about her in the Prologue. She has much experience with marriage and husbands and can talk about what women really want out of marriage. Students may point out that the old woman in the tale is wise and experienced, as the teller is, and teaches the knight the lesson the Wife has learned herself — that marriage is better when wives can "overbid" their husbands.
    Difficulty: *Challenging*   **Objective:** *Essay*
14. Students should point out that the Wife of Bath is a demanding woman who believes in equality in marriage. They may note that she represents sensuality, aggressiveness, vitality, and the value of life experience. Her character negatively reflects the fears that people

had about giving women any say or power in their lives or relationships, while her story reflects both the positive courtly ideals of knighthood and her own strong ideas about the role of women in marriage.

Difficulty: *Average*   **Objective:** *Essay*

Oral Response

15. Oral responses should be clear, well organized, and well supported by appropriate examples from the selections.

Difficulty: *Average*   **Objective:** *Oral Presentation*

Selection Test A, p. 127

Critical Reading

1. ANS: C	DIF: Easy	OBJ: Comprehension
2. ANS: A	DIF: Easy	OBJ: Reading Strategy
3. ANS: A	DIF: Easy	OBJ: Literary Analysis
4. ANS: B	DIF: Easy	OBJ: Interpretation
5. ANS: B	DIF: Easy	OBJ: Interpretation
6. ANS: C	DIF: Easy	OBJ: Comprehension
7. ANS: D	DIF: Easy	OBJ: Reading Strategy
8. ANS: A	DIF: Easy	OBJ: Interpretation
9. ANS: C	DIF: Easy	OBJ: Comprehension
10. ANS: B	DIF: Easy	OBJ: Literary Analysis
11. ANS: D	DIF: Easy	OBJ: Interpretation

Vocabulary and Grammar

12. ANS: D	DIF: Easy	OBJ: Vocabulary
13. ANS: C	DIF: Easy	OBJ: Vocabulary
14. ANS: A	DIF: Easy	OBJ: Grammar

Essay

15. The tale told by the Wife of Bath is consistent with the background given about her in the Prologue. She is a wife with lots of experience with marriage and husbands, as well as with other men during her youth. She has the experience to talk about what women really want out of a marriage and how they are treated by men. She certainly would have a strong opinion about the relationship between husbands and wives.

Difficulty: *Easy*

Objective: *Essay*

16. Students should understand that the woman's appearance as old and ugly is another test for the knight. She wants to learn whether he is interested in appearances or if he is also interested in other values, such as her faithfulness. When he shows that he has learned what women desire and is willing to give it to his wife, she rewards him with all he desires.

Difficulty: *Easy*

Objective: *Essay*

17. Students should point out that the Wife of Bath is a demanding woman who believes in equality in marriage. They may note that she represents sensuality, agressiveness, vitality, and the value of life experience.

Difficulty: *Easy*

Objective: *Essay*

Selection Test B, p. 130

Critical Reading

1. ANS: C	DIF: Challenging	OBJ: Literary Analysis
2. ANS: B	DIF: Average	OBJ: Interpretation
3. ANS: A	DIF: Average	OBJ: Interpretation
4. ANS: A	DIF: Challenging	OBJ: Interpretation
5. ANS: B	DIF: Average	OBJ: Comprehension
6. ANS: A	DIF: Average	OBJ: Comprehension
7. ANS: B	DIF: Average	OBJ: Literary Analysis
8. ANS: C	DIF: Average	OBJ: Reading Strategy
9. ANS: C	DIF: Average	OBJ: Comprehension
10. ANS: B	DIF: Challenging	OBJ: Interpretation
11. ANS: D	DIF: Average	OBJ: Reading Strategy
12. ANS: C	DIF: Average	OBJ: Reading Strategy

Vocabulary and Grammar

13. ANS: C	DIF: Average	OBJ: Vocabulary
14. ANS: D	DIF: Average	OBJ: Vocabulary
15. ANS: B	DIF: Average	OBJ: Vocabulary
16. ANS: A	DIF: Challenging	OBJ: Grammar
17. ANS: C	DIF: Challenging	OBJ: Vocabulary

Essay

18. Students should note that "The Wife of Bath's Tale" is set in the time of King Arthur, a time, the Wife tells us, when elves still danced in the meadows and when women could not walk alone safely for fear of fairies and incubuses. It was also a time of knights who were chivalrous. These are all key features of the plot. The protagonist is a knight who acts dishonorably but then is honorable enough to respect his promise to return and face the queen. The setting in this time of magic also makes the transformation of the old woman more believable. If the setting were changed, it would require a complete change in characters, since knights did not live at other times and elves disappeared with the coming of the friars.

Difficulty: *Average*

Objective: *Essay*

19. Most students will agree that the Wife of Bath shares some of the convictions of twenty-first century women but may not have quite the same views. According to her story, what women want most is to rule their hus-

bands. In return, she implies that women should be willing to do anything to satisfy their husbands. Many modern women might say they do not want to control their husbands but to have equality with them. They might also argue that they prefer having their husband's respect rather than trying to satisfy their husbands' every wish. Men, of course, would generally object to allowing themselves to be ruled by their wives, but they would also appreciate having beautiful and faithful wives who were willing to do anything to make them happy.

Difficulty: *Average*

Objective: *Essay*

20. Students should point out that the Wife of Bath is a demanding woman who believes in equality in marriage. They may note that she represents sensuality, agressiveness, vitality, and the value of life experience. Her character negatively reflects the fears that people had about giving women any say or power in their lives or relationships, while her story reflects both the positive courtly ideals of knighthood and her own strong ideas about the role of women in marriage.

Difficulty: *Average*

Objective: *Essay*

Literary Analysis: Comparing Frame Stories, p. 133

Sample Answers

The Canterbury Tales

Main frame: In fourteenth-century England, a group of travelers is making a pilgrimage to Canterbury to receive a blessing at the shrine of St. Thomas à Becket.

Premise for storytelling: Each pilgrim is invited to tell two stories on the way to Canterbury and two more on the return trip, with the best storyteller being treated to dinner by the others.

Effect of premise: The premise provides a context for a great variety and richness of stories from different times and places.

The Decameron:

Main frame: During the Black Death in fourteenth-century Italy, a group of seven women and three men is fleeing from the plague in crowded Florence, seeking refuge in a countryside villa for two weeks.

Premise for storytelling: to pass the time, each member of the group tells one story for each night spent in the villa, each on a different topic.

Effect of premise: Allows for a great variety of topics and themes in the stories told.

Vocabulary Builder, p. 134

Sample Answers

A. 1. impertinence
2. deference
3. frugally

4. courtly
5. despondent
6. affably

B. 1. D; 2. B; 3. D; 4. C; 5. A

Selection Test, p. 139

Critical Reading

1. ANS: C	DIF: Average	OBJ: Literary Analysis
2. ANS: A	DIF: Average	OBJ: Comprehension
3. ANS: D	DIF: Average	OBJ: Interpretation
4. ANS: C	DIF: Average	OBJ: Interpretation
5. ANS: C	DIF: Challenging	OBJ: Interpretation
6. ANS: B	DIF: Average	OBJ: Comprehension
7. ANS: D	DIF: Challenging	OBJ: Literary Analysis
8. ANS: B	DIF: Average	OBJ: Comprehension
9. ANS: C	DIF: Challenging	OBJ: Interpretation
10. ANS: A	DIF: Average	OBJ: Literary Analysis

from Sir Gawain and the Green Knight, translated by Marie Borroff
from Morte d'Arthur by Sir Thomas Malory

Vocabulary Warm-up Exercises, p. 139

A. 1. slumbering
2. accorded
3. almighty
4. marvel
5. puny
6. swooned
7. fused
8. hermits

B. Sample Answers
1. The barren tree didn't produce any fruit.
2. The child who hated sweets drank her tea sans sugar.
3. The reporter displayed his arrogance by refusing to apologize for his mistakes.
4. Visitors were not authorized to enter the restricted area of the power plant.
5. Paul was dismayed to hear he had lost the lottery.
6. The car accident was caused by the driver's wilful running of a red light.
7. The world-famous sculptor condescended to teach a class at our local art studio.

Reading Warm-up A, p. 140

Sample Answers

1. (loyalty, honor, self-sacrifice and defense of the weak); An antonym for *fused* is *separated.*
2. (when battles were fought in their name); *Swooned* means "fainted."

3. (the knight's beloved); It was also expected to make the knight's beloved <u>be in awe</u> at his attempts to be worthy of her.

4. (matrimonial decisions); *Accorded* means "given what is due or appropriate."

5. (the future husband and wife); *slumbering* means "sleeping or dozing."

6. (a wealthy father); A <u>hermit</u> might be found living in the wilderness or any area far away from civilization, society, and other people.

7. (expect her to marry); A <u>puny</u> sum is a little bit of money. Fifteen cents is a very *puny* sum.

8. (Money); <u>almighty</u> means "all powerful."

Reading Warm-up B, p. 141

Sample Answers

1. <u>sans a chair, and contained little more than a phone and a computer</u>. The farmer's fields stood out from the others because they were *empty* of trees or crops.

2. (a chair) The most popular restaurant in our small town has a counter but is <u>sans</u> booths.

3. <u>. . . so he set about making his cubicle more personal with a trophy from his high school swimming team, a comical mouse pad, and a photo of his girlfriend</u>. *Satisfied* is an antonym for *dismayed*.

4. (Greg) Nobody really likes being <u>condescended</u> to.

5. <u>coffee machine . . . copier</u> You need to be *authorized* or have official permission to drive, hunt, or fish.

6. (Judy, the receptionist) A synonym for *arrogance* is *haughtiness*.

7. (Mr. Bernhardt) Greg was astonished that Mr. Bernhardt would tolerate Judy's display of arrogance and *deliberate* rudeness.

8. <u>. . . he brought Judy a cup</u> A person who is *groveling* might beg for a chair, any chair to be brought to his empty office.

Literary Analysis: Medieval Romance, p. 142

Sample Answers from *Sir Gawain and the Green Knight:*

1. The Green Knight himself—given his size, color, and ability to disguise himself—is an example. Another is the green girdle; although in fact it was part of the Green Knight's scheme and probably not magical after all, the girdle still conveyed a sense of the supernatural earlier in the story.

2. At Arthur's court, the knights are dressed in armor, sitting on a high dais. The New Year's Eve feast was very elaborate, "With all dainties double, dishes rare, / With all manner of meat and minstrelsy both . . ."

3. Gawain courageously offers to take Arthur's place. He also courageously presents himself at Green Chapel even though he fears the place is inhabited by Satan.

4. Traveling in search of Green Chapel and finding a wondrous castle where Gawain stays with "strangers" can be viewed as examples of a hero engaged in adventure.

Sample Answers from *Morte d' Arthur:*

1. King Arthur dreams a wonderful dream full of rich detail and supernatural elements such as hideous black water, serpents, and worms. Sir Lucan reminds Arthur of his dream and what the spirit of Sir Gawain has taught him.

2. Courtly life is seen in the number of lords, ladies, and knights that appear.

3. Sir Gawain refers to all of the ladies he has fought for and the fact that God has given them grace.

4. A sense of adventure permeates the story as Mordred controls England when Arthur returns and a battle ensues. Just before Gawain dies, he manages to send word to Lancelot that Arthur needs help.

Reading Strategy: Summarize, p. 143

Sample Answers

Key Ideas and Events: Sir Lucan left because he was hurt very badly. He saw pillagers and robbers who killed people after they robbed them. He told the king what he saw.

Summary: Sir Lucan was badly hurt, so he left. As he walked he saw pillagers and robbers stealing from the nobles. As soon as he could, he told the king about it.

Vocabulary Builder, p. 144

A. Sample Answers

1. Because of his *adroitness* with a football, Charley was able to make the football team. *or* Because of his *maladroitness* with a football, Charley was unable to make the football team.

2. Amber was very *adroit* at gymnastics, so she knew she might go to the Olympics. *or* Amber was very *maladroit* at gymnastics, so she knew she would never go to the Olympics.

3. correct

4. Tad prides himself on his *adroitness*, having never broken a leg in all his years as a skier.

B. 1. assay; 2. feigned; 3. righteous; 4. adjure; 5. peril; 6. adroitly; 7. entreated; 8. largesse; 9. interred

Enrichment: Film Depictions of King Arthur, p. 146

Sample Answer

Student responses will depend upon the versions of the King Arthur story they choose to compare and contrast.

Open-Book Test, p. 147

Short Answer

1. He is confident, courteous, and commanding. He plays host to the Green Knight and deals firmly with his guest.
   Difficulty: *Average*   **Objective:** *Interpretation*

2. There is no damsel in distress or doomed love in the excerpt.
   Difficulty: *Easy*   **Objective:** *Interpretation*

3. A horseman whose skin is green comes into King Arthur's hall, where the king's guests are gathered. He asks to speak to the leader of the group, and everyone is silent, stunned by his actions and his color.

   Difficulty: *Average*   **Objective:** *Reading*

4. He is ashamed that he kept the girdle that the Green Knight's wife gave to him.

   Difficulty: *Easy*   **Objective:** *Interpretation*

5. When King Arthur's sword is thrown into the lake, a hand rises up and catches it, which is a magical occurrence.

   Difficulty: *Easy*   **Objective:** *Literary Analysis*

6. King Arthur ran toward Sir Mordred with his spear and stabbed him under his shield, and Sir Mordred hit the king on the head with his sword. Then Sir Mordred died, and King Arthur fell in a faint.

   Difficulty: *Average*   **Objective:** *Reading*

7. Sir Gawain keeps the magic girdle. This breaks his promise and shows that he is fearful of death, both of which go against the ideals of chivalry. Sir Bedivere does not throw the sword into the lake at first, disobeying his lord.

   Difficulty: *Challenging*   **Objective:** *Literary Analysis*

8. Gawain goes to meet the Green Knight a year after their first encounter.

   Gawain allows the Green Knight to try to kill him.

   Gawain insists on facing the Green Knight in Arthur's place.

   Sir Bevidere finally throws Excalibur into the lake.

   Arthur knows Mordred will kill him but faces him anyway.

   The ladies and knights give Arthur the death he wants.

   Difficulty: *Average*   **Objective:** *Literary Analysis*

9. Both tales focus on the principles of chivalry and the importance of honorable behavior.

   Difficulty: *Average*   **Objective:** *Interpretation*

10. He pretended to be brave because a knight should not be fearful, and he didn't want the Green Knight to know he was afraid.

    Difficulty: *Average*   **Objective:** *Vocabulary*

Essay

11. Students should include at least one example of a realistic and a supernatural detail from each selection. They may note Sir Gawain's beheading of the Green Knight or the description of the battle between Arthur and Mordred as realistic details. They may note the Green Knight picking up his head and the king's prophetic dream as supernatural details. Students may feel that the supernatural details make the stories less believable but more fun to read.

    Difficulty: *Easy*   **Objective:** *Essay*

12. Students should realize that the character of King Arthur is portrayed consistently in the two stories. They might point out that King Arthur shows he is supportive, brave, wise, shrewd, and honorable and use examples from both tales to illustrate these traits.

    Difficulty: *Average*   **Objective:** *Essay*

13. Students should point out that the chivalric code combined Christian values and the virtues of being a warrior. Knights were to be brave, honest, loyal, to right wrongs and defend the weak. Students' responses will vary depending on which characters they select but should reflect the code of chivalry. They should note that Gawain's self-protectiveness and Sir Bedivere's breach of loyalty lead those knights to violate the code; the Green Knight's and Arthur's forgiveness and the fact that the knights eventually do the right thing resolve the conflicts.

    Difficulty: *Challenging*   **Objective:** *Essay*

14. Students should note that Gawain is brave, adventurous, and loyal. However, he breaks his promise to give back the girdle because he is fearful of dying. They should point out that Bedivere is loyal, loving, and courageous. However, when Arthur tells him to throw Excalibur into the lake, he does not immediately do so and he lies about it. Students may feel that the result of these unchivalric actions is to allow the reader to see the knights as more fully human, with human flaws.

    Difficulty: *Average*   **Objective:** *Essay*

Oral Response

15. Oral responses should be clear, well organized, and well supported by appropriate examples from the selections.

    Difficulty: *Average*   **Objective:** *Oral Presentation*

Selection Test A, p. 150

Critical Reading

1. ANS: A	DIF: Easy	OBJ: Reading Strategy
2. ANS: C	DIF: Easy	OBJ: Comprehension
3. ANS: D	DIF: Easy	OBJ: Comprehension
4. ANS: B	DIF: Easy	OBJ: Reading Strategy
5. ANS: A	DIF: Easy	OBJ: Interpretation
6. ANS: B	DIF: Easy	OBJ: Literary Analysis
7. ANS: D	DIF: Easy	OBJ: Comprehension
8. ANS: C	DIF: Easy	OBJ: Comprehension
9. ANS: B	DIF: Easy	OBJ: Literary Analysis
10. ANS: A	DIF: Easy	OBJ: Interpretation
11. ANS: A	DIF: Easy	OBJ: Interpretation
12. ANS: C	DIF: Easy	OBJ: Comprehension

Vocabulary and Grammar

13. ANS: B	DIF: Easy	OBJ: Vocabulary
14. ANS: A	DIF: Easy	OBJ: Vocabulary
15. ANS: D	DIF: Easy	OBJ: Grammar

Essay

16. Students should respond to the questions and also include at least one example of a realistic detail and one supernatural detail from each selection. An example from *Sir Gawain and the Green Knight* of a realistic detail includes the description of Sir Gawain beheading the Green Knight. An example of a supernatural event includes the Green Knight picking up his head, which then speaks. An example of a realistic detail from *Morte d'Arthur* includes the description of King Arthur's fight with Mordred. An example of a supernatural detail includes King Arthur's prophetic dream.
   Difficulty: *Easy*
   Objective: *Essay*

17. Students should recognize that the character of King Arthur is consistent between the two tales. As an example, they might point out that King Arthur supports his knights when he encourages Sir Gawain to enter the contest with the Green Knight, is brave when he attacks Mordred, is wise when he listens to the message in his dreams, is smart when he tells his men to be ready to attack if one of Mordred's men draws a sword, and is honorable because he appreciates the loyalty of his knights.
   Difficulty: *Easy*
   Objective: *Essay*

18. Students should note that Gawain is brave, adventurous, and loyal. They should point out that Bedivere is loyal, loving, and courageous.
   Difficulty: *Easy*
   Objective: *Essay*

Selection Test B, p. 153

Critical Reading

1. ANS: B   DIF: Average   OBJ: Reading Strategy
2. ANS: C   DIF: Average   OBJ: Comprehension
3. ANS: D   DIF: Average   OBJ: Literary Analysis
4. ANS: A   DIF: Easy   OBJ: Interpretation
5. ANS: B   DIF: Average   OBJ: Literary Analysis
6. ANS: D   DIF: Easy   OBJ: Reading Strategy
7. ANS: C   DIF: Easy   OBJ: Comprehension
8. ANS: B   DIF: Challenging   OBJ: Interpretation
9. ANS: C   DIF: Average   OBJ: Interpretation
10. ANS: D   DIF: Average   OBJ: Interpretation
11. ANS: C   DIF: Average   OBJ: Literary Analysis
12. ANS: C   DIF: Challenging   OBJ: Comprehension
13. ANS: B   DIF: Challenging   OBJ: Reading Strategy

Vocabulary and Grammar

14. ANS: D   DIF: Easy   OBJ: Vocabulary
15. ANS: C   DIF: Average   OBJ: Grammar
16. ANS: B   DIF: Easy   OBJ: Grammar
17. ANS: D   DIF: Average   OBJ: Vocabulary
18. ANS: C   DIF: Challenging   OBJ: Vocabulary

Essay

19. Students should realize that the character of King Arthur is portrayed consistently in the two stories. They might point out that King Arthur shows he is supportive when he encourages Sir Gawain to enter the contest with the Green Knight, brave when he attacks Mordred, wise when he listens to the message in his dreams, shrewd when he tells his men to be ready to attack if one of Mordred's men draws a sword, and honorable because he truly appreciates the loyalty of his knights.
   Difficulty: *Average*
   Objective: *Essay*

20. Developed by feudal nobles, the chivalric code combined Christian values and the virtues of being a warrior. Knights were to be brave, honest, and loyal; to right wrongs and selflessly defend the weak. Students' responses will vary depending upon which characters they select but should reflect the code of chivalry. They should note that Gawain's self-protectiveness and Sir Belvidere's less-than-unquestioning loyalty both lead them to violate the code; the Green Knight's and Arthur's forgiveness, and the fact that the knights eventually "get it right," resolve the conflict.
   Difficulty: *Challenging*
   Objective: *Essay*

21. Students should note that Gawain is brave, adventurous, and loyal. However, he breaks his promise to give back the girdle because he is fearful of dying. They should point out that Bedivere is loyal, loving, and courageous. However, when Arthur tells him to throw Excaliber into the lake, he does not immediately do so and he lies about it. Students may feel that the result of these unchivalric actions is to allow the reader to see the knights as more fully human, with human flaws.
   Difficulty: *Average*
   Objective: *Essay*

Vocabulary Builder, p. 157

Selection Test, p. 158

Critical Reading

1. ANS: B   DIF: Easy   OBJ: Literary Analysis
2. ANS: A   DIF: Average   OBJ: Literary Analysis
3. ANS: D   DIF: Average   OBJ: Literary Analysis
4. ANS: C   DIF: Challenging   OBJ: Literary Analysis
5. ANS: A   DIF: Average   OBJ: Literary Analysis
6. ANS: B   DIF: Average   OBJ: Literary Analysis
7. ANS: A   DIF: Average   OBJ: Literary Analysis
8. ANS: B   DIF: Challenging   OBJ: Literary Analysis

9. ANS: A   DIF: Average   OBJ: Literary Analysis
10. ANS: C   DIF: Easy   OBJ: Literary Analysis

Writing About Literature—Unit 1

Analyze Literary Periods: Integrating Grammar Skills, p. 160

Sample Revisions

1. The knight in *The Canterbury Tales* displays idealized values of his class, such as modesty, courtesy, and generosity.
2. Unlike the Wife of Bath, the Prioress is sentimental and tenderhearted.
3. Although the Monk has supposedly taken a vow of poverty, he owns fine clothes, wears gold jewelry, and owns horses and hunting dogs.
4. Because the Cleric is devoted only to his studies, he doesn't care about his appearance or his social life.
5. In the 1380s, when Chaucer was writing, ideals of chivalry were already dying.

Writing Workshop—Unit 1

Autobiographical Narrative: Integrating Grammar Skills, p. 161

A. 1. incorrect
2. correct
3. correct
4. incorrect
5. incorrect

B. 1. The summer I went to baseball camp, I never dreamed I would learn so much.
2. When I am learning a new skill, I need hours of practice to finally master it.
3. correct
4. Today, when I see little kids on the playground, I remember how important my earliest friendships were to me when I was a kid.
5. correct

Vocabulary Workshop—1, p. 163

A. 1. **shield** Middle English schelde < Old English *scield*, akin to German *schild* < Indo-European *skelp*, to cut, divide
2. **destiny** Middle English *destine* < Old French *destiner* < Latin *destinare*, to fasten down, secure
3. **fame** Middle English < Old French < Latin *fama*, reputation
4. **hero** Latin *heros* < Greek *heros* < Indo-European base *ser-*, to protect

5. **dragon** Middle English *dragoun* < Old French *dragon* < Latin *draco* < Greek *drakon* < Indo-European base *derk-*, to see
6. **sword** Middle English < Old English *sweord* < Indo-European base *swer-*, to cut

B. 1. **shield:** buckler, bulwark, escutcheon
His courage acted as a *bulwark* against disaster.
2. **destiny:** fortune, karma, doom
It was her *karma* and could not be avoided.
3. **fame:** celebrity, distinction, eminence
In an age of *celebrity*, people are famous for being famous.
4. **hero:** champion, exemplar, paladin
Children want to imitate the deeds of an *exemplar*.
5. **dragon:** monster, behemoth, beast
They faced the *behemoth* and destroyed it.
6. **sword:** blade, cutlass, bodkin
Hamlet thought about using a bare *bodkin*.

Benchmark Test 2, p. 165

MULTIPLE CHOICE

1. ANS: A
2. ANS: D
3. ANS: A
4. ANS: A
5. ANS: C
6. ANS: B
7. ANS: D
8. ANS: B
9. ANS: A
10. ANS: C
11. ANS: C
12. ANS: C
13. ANS: A
14. ANS: D
15. ANS: B
16. ANS: B
17. ANS: C
18. ANS: B
19. ANS: D
20. ANS: C
21. ANS: D
22. ANS: D
23. ANS: A
24. ANS: B
25. ANS: C
26. ANS: B

27. ANS: A
28. ANS: D
29. ANS: A

ESSAY

30. Students should clearly state their opinion of the criticism and provide strong support for their opinion based on details and examples from the passage.

31. Students' interior monologues should be written in the first person. Students should describe thoughts and feelings related to the possibility of winning or losing the school election, using language that is lively and interesting to readers.

32. Students should create a graphic organizer that shows the main characters, setting, and sequence of events in an incident from their lives. Below the graphic organizer, they should clearly explain, in one sentence, an insight related to the incident.

Vocabulary in Context, p. 171

MULTIPLE CHOICE

1. ANS: B
2. ANS: D
3. ANS: C
4. ANS: C
5. ANS: A
6. ANS: C
7. ANS: D
8. ANS: D
9. ANS: B
10. ANS: D

11. ANS: A
12. ANS: D
13. ANS: C
14. ANS: B
15. ANS: D
16. ANS: B
17. ANS: D
18. ANS: B
19. ANS: C
20. ANS: A